# SPELLING
# IMPROVEMENT
### A PROGRAM FOR SELF-INSTRUCTION

| DATE | | |
|------|------|------|
|  |  |  |
|  |  |  |
|  |  |  |
|  |  |  |
|  |  |  |
|  |  |  |
|  |  |  |
|  |  |  |
|  |  | MAR 9 0 |
|  |  |  |
|  |  |  |

# FOURTH EDITION

# SPELLING IMPROVEMENT

## A PROGRAM FOR SELF-INSTRUCTION

# PATRICIA M. FERGUS, Ph.D.

Consultant in Business and Industrial Writing
Professor Emerita,
Mount Saint Mary's College
Emmitsburg, Maryland

McGraw-Hill Book Company

New York   St. Louis   San Francisco   Auckland   Bogotá
Hamburg   London   Madrid   Mexico   Montreal
New Delhi   Panama   Paris   São Paulo   Singapore   Sydney
Tokyo   Toronto

# SPELLING IMPROVEMENT
## A PROGRAM FOR SELF-INSTRUCTION

67890 HALHAL 898

ISBN 0-07-020476-4

This book was set in Helvetica by
Monotype Composition Company, Inc.
The editors were Marian D. Provenzano and James R. Belser;
the designer was Janice Noto;
the production supervisor was Diane Renda.
Halliday Lithograph Corporation was printer and binder.

**Library of Congress Cataloging in Publication Data**

Fergus, Patricia M.
    Spelling improvement

    Includes index.
        1. English language—Orthography and spelling.
2. Vocabulary.   I. Title.
PE1143.F4   1983      428.1        82-9971
ISBN 0-07-020476-4                 AACR2

# CONTENTS

# PREFACE

Like its predecessors, the fourth edition places prime importance on spelling as a multisensory process and as a tool of language—an integral part of written communication. However, as time and usage have a habit of revealing the necessity for change, several modifications were deemed appropriate and desirable. Appendix A and Chapter 3 of the third edition are now presented as Part One, "A Multisensory Approach to Spelling," followed by Part Two, "Sound and Spelling," Part Three, "Meaning and Spelling (including the chapter on prefixes), and Part Four, "Rules and Spelling." A new, more easily administered and scored diagnostic test, and either new or revised chapter, part, and final tests replace those of the previous edition.

Adding word origins, examples, and illustrative material while retaining the compactness of the third edition proved to be quite a challenge—one I have tried to meet successfully. For one main reason, only a minimum of "basics" is presented: the text is directed to persons who misspell words for a variety of reasons but who already have a measure of visual and auditory perception and discrimination as well as a measure of reading competency. The text can certainly be used in a remedial setting (clinic, laboratory, and the like), but it should not be categorized as a remedial text. It offers specific help to persons having spelling problems (not necessarily severe) by diagnosing sixteen problem areas, guiding users through chapters relating to their particular difficulties, and testing their progress throughout. In addition, by frequently referring them to the dictionary, it promotes the "dictionary habit."

Although the format remains the same, more varied frames requiring more varied responses have been added, especially in the chapter reviews and tests, and some words have been replaced by others of greater practical value.

Linguistic change has been emphasized by the inclusion of the process of assimilation in several chapters and by the addition of a special list of prefixes and their variant spellings in Chapter 7. Chapter 4 concentrates only on the problems created by the unstressed vowel (the schwa).

New to this edition is an Instructor's Guide, which presents suggestions for teaching spelling, illustrations of word-building and word origins, additional tests (dictation and proofreading), suggestions for teacher-made tests, spelling games and puzzles, and special spelling lists (words in the text plus selective business and legal terms).

In preparing this edition, I am reminded of my indebtedness to the reviewers who painstakingly read the third edition and offered many useful suggestions for change; to the many students and teachers who studied the text and offered cogent comments; and to Nancy Schommer, who made the preparation of the revision and the Instructor's Guide easier by sharing her insights into student perspectives and her firsthand experiences as both a teacher and a student.

**Patricia M. Fergus**

# INTRODUCTION

## THE ENGLISH WRITING SYSTEM

A writing system develops chiefly from attempts to standardize and innovate and from the political and educational movements rather than from the linguistic process itself. The English language has had an interesting development. It was introduced in its earliest form from about the middle of the fifth century by the Angles, Saxons, and tribes from the northern part of Germany. These invaders eventually founded kingdoms of their own, and from the language of these Teutonic settlers developed the national tongue. This Anglo-Saxon period, usually called "the Old English period," extended until about 1100, when "the Middle English period" began, which continued until 1500.

Of the three English periods—Old, Middle, and Modern— the Middle period had the most effect on the writing system as we know it today. There were gradual changes in spelling to correspond better with various sounds. There were sometimes several different developments of phonemes which produced striking inconsistencies in modern English spelling, one of the most interesting yet plaguing being *gh* (*through, rough, caught*).

From the twelfth century until well into the fourteenth, many who wrote in English were extremely proficient in French and brought many of the aspects of the French language into English. For example, they borrowed the French *ou* to replace the English *u* (as in *house* or *found*); they borrowed whole words from the French; and they replaced many English characters with those from the French.

Greek words were also borrowed during this period, and although the Greek alphabet was related historically to the

Latin alphabet, it was different enough to cause some problems. The Greek letters had to be represented by Roman letters, and in this representation decisions had to be made about the original or altered pronunciation and spelling. The familiar silent *p* at the beginning of such words as *psychology* and *pneumonia* or the "f" sound of *ph* in *philosophy* and *sophomore* can be linked to this period of borrowing from the Greek.

In the latter part of the Middle English period Latin loan words remained virtually unchanged, resulting in the addition of more rules to those already in use from Old English and French. An interesting point concerning Latin and French during this period of development is the spelling of several English suffixes. *Able* and *ible,* which often cause spelling difficulties today, were the French spellings from the Latin *abilis* or *ibilis,* the choice of which depended on the stem vowel of the Latin verb. Two other suffixes, *ance* and *ence,* are derived from the Latin verb endings *antem* and *entem,* but they have no relationship to phonological or grammatical systems of English today. Not only do we have problems with suffixes, but we also have silent letters which either have carried over from the Old English period or were put back into words like dou*b*t and de*b*t by scholars who wanted the Latin derivation to be apparent.

The period generally from about 1350 to 1550 is considered the transition from Middle to Modern English, and it is in this stage that we have the Great Vowel Shift. Here the long stressed vowels moved forward in the mouth; for example, the *i* which was pronounced as a long *e* became the I that we know today as the personal pronoun. It was also at this time that the printing houses (printing having been brought into England by William Caxton in the midst of the shift) endeavored to standardize the spelling of many words and conventions, such as the initial and medial use of *i,* the final use of *y,* and the reduction of double consonants, but at the same time tended to retain some of the Middle English spelling. What resulted is obvious today: Some of our biggest problems in spelling are due to the variance between pronunciation and graphic presentation

A few examples will illustrate this variance. Consider *sword* and *two*—the *w,* which earlier represented a semivowel, has ceased to be pronounced, but the letter remains. Or consider *climb* and *dumb*—the *b* is not pronounced, yet the letter remains. The final *e* has varied from period to period, sometimes sounding like an unstressed vowel, sometimes not sounding, appearing at the end of a word because of a printer's whim to fill out a line. Today the diacritic *e* in the final position, although not pronounced, has specific functions: (1) to make the preceding vowel long (tōne, cāke, dīke); (2) to help produce the "v" sound in words like *stove* or *nave;* (3) to help indicate a final "s" sound (pea*ce*) or a final "z" sound (mu*se*).

Research in linguistics has shown that the English lan- guage is more phonetic than we realize (approximately eighty-five percent), and that a number of spelling patterns are predictable. Because the language is quite phonetic and patterns are predictable, we *can* spell correctly. True, some words may stump us for a while, but with so many helpful guides, we should not misspell any words for long.


## REASONS FOR INCORRECT SPELLING

One reason touched on earlier is the variance between pronunciation and graphic presentation. Another is a lack of knowledge about the consistency of the language. For instance, the "s" sound is usually written *s* at the beginning of a word (*s*ad), but *ss* at the end (me*ss*). When followed by *i, e,* or *y, c* nearly always has the "s" sound (*ci*ty, *ce*ll, *cy*cle). When followed by *a, o,* or *u,* it has a "k" sound (*ca*mp, *co*urt, *cu*p), except when combined with *h* to rep- resent *ch* (*ch*urch, *ch*erry, cin*ch*). The "k" sound at the beginning of a word when followed by *i* or *e* is written *k* (*ki*ll, *ke*nnel); at the end it is usually spelled *ck* in a one-syllable word (che*ck*) or in stressed syllables (kni*ck*knack), but *c* in unstressed syllables (atti*c*, traffi*c*). *Q* is always followed by *u* to sound like "kw" (*qu*it, *qu*ack).

And there are other reasons for problems in spelling. Some sounds, like the long a (lābor) can be represented in writing by more than one spelling: *ai* (st*ai*n), *ei* (w*ei*gh), *ay* (d*ay*), or *a* (r*a*diant). Many multisyllabic words have a schwa (unstressed vowel) that can be spelled with different vowels: mandat*o*ry, def*i*nite, ben*e*fit, bott*o*m. The combination of *e* and *i* also causes problems: when is it *ie* and when is it *ei?* Then there are words borrowed from other languages, some still in their native spelling (*kimono, kindergarten, restaurant*). All in all, words can perplex us for many reasons.

But the language is not totally at fault. Frequently we do not know the meanings of words or parts of words. We have poor study habits and we are careless. We mispronounce words, we fail to enunciate clearly, we do not use our eyes and ears to discriminate. We may add or omit syllables. We may even slur vowels, consonants, or syllables. Although most of us have two patterns of oral expression (formal and informal), the choice depending upon circumstances, we must remember that written expression does not have two patterns of spelling correctly. Dr. Samuel Johnson, author of the *Dictionary of the English Language* (1755), aptly described the problem of two pronunciations, one colloquial and cursory, the other regular and solemn: "The cursory pronunciation is always vague and uncertain, being made different in different mouths by negligence, unskilfulness, or affectation. The solemn pronunciation, though by no means immutable and permanent, is yet always less remote from the orthography, and less liable to capricious innovation." We may talk with a close friend (informally) about the failings of "goverment," but when we write to the mayor (formally) we had better discuss the failings of "government."

## NEED FOR CORRECT SPELLING

Fortunately or unfortunately, we can be judged and usually are judged by our ability to spell. High school and college instructors return papers marked with "sp" in the margins, applicants miss job opportunities, and employees miss promotional opportunities. But worse than this, many of us miss opportunities for communication. To properly express ourselves, we need all the tools of language, and spelling is a mighty important tool. It has one primary function: to make reading what we write easier to read. If we write for ourselves, we can spend time deciphering incorrectly spelled words. But if we write for others—and this is what communication is all about—we can press our luck too far. Readers do not want to plow through misspelled words that hinder the flow of thought, and alienation of even one reader is what no writer can afford.

Inasmuch as research indicates that good spellers have a method for spelling, the book presents a five-step method of syllabication as a basis for studying words in the text and for later independent study. It is true that not all people learn by one method, but the multisensory approach offered here is well suited to all: we see the word, listen as we say it, and write it. The approach is visual, auditory, and kinesthetic.

Because a knowledge of word origins and of word-building is important not only in understanding a language but in spelling it, a second purpose is to show the relationship between this knowledge and spelling, and to increase both writing and spelling vocabularies. The size of a text necessarily limits the amount of material, but as many etymological references as possible have been included.

The text is not a panacea for all spelling ills, but for those who misspell words like *occurrence, definite, loneliness,* and *affect,* it offers concrete help to overcome such difficulties. It establishes a solid basis for independent study by making users aware that spelling is a multisensory process, that word origins, word-building, sound, and meaning are all part of learning to spell correctly.

A last purpose is the piquing of the users' curiosity to explore. The English language is a fascinating subject, and the more we delve into origins, patterns, and principles, the more we understand the language. The total fulfillment of this purpose, however, will depend on the extent of the commitment to spell well. It is hoped that the book sufficiently piques the users' curiosity so that learning more about the language becomes an enjoyable and stimulating challenge.

## FEATURES OF THE BOOK

Through the technique of programming, users, at their own pace, apply what they learn by spelling correctly a large number of words in the program plus other words representing similar problems. Special features are:

**1.** The text is a unified instructional system, and owing to the completeness of each chapter, it has an inherent flexibility— users can study the whole program or particular sections only. So as to provide themselves with a method for studying spelling, however, all users should work through Chapters 1 and 2 before proceeding to the rest of the program or any part of it. Because of the many etymological references in the book, it is strongly recommended that users study the entire text to make doubly sure that no misspelled words will appear in any of their written work. Too, seldom does a person have a single area for improvement.

**2.** Reasons for misspelling are emphasized throughout, with users becoming aware (perhaps for the first time) of the roles that sound, word origin, and meaning play in the spelling process.

**3.** Each chapter introduction presents behavioral objectives so that users know exactly what they are to accomplish by the end of the chapter.

**4.** Built into the text is a complete testing program. A diagnostic test pinpoints problems, or potential problems; chapter pretests offer a detailed diagnosis and a basis for comparison with the posttests; reviews, strategically placed for completion of short learning units, allow for immediate testing; chapter posttests indicate immediate progress; tests for Parts One, Two, Three, and Four provide further indication of progress; a final test shows the overall accomplishment. With the exception of those portions of tests requiring the dictionary, answers to all tests are in the appendix.

**5.** Most of the words in the program appear in numerous lists of words commonly misspelled by high school and college students and by adults in business. Inasmuch as a number of them are defined and presented in context, the program builds vocabulary and improves spelling. Of especial importance are the references to the origins of words; these can increase users' knowledge of the English language and also pique their curiosity about language in general.

## TO THE USER

**1.** *Studying the text.*
a. If you have not already done so, read the Preface and the Introduction for a brief overview.
b. Complete the diagnostic test (read the introductory and explanatory material carefully).
c. Regardless of your strengths, you should establish a solid basis for spelling by learning the multisensory approach in Chapters 1 and 2. Once you have completed Part One, continue with the program or appropriate chapters or parts according to the results of the diagnostic test. Wherever you start, take the chapter pretest—if you have 90 percent of the answers correct, you may bypass the chapter. If you work the chapter, complete the posttest to note improvement. The chapters have several reviews, so you may wait one or two days or longer before taking the posttest. Whether you bypass any chapters or not, complete the Part tests and the final examination—you may delay these tests for a better indication of your progress and final accomplishment.
d. Even if you misspell only one or two words on the pretest (and bypass the chapter) and on the posttest, check the index (or the dictionary) and reread the appropriate section in the text.

**2.** *Responding.* As one frame is dependent on another for understanding and progress, you should work carefully and at times slowly. In other words, you must apply what you learn. Several types of frames require different responses, such as filling in letters; discriminating between groups of words; writing of single words, parts of words, or a phrase or two. Even though you can answer some frames quickly with just mental responses, it is better to write the words and "feel" them.

Each frame is numbered and may require more than one response. If dotted lines appear in a frame, write your answer(s) for questions up to those lines and check to see if you are correct—then go to the next part of the same frame. If a frame requires more than one response and does not have dotted lines, answer all parts and then check.

If you have a wrong answer, reread the frame. Do not hesitate about going back over a frame or two—there is no penalty for rereading. If you miss a question or two (or parts of a question) in a review, return to the beginning of that particular unit or to the specific frames pertinent to the wrong answer, and refresh your memory. It may be necessary to reread only a few frames for a better start.

Because the answers are immediately available, it is possible to cheat. However, eyes that wander will not improve your spelling, so cover the answer(s) with a small card ( a 3 by 5 will do), sliding it down as you check the answer(s) for one frame but not revealing the answer(s) for the next frame.

**3.** *Timing.* Each chapter is divided into short units of material with a review for each unit. If time prevents you from finishing a chapter, stop after a review so as not to break the continuity. Otherwise, you may be forced to try picking up where you left off or to return to the beginning and reread.

Because this is programmed material, work as rapidly or as slowly as you wish or as the material demands.

Not all frames are the same length, so do not anticipate finishing the same number in the same length of time. Some requiring discrimination and application take longer than others requiring a letter or a single word.

The "dictionary habit" is a must for efficient spelling, efficient writing, and efficient reading. If you do not already have the habit, you will be introduced to it here because some frames and parts of tests require use of the dictionary. Make a habit of consulting the dictionary to check meanings and pronunciation of words, familiar or unfamiliar.

# DIAGNOSTIC TEST

Proofreading an original composition is undoubtedly the ultimate test of spelling efficiency. Inasmuch as accurate proofreading entails reading words, not necessarily whole thoughts, a list of correctly and incorrectly spelled words can serve as a diagnostic indicator. But remember this: the diagnostic test is simply that, nothing more. There are no passing scores, no levels to attain; there are just words to spell so that existing or potential problems can be identified, treated, and cured.

The best way to take the test is to work quickly but conscientiously. Do not guess or hesitate unduly. Puzzling over any part of a given word means you do not have that word at your fingertips. The test must show all the words you consistently misspell or are apt to misspell.

To provide maximum coverage within a minimum of space and time of all the aspects of spelling covered in this text, ten representative words for each chapter in Parts Two, Three, and Four are included in the test, a total of 150 words. They were selected for their ability to pinpoint areas in which you have a problem or a potential problem. There are no words for Part One, as every user should work through Chapters 1 and 2 to establish a multisensory method for studying spelling.

## DIRECTIONS

Check all the *misspelled* words and write them correctly.

**PART TWO**

1. finally _____
2. hundred _____
3. envirnment _____
4. maintainance _____
5. candidate _____
6. atheletics _____
7. labratory _____
8. pronounciation _____
9. surprise _____
10. mischievious _____
11. comparitive _____
12. benefit _____
13. specimen _____
14. similiar _____
15. familiar _____
16. sophmore _____
17. privilege _____
18. catagory _____
19. grammar _____
20. seperate _____
21. indictment _____
22. corps _____
23. rythm _____
24. subtle _____
25. doubt _____
26. discern _____
27. mortgage _____
28. sychology _____
29. Wensday _____
30. debtor _____
31. existance _____
32. guidance _____
33. criticize _____
34. permanant _____
35. irresistible _____

36. noticable   _____
37. analize   _____
38. desirable   _____
39. eminent   _____
40. licence   _____

**PART THREE**

41. discription   _____
42. unnecessary   _____
43. disolution   _____
44. recommendation   _____
45. dissapoint   _____
46. collection   _____
47. comence   _____
48. persuade   _____
49. accumulate   _____
50. dispise   _____
51. recede   _____
52. excede   _____
53. succede   _____
54. supersede   _____
55. intersede   _____
56. antecede   _____
57. conceed   _____
58. procede   _____
59. cede   _____
60. precede   _____
61. lead (past tense of lead)   _____
62. council (group of people)   _____
63. later (second of two things mentioned)   _____
64. complement (praise)   _____
65. waiver (relinquishment of a right)   _____
66. grate (to scrape)   _____
67. stationery (not movable)   _____
68. discreet (prudent)   _____

69. breath (inhale and exhale) _____

70. principle (head or chief) _____

71. morale (well-being) _____

72. advice (to counsel) _____

73. discus (talk over) _____

74. affect (result) _____

75. allusion (reference) _____

76. loose (to misplace) _____

77. adverse (hostile) _____

78. adept (skilled) _____

79. angle (supernatural being) _____

80. human (compassionate) _____

**PART FOUR**

81. foriegner _____

82. belief _____

83. counterfeit _____

84. seize _____

85. seige _____

86. ancient _____

87. wierd _____

88. handkerchief _____

89. deceit _____

90. freindship _____

91. preferred _____

92. rebutal _____

93. batting _____

94. admittance _____

95. occurence _____

96. begining _____

97. cannery _____

98. benefitted _____

99. profiting _____

100. stoper _____

101. excitement _____

102. coming _____

103. disciplinary _____

104. adequatly _____

105. desireous _____

106. losing _____

107. writting _____

108. singeing (burning) _____

109. shiney _____

110. advising _____

111. occupying _____

112. business _____

113. replys _____

114. disobeying _____

115. buoyant _____

116. certifyable _____

117. accompaning _____

118. dutyful _____

119. happiness _____

120. studing _____

121. boisterous _____

122. truely _____

123. immediatly _____

124. murderous _____

125. copeous _____

126. tortuous (twisting) _____

127. sincerly _____

128. surely _____

129. wholely _____

130. grievious _____

131. calfs _____

132. Negros _____

133. heros _____

134. pennies _____

135. batterys _____

136. elfs _____

137. criteria _____

138. rodeos _____

139. potatoes _____

140. crisis (plural form) _____

141. dont (contraction) _____

142. youre (contraction) _____

143. friends' (possessive plural) _____

144. Diller and Dollar's store (joint ownership) _____

145. Jackie's and Mabel's reports (single ownership) _____

146. its (contraction) _____

147. church's (possessive singular) _____

148. princesses' (possessive plural) _____

149. mans' (possessive singular) _____

150. womens' _____

Now that you have completed the test, compare your answers with the key in the appendix, checking (√) the wrong answers. Your total score will show how well you did overall. For example, if you missed 75 out of 150, you had 50 percent wrong (and 50 percent right); if you missed 50 out of 150, you had 33 percent wrong (and 66 percent right).

Once you have this score, total the words missed for each chapter according to the chart below.

**PART TWO   SOUND AND SPELLING**

| ITEMS | NO. MISSED | CHAPTER | PROBLEM AREA |
|-------|-----------|---------|--------------|
| 1–10 | _____ | 3 | Pronunciation and Enunciation |
| 11–20 | _____ | 4 | The Unstressed Vowel |
| 21–30 | _____ | 5 | "Silent" Letters |
| 31–40 | _____ | 6 | Sound-Alike Suffixes |
| Total | _____ | | |

**PART THREE   MEANING AND SPELLING**

| | | | |
|-------|-----------|---------|--------------|
| 41–50 | _____ | 7 | Prefixes |
| 51–60 | _____ | 8 | "Seed" Roots |
| 61–70 | _____ | 9 | Homonyms |
| 71–80 | _____ | 10 | Similar Words |
| Total | _____ | | |

## PART FOUR   RULES AND SPELLING

| ITEMS | NO. MISSED | CHAPTER | PROBLEM AREA |
|-------|-----------|---------|--------------|
| 81–90 | _____ | 11 | *IE-EI* |
| 91–100 | _____ | 12 | Doubling the Final Consonant |
| 101–110 | _____ | 13 | The Final *E* |
| 111–120 | _____ | 14 | The Final *Y* |
| 121–130 | _____ | 15 | *Ly* and *Ous* |
| 131–140 | _____ | 16 | Plurals |
| 141–150 | _____ | 17 | The Apostrophe |
| Total | _____ | | |

**ALL PARTS TOTAL**   _____

Below is a sample tally for Part Two of one user's diagnostic test.

| ITEMS | NO. MISSED | CHAPTER | PROBLEM AREA |
|-------|-----------|---------|--------------|
| 1–10 | 6 | 3 | Pronunciation and Enunciation |
| 11–20 | 5 | 4 | The Unstressed Vowel |
| 21–30 | 2 | 5 | "Silent" Letters |
| 31–40 | 4 | 6 | Sound-Alike Suffixes |
| Total | 17 | | |

Out of 40 words this user missed 17 or approximately 43 percent—not too bad, but if you look at Items 1 to 20, you will notice 11 errors, or over half. Here are the user's weaknesses. However, he or she missed 4 out of 10 in Items 31 to 40, slightly less than 50 percent, so this category also constitutes a weakness. All told, this user needs special work on pronunciation and enunciation (Chapter 3), the unstressed vowel (Chapter 4), and sound-alike suffixes (Chapter 6). There were only two errors in Items 21 to 30, so the user has some strength in "silent" letters (Chapter 5).

Now that you have all your scores (total, parts, and chapters), you have an excellent profile of your strengths and weaknesses. You know the areas where you can improve your spelling performance, and whether your strengths and weaknesses are in sound and spelling, meaning and spelling, or rules and spelling.

From here proceed to Part One and complete Chapters 1 and 2; then you may proceed to the rest of the program in order (Chapters 3 through 17), or start with those chapters for which you have the greatest number of errors as indicated by your scores, working down to those with the least errors. Wherever you start, take the chapter pretest, study the chapter conscientiously, and take the posttest.

*Remember, you can improve your spelling! Many other hundreds of persons have done just that!*

# PART ONE

## A MULTISENSORY APPROACH TO SPELLING

# CHAPTER ONE
## GUIDELINES FOR SYLLABICATION

To be correctly spelled, some words seem to defy rules, pronunciation guides, or meaning guides, and about the only way to master them is to divide them into syllables. This does not mean that only these words should be syllabified; on the contrary, syllabication is a good basis for spelling many words, particularly unfamiliar ones.

Of the several methods of syllabication the one presented here is a graphic presentation, not a phonetic one. Not that sound is unimportant. Indeed it is, but to give you a phonetic system without being able to assume that you have studied linguistics would be assuming too much.

The graphic system does take pronunciation and the various characteristics of the English language into account, and because it demands some knowledge of vowel sounds, stress, and the components of words, this chapter will present the basic material as concisely as possible. You will become familiar with long and short sounds of vowels, semivowels, diphthongs, and the stress in syllables. Further, you will apply specific guidelines in the dividing of words of two or more syllables. By the end of the chapter you will confidently divide a word into its parts.

One last word: these guidelines are simply that. They are not hard and fast rules, but aids. They will, however, help you to spell correctly and to follow the syllabication in any standard dictionary. If you already know about vowels, consonants, diphthongs, stress, and the like, you can begin with frame 13. If you are unfamiliar with this material, or if you want a short refresher, start at the beginning of the chapter.

## PRETEST

Divide these words into syllables. To indicate the separation between syllables, leave a space in between: con   fer   ence

1. necessary     _____
2. manufacture     _____
3. vowel     _____
4. accommodate     _____
5. carpenter     _____
6. rapid     _____
7. consideration     _____
8. antipathy     _____
9. geology     _____
10. rubble     _____
11. reference     _____
12. accumulate     _____
13. delude     _____
14. pilot     _____
15. sophomore     _____
16. antibody     _____
17. consonant     _____
18. appearance     _____
19. tribulation     _____
20. rivalry     _____

a. C
b. C
c. C
d. S
e. S
f. V
g. C
h. V

**1.** Of the twenty-six letters of the English alphabet five can be classed as vowels, three as semivowels, and the rest as consonants. The vowel sounds are represented by the letters *a, e, i, o, u;* the semivowels by *w, h, y;* and the consonants by the other letters, like *b, c, d, g, s.*
Indicate by V, S, or C whether the following letters represent vowels, semivowels, or consonants.

a. s_____    c. b_____    e. h_____    g. x_____
b. p_____    d. w_____    f. e_____    h. a_____

*i   o   u*

**2.** In the preceding frame you checked *a* and *e* as vowels. You were correct. Name the other three: _____

*y*

**3.** You checked *w* and *h* as semivowels, and again you were correct. What is the third semivowel? _____

*a   e   i   o   u*
*w   h   y*

**4.** List all the vowels and semivowels: _____
_____.

b.  d.  e.  g.  h.

**5.** Identify the consonants.

a. a_____    c. u_____    e. b_____    g. f_____
b. g_____    d. s_____    f. h_____    h. k_____

A.
· · · · · · · · · · · · ·
yes

**6.** For the vowels there are long and short sounds and diphthongs. The long sounds are usually higher, longer, and tenser than the short sounds. Pronounce these words: *bite* and *bit.* Yes, the *i* in *bite* is higher, longer, and tenser than the *i* in *bit,* so it is the long sound. Since the *i* in *bit* is not nearly as long, high, or tense, it is the short sound. Diphthongs are speech sounds moving from one vowel to another vowel or to a semivowel within the same syllable. Take the words *boil* and *toy.* Pronounce them slowly—the vowels *oi* and the vowel *o* and semivowel *y* blend together. Pronounce these two groups of words, then answer this question: Which group has the long sound of the vowels? _____

| A. | B. |
|----|----|
| Pete | bit |
| rate | top |
| beet | met |
| proof | hat |
| stone | but |
| night | knit |
| rude | rut |

· · · · · · · · · · · · · · · · · · · · · · · · · · · · · · · · · · · · · · · ·

Do the underlined portions in these words qualify as diphthongs? _____

spout        plow

a. S
b. L
c. D
d. L
e. D
f. S

**7.** Now identify whether the underlined portions are long or short vowels, or diphthongs. Use L, S, or D as indicators.

a. bitter        _____        d. frame        _____

b. key        _____        e. pout        _____

c. boil        _____        f. butter        _____

a. L
b. D
c. L
d. L
e. L
f. D
g. L
h. D

**8.** Sometimes two vowel letters result in a long vowel sound. To distinguish between the long vowel and the diphthong remember that a long sound is *one* sound, whereas a diphthong is a *movement* from one vowel sound to another or to a semivowel. Here are two words: *freight* and *mate.* Both have the long *a* sound. In the first, two vowels (*ei*) constitute the single sound; in the second, the single vowel *a.* In the words *toil* (two vowels) or *boy* (vowel and semivowel) you have diphthongs, as there is a movement from *o* to *i* and from *o* to *y.*
Pronounce each word below, then identify whether the underlined portion is a long sound (L) or a diphthong (D).

a. believe        _____        e. meat        _____

b. boisterous        _____        f. poise        _____

c. boat        _____        g. main        _____

d. reindeer        _____        h. plow        _____

b. V
c. C
d. V
e. D
f. V
g. C
h. D

long *e*
suffix (or ending)

a. 2
b. 3
c. 1
d. 2
e. 2
f. 5
g. 1
h. 3
i. 2

**9.** The *semi* in *semivowel* suggests that semivowels are and they are not vowels. This is correct because in most systems of classification *w, h,* and *y* are included with the consonants but are acknowledged as being capable of producing vowel sounds. As consonants they precede vowels, as in *way, you,* and *he*; as vowels they usually follow a simple vowel to help make a long vowel sound (*tow*) or a diphthong (*ploy*). The *y* can also be a full vowel with the long sound of *e*. If you pronounce *skinny* or *clammy,* you will hear the long *e* sound of *y*; its function, of course, is to serve as a suffix (or ending).

Now check which sound the underlined portions produce: C (consonant), V (vowel), and D (diphthong).

a. hoe _____    e. boy _____

b. lawyer _____    f. they _____

c. wide _____    g. yea _____

d. low _____    h. cow _____

**10.** Now pronounce these words:

gossipy    chunky    happy

What sound does the *y* have? _____
What is the function of the *y*? _____

**11.** There are several technical ways to define a syllable and its components, but suffice it to say that a syllable is the smallest phonological construction and usually consists of a pronounced vowel or diphthong or either one or more vowels with one or more consonants. Let us also say that a syllable can form a complete word or is part of a larger word. For instance, the word *bat* has one pronounced vowel (*a*) which is preceded by and followed by one consonant (*b* and *t*). The sounds produce just one syllable, in this case a complete word. Often such a word is called a one-syllable word. Now take the word *plow*—it has a diphthong instead of a single vowel—but together with the consonants *pl* it forms one syllable, and again a complete word.

If you add a suffix to a word, like *er* to *bat,* you get *batter.* Here you have two pronounced vowels (*a* and *e*) forming two syllables: bat ter. Root words, those words without any additions (prefixes or suffixes), can have more than one syllable, for example: *garden, loiter, establish.* In each word you have several pronounced vowels or diphthongs: gar den loi ter es tab lish. Sometimes a consonant can form a syllable without a vowel (called a syllabic consonant). Pronounce these words: *riddle, bottle.* Each has two syllables *rid dle bot tle,* with the second syllable having just an "l" sound.

In summing up, we can say that a syllable consists of either a vowel or a diphthong alone, a syllabic consonant, or either one or the other with one or more consonants. Now say the following words carefully, looking at and hearing the vowels. Then indicate the number of syllables in each.

a. summer _____    f. considerable _____

b. consonant _____    g. coat _____

c. hoe _____    h. disapprove _____

d. vowel _____    i. battle _____

e. shepherd _____

a. clámmy
b. repel´
c. none
d. accómmodáte
e. páddle
f. cońsonant
g. presefve
h. none

**12.** One last point to consider before studying the guidelines is the stress. Stress (or accent) is the prominence which develops from pronouncing one or more syllables more strongly than the other(s). One-syllable words have no stress, so let us turn to multisyllabic words. *Garden,* for instance, has two syllables and in pronouncing it you stress the first syllable: gaŕ den. In *establish* you stress the second: es taɓ lish. In the word *consideration,* however, you have more than one stress, resulting in what we call "major" ( ´ ) and "minor" ( ´ ) stress: con sid er á tion. But remember, there is never more than one major stress in a word.

Now indicate the stress or stresses in these words. Use the same marks shown above: the bold mark for major, a similar but lighter mark for minor. If the word has no accent, indicate "none."

a. clammy _____    e. paddle _____

b. repel _____    f. consonant _____

c. course _____    g. preserve _____

d. accommodate _____    h. club _____

a. vowels
b. long
c. is

**13.** Now we are ready for the guidelines. If a single consonant comes between two vowels, the first of which has a *long* sound and is *accented,* the consonant will usually go with the *second* vowel. Look at and pronounce *pilot.* The single consonant *l* comes between two vowels *i* and *o.* The first vowel has the long sound of *i* and carries the stress (pí lot). The consonant *l* will therefore go with the second vowel: pi lot.

Now pronounce the word *garden.* It has the stress on the first vowel, but between the two vowels (*a* and *e*) come two consonants (*r* and *d*). We cannot apply this guideline to this word. How about *money*? Again we have two vowels (*o* and *e*) and a single consonant (*n*) between the two vowels, but the first vowel (*o*) does not have the long sound. So this word cannot be divided like pilot. To divide words like pilot, we must look for these requirements:

a. It must have a single consonant between two _____.

b. The first vowel must have a (long, short) sound. _____

c. The first vowel (is, is not) stressed. _____

a. no
b. yes
c. no
d. yes
e. no
f. no

**14.** For each two-syllable word below, write yes or no to indicate whether it would be divided like pilot.

a. compel _____          d. local _____

b. native _____          e. rusty _____

c. dollar _____          f. palace _____

a. 1 and 2
b. 1 and 3
c. 1 and 3
d. 3

**15.** *Native* and *local* are syllabified like pilot, as they meet all the requirements. For the rest of the words in the above list, write the number of the reason(s) for their not meeting the requirements.

(1) two consonants between two vowels

(2) stress on second syllable

(3) short sound of first vowel

(4) a vowel between two consonants

a. compel _____          c. rusty _____

b. dollar _____          d. palace _____

a. fi  nal
b. na  tive
c. lo  cal
d. ri  val
e. fa  vor

**16.** Now divide these words into syllables, leaving a space to indicate the separation: pi lot.

a. final _____          d. rival _____

b. native _____          e. favor _____

c. local _____

do

**17.** We are ready for the second guideline: when a consonant comes between vowels, the first of which is *short* and *accented,* the consonant will usually go with the *first* vowel. *Modest* is a good example. The *d* comes between the *o* and *e*, the first vowel has a short sound of *o* and is accented, so the *d* goes with the first vowel (*o*) to form the first syllable: mod est. Pronounce these words:

palace        solid        ravel        tepid

They (do, do not) meet this guideline. _____

a. pal  ace
b. sol  id
c. rav  el
d. tep  id

a. ro  bust
b. rap  id
c. ten  or
d. me  ter
e. mon  ey
f. pu  pil
g. bo  nus
h. del  uge

a. pot  ter
b. jag  ged
c. pon  der
d. gos  sip
e. med  dle
f. hur  tle
g. car  pet
h. gin  ger

a. pre  fer
b. dis  miss
c. pro  ceed
d. dis  ap  pear
e. per  form
f. an  tith  e  sis

**18.** Now divide the following into syllables.

a. palace  _____     c. ravel  _____

b. solid  _____      d. tepid  _____

**19.** Test your skill by applying the guidelines presented thus far to these words.

a. robust  _____     e. money  _____

b. rapid  _____      f. pupil  _____

c. tenor  _____      g. bonus  _____

d. meter  _____      h. deluge  _____

**20.** Here is the third guideline: if a word has two consonants between two vowels, you usually divide between the consonants. For instance, in *garden* the *rd* comes between *a* and *e*. To divide you would separate the *r* and *d*: gar den. If a word ends in *le* the consonant preceding the *le* usually combines with the *le* to form a syllable. Take the word *turtle*. It ends in *le,* so the consonant immediately preceding it (*t*) goes with the *le* to form the second syllable: tur *tle.*
Keeping these guidelines in mind, divide the following:

a. potter  _____     e. meddle  _____

b. jagged  _____     f. hurtle  _____

c. ponder  _____     g. carpet  _____

d. gossip  _____     h. ginger  _____

**21.** As far as possible try to syllabify a word according to its structure, but always keep the pronunciation in mind. If the word contains a prefix (an element added to the beginning of a word), and this prefix sounds out a syllable, separate it from the root word: *dis* approve, *re* fer. Let us look at these words: *misspell, disappoint, antibody.* Each has a prefix (*mis, dis, anti*), so it can be separated from the root. But there is a difference: *mis* and *dis* have one syllable and *anti* has two. The proper syllabication then would be *mis* spell, *dis* ap point, *an ti* bod *y.* Here is another *anti: antipathy.* The prefix in this word is not pronounced the same as in *antibody,* so in *antipathy* the pronunciation must be followed for syllabication:

an  ti  bod  y        but        an  tip  a  thy

Say the following words aloud, then syllabify them.

a. prefer  _____     d. disappear  _____

b. dismiss  _____    e. perform  _____

c. proceed  _____    f. antithesis  _____

a. *ly*
b. *ness*
c. *ful   ness*
d. *y*
e. *ence*

**22.** You should also be able to distinguish suffixes (elements at the end of words) from the roots. For instance, *helpful, entirely,* and *consolable* each have a suffix: *ful, ly,* and *able.* Again we have two (*ful* and *ly*) that have one syllable each, and *able* that has two.

For the following words identify the suffix in each word. Remember that words can have more than one suffix.

a. happily _____    d. grumpy _____

b. trueness _____    e. existence _____

c. helpfulness _____

a. hap   pi   ly
b. true   ness
c. help   ful   ness
d. grum   py
e. ex   is   tence

**23.** Let us take the same words in frame 22 to syllabify. You have identified the suffixes, so now, remembering your guidelines, pronounce the words carefully and write the syllables.

a. happily _____    d. grumpy _____

b. trueness _____    e. existence _____

c. helpfulness _____

There are 2 conso-
nants (*st*) between 2
vowels (*i* and *e*).

**24.** Even though *existence* has a suffix (*ence*), why do you divide between the *st* for the second and third syllables?

_____

**REVIEW**

a. del   uge
b. stu   pid
c. por   tal
d. dou   ble
e. de   lude
f. pos   ture
g. re   vise
h. doubt   ful
i. stum   ble
j. hub   bub
k. jum   bo

**25.** Test your skill by dividing these words into syllables. Remember that pronunciation and stress are important.

a. deluge _____

b. stupid _____

c. portal _____

d. double _____

e. delude _____

f. posture _____

g. revise _____

h. doubtful _____

i. stumble _____

j. hubbub _____

k. jumbo _____

second

**26.** When a single consonant comes between two vowels, the first of which is long and accented (local), the consonant usually goes with the (first, second) vowel. _____

first

**27.** When a single consonant comes between two vowels, the first of which is short and accented (palace), the consonant usually goes with the (first, second) vowel. _____

*le*

**28.** If a word ends in *le,* the consonant preceding it goes with the _____ to form a syllable.

between

**29.** If two consonants come between two vowels, you usually divide _____ the consonants.

ac com mo date
accommodate

**30.** Before we work on longer words, a brief note on the process of assimilation (the modification of a sound to make it resemble an adjacent sound) is in order. Three words will illustrate: *appear, attend, annul.* The beginning of each word is really the prefix *ad,* but the sound of the *d* has been replaced by the sound of the letter in the beginning of the root: ad pear = *ap*pear; ad tend = *at*tend; ad nul = *an*nul. If you pronounce these words with the original prefix (*ad*) distinctly, you will have to do it slowly; if you say them quickly, you will notice how the *d* slides into the sound of the next letter, making the words much easier to say.

Our first longer word, *accommodate,* is an excellent example of assimilation; in fact, two prefixes precede the root, *ad* and *con,* which become ac com modate. The last part of the word can easily be divided according to the guidelines: mo date. Write the full syllabication of this word and then write it from memory: _____

_____.

3
first
soph o more

**31.** The word *sophomore* is also a good word to syllabify. How many pronounced vowels has it? _____ Coming as it does from the Greek, the *ph* sounds like the single letter *f*. Does the *ph* go with the first or second vowel? _____ Now divide the word into syllables. _____

sophomore

**32.** A second-year student in college is a so_____.

accommodate
sophomores

**33.** The new dormitory could not _____date any s_____s.

a. per  fec  tion
b. com  mit  tee
c. prep  a  ra  tion
d. ar  gu  ment
e. suc  ces  sion
f. spec  i  men

**34.** Here are some multisyllabic words to divide. Pronounce them carefully and then apply the guidelines.

a. perfection  _____
b. committee  _____
c. preparation  _____
d. argument  _____
e. succession  _____
f. specimen  _____

a. car  pen  ter
b. es  tab  lish  ment
c. lib  er  al
d. ac  cu  mu  late
e. sup  pli  cate
f. nec  es  sar  y
g. in  ef  fec  tive

**35.** Below is a list of questions to remind you of the guidelines for syllabication.

Is there a vowel between two consonants?
Is the first vowel long or short?
Are there two consonants between two vowels?
Is there a prefix or suffix in the word?
Does the word end in *le*?

Using these questions as reminders, divide the following words.
Don't forget to pronounce them.

a. carpenter  _____
b. establishment  _____
c. liberal  _____
d. accumulate  _____
e. supplicate  _____
f. necessary  _____
g. ineffective  _____

## POSTTEST

Divide these words into syllables. To indicate the separation, leave a space in between: gar  den  er.

1. controversy  _____
2. restaurant  _____
3. recurrence  _____
4. precede  _____
5. disappointment  _____
6. tremendous  _____
7. unnecessary  _____
8. description  _____
9. opportunity  _____
10. advantageous  _____

11. incidental  _____
12. documentary  _____
13. knowledge  _____
14. Wednesday  _____
15. psychology  _____
16. ridiculous  _____
17. achievement  _____
18. forgotten  _____
19. government  _____
20. procedure  _____

# CHAPTER TWO
## A FIVE-STEP METHOD FOR SPELLING

You have mastered the guidelines for syllabication, and are now ready to divide a number of words that are frequently misspelled. In doing so, you will learn a five-step method which will not only help you to spell the words in the chapter correctly, but will also give you a basis for tackling harder words later on. By the end of the chapter you will (1) use this multisensory method in spelling specific words; (2) recognize what elements to look and listen for; (3) spell many words in and out of context; and (4) reproduce words from definition clues.

**PRETEST**

Fill in the missing letters. Meanings are given to help you identify words.

1. in_____est                 concern, curiosity
2. embar_____                 make ill at ease
3. ir_____vant                not related
4. ser_____                   noncommissioned rank in Army
5. vil_____                    scoundrel
6. expe_____                   knowledge, skill
7. ac_____                     get possession of
8. im_____ately               right now
9. dis_____faction            displeasure
10. vac_____                   cleaning appliance
11. ap_____ent                readily seen or understood
12. con_____ience             comfort
13. pro____dure                  method of proceeding

14. oc_____ally     from time to time

15. disap_____     not come up to expectations

16. lon____ness     dejection and sadness

17. op_____nity     occasion

18. fin____cier     expert in finance

19. discrim____ation     prejudice

20. par____el     going same direction

21. ac_____late     amass, gather

22. disap_____     vanish

23. inter_____     break between

24. res_____     eating place

25. ap_____ciate     recognize, become aware of

26. ac_____ance     someone you know slightly

27. ex_____ation     act of explaining

28. ac_____plishment     act of succeeding

29. pos_____sion     ownership

a. both
yes
• • • • • • • • • • • • •
b. 4
4
short
• • • • • • • • • • • •
c. ac   com   plish
ment
d. accomplishment
• • • • • • • • • • • • •
e. accomplishment

**1.** Several words have what is called the "double consonant" difficulty: sometimes an extra consonant is added, other times a consonant is omitted. We shall eliminate the problem by establishing a procedure for dividing words into syllables.

(1) Look at the word carefully (look for familiar roots, prefixes, suffixes, double letters, and the like).

(2) Say the word distinctly and correctly. If you are not sure about the pronunciation, check the dictionary. Look for pronounced vowels as a guide to the number of syllables.

(3) Sound the word in syllables and then write it.

(4) Write the word from memory and check for the correct spelling.

(5) Use it in sentences. Be sure you know what the word means.

a. Now take the word *accomplishment*. Look at it carefully. Do you find a prefix or a suffix or both? _____
Do you find a double consonant? _____
• • • • • • • • • • • • • • • • • • • • • • • • • • • • • • • • • • • • • •

b. Now pronounce it. How many pronounced vowels does it have? _____ How many syllables are there? _____ Does the second syllable have a short or long sound of *o*? _____
. . . . . . . . . . . . . . . . . . . . . . . . . . . . . . . . . . . . . . . . . . . . .

c. Mentally sound the word as you write it in syllables:

_____ _____ _____ _____.

d. Write it quickly from memory:

_____.
. . . . . . . . . . . . . . . . . . . . . . . . . . . . . . . . . . . . . . . . . . . . .

e. Use it in one or more sentences. The professor told me that my reaching the quota was quite an _____

_____.

look
say (pronounce)
in syllables
in sentences

**2.** To review the procedure: you first _____ at the word carefully, then _____ it distinctly, sound out and write the word (as a whole, in syllables) _____, write it from memory and check the spelling, and finally use it (in phrases, in sentences) _____.

4
ac  cu  mu  late

**3.** Here is the second word, *accumulate,* which means to amass or gather. Perform the first two steps on your own. How many syllables are there? _____ What are they? _____

accumulate

**4.** Write the word from memory: _____.

a. accumulate
b. accumulate

**5.** Now use it in context:

a. Jane's father exclaimed, "How many books did you _____ in a year!"

b. This house can _____ more dust than any other I've known.

ap  pre  ci  ate

**6.** The next four words also have a double consonant difficulty. The first is *appreciate.* In mastering the spelling of this word, you first look at it carefully, pronounce it distinctly, and then divide it into syllables: _____

_____.

appreciate

**7.** The word which means to estimate the value of something or to fully realize a situation is _____.

appreciate
appreciate

**8.** Even though I haven't been poverty-stricken, I think I can _____ the dire problems involved.
                              realize
    Professors _____ the efforts of their
                          value
students.

3
*p*
• • • • • • • • • • • • • •
ap   par   ent
apparent

apparent
apparent
apparent

*c*
oc   ca   sion   al   ly

occasionally
occasionally
occasionally

op   por   tu   ni   ty

a. opportunity
b. opportunity

occasional*ly*

a. accumulate
b. occasionally
c. appreciate
d. accomplishment
e. opportunity
f. apparent

**9.** On your own perform the first two steps with the word *apparent.* It has _____ syllables and a double conso- nant _____ near the beginning of the word.
• • • • • • • • • • • • • • • • • • • • • • • • • • • • • • • • • • • •
Perform the third step: _____.
And now the fourth: _____.

**10.** To be readily understood is the definition of the word
_____.
That he has a mastery of his subject is _____.
Are my feelings about religion that _____?

**11.** Look carefully at the adverb *occasionally.* It has only one *s* but it has two _____'s.
Now divide it into syllables: _____.

**12.** Write it quickly from memory: _____.
Now use it in these sentences:
I go to the theater _____.
Will you accompany me _____ to the symphony concerts?

**13.** Here is the word *opportunity.* Look at it . . . pronounce it . . . and remembering the guidelines for a long and short vowel, divide it into syllables: _____
_____.

**14.** Combine the fourth and fifth steps:
a. The noun that means a suitable occasion or time is
_____.
b. Will we ever have an _____ to meet the famous pitcher?

**15.** Fill in the missing letters: oc__asional_____.

**REVIEW**

**16.** From the meaning clues supply the appropriate words you have just studied.
a. The verb meaning to amass is _____.
b. We used to drive to the ranch every Sunday; now we go only _____.
c. No matter what the outcome is, I do _____
value
your efforts to promote the campaign.

d. After reviewing Jim's work in art history, the instructor said, "That's quite an _____!"

successful completion

e. I've never had the _____ to attend

occasion

a drama festival.

f. She made her intentions quite _____.

readily understood

first
4
dis sat is fac tion

**17.** Here are four words with the same beginning, the prefix *dis*. Remember that a prefix is a separate unit, so the addition of a prefix usually does not disturb the word or the prefix. The noun *dissatisfaction* is simply the combination of *satisfaction* and *dis* (meaning not), so the whole word means a state of not being satisfied, or displeasure. Look at the word carefully and then pronounce it.

Which syllable is the prefix? _____
How many other syllables are there? _____
Write the word in syllables: _____.

a. dissatisfaction
b. dissatisfaction

**18.** Use the word in these contexts:

a. To have a feeling of displeasure is to have one of

_____.

b. Mr. Brown registered his _____ by shouting at the delegate.

dissatisfaction

**19.** The new wage proposals caused the most _____ _____ among the lowest paid drivers.

prefix
crim i na tion

**20.** Perform the first two steps for this word: *discrimination*. *Dis* is a (prefix, suffix) _____. Now divide the rest of the word into syllables, watching your vowel sounds:

_____.

discrimination

**21.** This word has two common meanings. The first is an act of prejudice: There is too much _____ between the races and sexes.

discrimination

**22.** Another meaning is the ability to see fine distinctions: In his reviews of operatic performances, Mr. Bucher shows a keen _____.

dis
p

**23.** *Disappoint* and *disappear* have two similarities: both have the prefix _____ and both have a double _____ in the root.

dis  ap  point
dis  ap  pear

**24.** Now pronounce the words and separate each into syllables: _____
_____.

a. disappear
b. disappoint
c. disappoint
d. disappear

**25.** Read the sentences and write the correct one of these two words for each.

a. Perhaps I can catch them before they _____ from sight.

b. If you don't go with me, you will _____ me.

c. When students do not work hard, they often _____ _____ their teachers.

d. In time the trumpeter swan may _____.

im  me  di  ate  ly

**26.** The next group of words also has double consonant difficulties. The first is *immediately*. Perform the first two steps . . . now divide it into syllables: _____
_____.

immediately

**27.** To respond without hesitation or delay is to answer _____.

immediately

**28.** The children were trained to reply _____.

3
s

**29.** The second word in this group is *possession*. Look . . . pronounce . . . how many syllables does the word have? _ There are two sets of __'s.

pos  ses  sion

**30.** Now divide it: _____.

possessions

**31.** A few clothes and a toothbrush comprise his worldly _____.

possession

**32.** There is an old saying that _____
ownership
is nine-tenths of the law.

yes
l
par  al  lel

**33.** Perform the initial steps for this word: *parallel.*

Does it have a double letter? _____
What is it? _____
What are the syllables? _____

second  third

**34.** One of the double letters completes the _____ syllable and the second begins the _____ syllable.

*II*

parallel

em bar rass

embarrass

embarrass

a. dissatisfaction
b. disappear
c. parallel
d. possession
e. discrimination
f. immediately
g. embarrass
h. disappoint

**35.** The two *l*'s standing so nicely together match the geometric definition of the word: two (or more) straight lines that do not intersect. Look for the straight lines in para_____ el.

**36.** This word also means having comparable parts: The construction of the two sentences is _____.

**37.** The word *embarrass* can best be spelled correctly by dividing it into syllables. But first look at it . . . then pronounce it : . . and now divide it: _____.

**38.** To cause someone to be ill at ease or to hamper with financial difficulties are definitions of the word _____
_____.

**39.** Jack's intention was to _____ the assembly.

**REVIEW**

**40.** From the clues presented in each sentence, write the correct word for each.

a. Reverend Dunn showed his _____
                                                        displeasure
with the program by closing the hall.

b. The minute I suggest their doing the dishes, they _____.
              vanish

c. Your red dots are not _____.
                                        comparable

d. How many appliances do you have in your pos_____
_____?

e. Now there are laws against _____.
                                            prejudice

f. May I return the book tomorrow or do you want it _____?
              right now

g. I was afraid to tell her because I might _____
                                                              put ill at ease
her.

h. I surely hope Mrs. Brown doesn't _____
                                                            fail to meet expectations
me.

first
1
2
ac quire
ac quain tance

**41.** Two words often misspelled have the same beginning: *acquire* and *acquaintance.* The misspelling is caused partly by poor pronunciation and partly by not studying the word. Perform the first two steps on your own.

Since *ac* is the prefix, it is the ⎯⎯⎯⎯⎯ syllable in each word.

How many syllables are left in acquire? ⎯⎯⎯ in acquaint-ance? ⎯⎯⎯

Now syllabify the two words: ⎯⎯⎯⎯⎯⎯⎯⎯⎯⎯⎯⎯ and ⎯⎯⎯⎯⎯⎯⎯⎯⎯⎯⎯⎯⎯⎯⎯⎯.

acquire

**42.** If Mr. Hancock wants to get possession of 10 percent of his company's stock, he wants to ⎯⎯⎯⎯⎯⎯⎯it.

acquaintance

**43.** A person you know less intimately than a friend is called an ⎯⎯⎯⎯⎯⎯⎯⎯⎯⎯.

a. acquire
b. acquaintance
c. acquaintances
d. acquire

**44.** Write the correct word of these two in the following sentences.

a. Randy wants to ⎯⎯⎯⎯⎯⎯⎯⎯⎯⎯⎯⎯two lakeshore lots.

b. Jack is not a friend; he is only an ⎯⎯⎯⎯⎯⎯⎯⎯.

c. Most people have quite a few ⎯⎯⎯⎯⎯⎯⎯⎯.

d. Tom has worked hard to ⎯⎯⎯⎯⎯⎯all his trophies.

prefix (or *ir*)
3
(ir) rel e vant

**45.** Perform the first two steps for *irrelevant* (*ir* is a variant of the prefix *in,* meaning not).

What constitutes the first syllable? ⎯⎯⎯⎯⎯⎯
How many more syllables are there? ⎯⎯⎯
What are they? ⎯⎯⎯⎯⎯⎯⎯⎯⎯

irrelevant

**46.** Write the word from memory: ⎯⎯⎯⎯⎯⎯⎯⎯⎯.

irrelevant

**47.** That which has no bearing on a particular case is ⎯⎯⎯⎯⎯⎯⎯⎯.

irrelevant

**48.** The teacher commented that some of my evidence was ⎯⎯⎯⎯⎯⎯⎯⎯.

2
I
r
in ter rupt

**49.** The word *interrupt* is derived from the Latin *inter,* meaning between, and *rumpere,* to break. Look at and pronounce the word carefully.

How many syllables does the prefix have? ⎯⎯⎯
How many remaining syllables are there? ⎯⎯⎯
What letter ends the prefix and also begins the root? ⎯⎯⎯
Write the syllables: ⎯⎯⎯⎯⎯⎯⎯⎯⎯⎯⎯.

interrupt

**50.** The word meaning to stop or break the continuity of is

_____.

interrupt

**51.** If you "break between" two persons carrying on a conversation, you will _____ them.

interrupt
irrelevant

**52.** The chairperson threatened to _____
the delegate's speech if some of the points were _____

_____.
  not related

3
e
long
3
yes; 2 suffixes (ly, ness)

**53.** Pronounce this word carefully: _loneliness,_ meaning the state of being lonely.

How many pronounced vowels does it have? _____
What vowel is not pronounced? _____
The function of this vowel is to give the first vowel a (long, short) sound. _____
How many syllables are there? _____
Are there added elements (prefix or suffix)? _____

lone  li  ness

**54.** Now for the syllables: _____.

loneliness

**55.** If one is dejected, perhaps a bit sad, one is lonely; the state of being dejected is called _____.

loneliness

**56.** Although surrounded by many friends, Sam lives a life of _____.

ex  pla  na  tion
pro  ce  dure

**57.** The spelling of these next words depends on your pronunciation of them and on your looking at them closely. Take _explanation_ first and perform the first two steps. Then do the same for _procedure._ If you have done your work carefully, you can now divide them easily: _____

_____.

explanation
procedure

**58.** Write both words from memory: _____

_____.

ex  pla  nation
pro  ce  dure

**59.** Notice that the last syllable of the verb _explain_ is not spelled like the second syllable of the related noun: ex____ nation. Neither is the last syllable of _proceed_ spelled like the second syllable of its related noun: pro____dure.

explanation
procedure

**60.** To explain a point is to offer an _____;
a manner of proceeding is called a _____.

a. explanation
b. procedure
c. explanation
procedure

**61.** Choose one or the other of these two words to fit the sentences below.

a. I doubt if he can give me a good _____.
b. I wonder what _____ he will initiate.
c. The noun that relates to explain is _____;
the one that relates to proceed is _____.

## REVIEW

a. irrelevant
b. acquaintance
c. loneliness
d. procedure
e. acquire
f. explanation
g. procedure

**62.** From the contexts, write the appropriate words.

a. If a point is not related, it is _____.

b. Someone you know slightly can be called an _____

_____.

c. The doctor cannot rouse him from his state of _____

_____.
        dejection

d. What will be the _____ at the convention?
                    method

e. How long will it take to _____ the property?
                          possess

f. He gave a lengthy _____ of the new
law.

g. Are you sure this is the right _____?
                              manner of proceeding

4
ex
ence

**63.** The word *experience* can present a problem, but only momentarily. First look at it, then pronounce it.

How many syllables has it? _____
What is the prefix? _____
What is the suffix? _____

e

**64.** We have the first and last syllables—now to divide to make the second and third: ex   peri   ence. Pronounce it again. Although the first vowel does not have a long sound as the *r* colors it, it is closer to this sound than to the short sound of *e*. Therefore, to get the second syllable you would divide after which letter? _____

ex   pe   ri   ence

**65.** Now divide the whole word: _____.

experience

**66.** An event lived through is the definition of the word

_____.

experience

**67.** A person can also _____ a feeling of loneliness.

3
*con*
*ience*
*ven*

**68.** Although the last part of the word *convenience* is similar to *experience,* it is not pronounced the same. The last syllable (*ience*) has the sound of "yens." With this difference in mind, perform steps (1) and (2).

How many syllables are there? _____
The first syllable is the prefix _____.
The last syllable is _____.
The middle syllable is _____.

con   ven   ience

**69.** Now write the three syllables: _____.

convenience

**70.** A personal comfort, or something that increases comfort, like a toaster or fry pan, is a _____.

convenience

**71.** Because many packaged foods are easy to prepare, they're often called _____ items.

2
first /
vil   lain

**72.** Look at and pronounce this word: *villain.*

How many syllables are there? _____
Where do you divide after the first? _____
Divide the word into syllables: _____.

villain

**73.** A scoundrel can be called a _____.

villain

**74.** In a melodrama the character usually hissed at and booed by the audience is the _____.

3

**75.** *Interest* can be pronounced correctly with two or three syllables. But the spelling always has how many syllables? _____

interest

**76.** To hold the attention of a person is to in_____ him.

interest

**77.** A feeling of curiosity or fascination is the definition of the noun _____.

vac   u   um

**78.** Like *interest,* the word *vacuum* can be pronounced in two or three syllables, but to spell it correctly you must divide it graphically into three parts. Apply your guidelines and divide this word: _____.

vacuum
vacuum

**79.** A space empty of matter is called a vac_____. A feeling of emptiness can be known as a _____.

vacuum

**80.** The electric appliance to clean rugs is also called a _____.

*res*
*tau   rant*

**81.** Two words, derived from Old French, have retained the spelling characteristics of the French language. The first is *restaurant.* If you remember the guideline about two consonants between two vowels, you can form the first syllable easily. What is the first syllable? _____.
The rest of the word falls naturally into two syllables: _____ _____.

restaurant

**82.** An eating place is called a _____.

*fin*
*an   cier*

**83.** The second word that has retained the French spelling is *financier,* an expert in financial affairs. The short vowel at the beginning gives the clue to the first syllable: _____.
The rest of the word is easy to divide: _____ _____.

financier

**84.** An expert in large-scale money affairs is known as a _____.

financier

**85.** J. P. Morgan was a famous American _____.

3
is not
2
vowel is the same—
sergeant, servire

**86.** *Sergeant* also has a French "flavor" as its derivation goes back to Old French; however, its basic origin is the Latin verb *servire,* to serve. Pronunciation alone will not give you the necessary clues to correct spelling, so observe it closely.

How many vowels does it have? _____
The *a* in the second syllable (is, is not) pronounced?
How many syllables are there? _____
What is the relationship of the first vowel in *sergeant* to the original Latin verb? _____

ser   geant

**87.** Now divide the word: _____ _____.

sergeant

**88.** One of the noncommissioned officer ranks in the Army is that of _____.

a. experience
b. villain
c. interest
d. convenience
e. sergeant
f.  restaurant
g. financier
h. vacuum

## REVIEW
**89.** From the clues given below write the correct word for each sentence.

a. John could not get the teaching position because he lacked ex_____.

b. The role I like to portray best is the _____.

c. I don't have any in_____ in collecting stamps.

d. Living a block from the store is a _____.

                                  comfort

e. Lance was promoted to s_____.

f. Dining at a _____ is expensive.

g. An expert in financial affairs is a _____.

h. My niece bought a new _____.

                              rug cleaner

# POSTTEST

A. Write the complete word. The beginning of each word and the meaning are given to help you identify them.

1. vac_____ cleaning appliance
2. vil_____ scoundrel
3. in_____ concern
4. s_____ noncommissioned officer rank
5. em_____ make ill at ease
6. ac_____ get possession of
7. dis_____ vanish
8. ex_____ knowledge, skill
9. im_____ this minute
10. pro_____ method of proceeding
11. oc_____ now and then
12. lo_____ state of dejection
13. fin_____ financial expert
14. ap_____ readily seen
15. dis_____ prejudice
16. ac_____ amass, gather
17. op_____ occasion
18. con_____ comfort
19. inter_____ break between
20. ac_____ person slightly known
21. dis_____ displeasure
22. res_____ eating place
23. ap_____ be aware of
24. dis_____ fail to come up to expectation

25. ex_____ act of explaining

26. ac_____ment act of succeeding

27. par_____ same direction, similar

28. pos_____ ownership

29. ir_____ not related

B. Here are new words for you to syllabify. Remember the guidelines and follow the five-step method, leaving a space between each syllable as you write. When you finish, check your dictionary. If the word is unfamiliar, check the meaning as well.

30. quandary _____

31. impostor _____

32. shepherd _____

33. consensus _____

34. pronunciation _____

35. concession _____

36. grammar _____

37. disputatious _____

38. dictionary _____

39. physician _____

40. therapy _____

41. abrupt _____

42. thesaurus _____

43. beneficial _____

44. acquittal _____

45. disbursement _____

46. franchise _____

47. confident _____

48. assignment _____

49. silhouette _____

50. assimilation _____

# TEST
## PART ONE

Test your skill by dividing these words into syllables.

1. perception _____
2. brilliant _____
3. fascinate _____
4. perseverance _____
5. mediocre _____
6. biography _____
7. encyclopedia _____
8. transition _____
9. inhabitant _____
10. penicillin _____
11. reminisce _____
12. vaccinate _____
13. momentum _____
14. category _____
15. exaggerate _____
16. specifically _____
17. reconcile _____
18. traceable _____
19. physical _____
20. endorsement _____

# PART TWO
## TWO
### SOUND AND SPELLING

# CHAPTER THREE

## PRONUNCIATION AND ENUNCIATION

Words can be misspelled because they are not pronounced correctly. Some are mispronounced, with syllables added or omitted; others are not enunciated distinctly. The words in this chapter have been selected not only for their frequency in being misspelled, but also for their usefulness in illustrating that faulty pronunciation can cause spelling problems. Since specific words comprise the material for you to work with, the objectives of the chapter will be directly concerned with them: you will (1) pronounce the words correctly, observing the troublesome spots; (2) master their spelling; (3) use them in and out of context; and (4) establish the habit of pronouncing all words distinctly.

### PRETEST

Complete the words below. The definitions will help you to identify them.

1. hin_____ance          obstruction
2. rec_____nize          acknowledge
3. ath_____         competitor in sports
4. misch_____ous      playful
5. light_____ing         making lighter
6. trag_____          dramatic, calamitous event
7. chim_____          passage for smoke and gas
8. temper_____    degree of hotness and coldness
9. ath_____ics        competitive sports
10. li_____ble           responsible for
11. fin_____ly           last, at the end

12. dis____trous          calamitous

13. veg_____       edible plant

14. light_____        electrical discharge

15. prej_____      adverse judgment, bias

16. fed____al             connected with central political authority

17. remem____ance         reminder or token

18. griev_____         serious

19. temper_____      disposition

20. quan____ty            number or amount

21. gov____ment           process of running political units

22. envi_____ment      surroundings

23. back_____      education, experience

24. gra____tude           thankfulness

25. hun_____         100

26. ag_____      make worse

2
3

**1.** In the first group are words in which an extra syllable is often added. Take *athlete* and *athletics.* You will sometimes hear them pronounced this way: "ath a lete" and "ath a let ics." These pronunciations are wrong, of course, as *athlete* has just _____ syllables and *athletics* only _____.

ath   lete
ath   let   ics

**2.** Pronounce the syllables carefully, then write them: _____ _____ and _____ _____ _____.

athlete
athletics

**3.** One who takes part in sports is an _____, and the name for competitive sports is _____.

2
3

**4.** Here is another pair: *grievous* and *mischievous.* Often they are pronounced with an extra syllable, but if you say them correctly—griev ous and mis chie vous, you will hear only _____ syllables in *grievous* and _____ in *mischievous.*

griev   ous
mis   chie   vous

**5.** Pronounce them once more and complete the syllables: _____ _____ and _____ _____ _____.

mischievous
grievous

**6.** It was not a harmful prank, just a mis_____ one. The two brothers were responsible for the gr_____ deed.

mischievous
grievous

**7.** The _____ child did not commit a _____ sin.

3

**8.** The following words have a common problem. Because they can remind you of a related word, you may include a part of that related word in the pronunciation and then spell it wrong. Take *disastrous* (dis as trous), meaning calamitous. Because the noun *disaster* comes to mind, you could easily say and spell it this way: "dis as ter ous." Correctly pronounced and spelled, this word has how many syllables? _____

disastrous

**9.** The results of the election were disas_____.

disastrous

**10.** The epidemic of sleeping sickness produced _____ _____ results.

is not

**11.** Pronounce it once more. There (is, is not) a syllable that sounds like "ter" in this word. _____

2
drance

**12.** Like *disastrous,* the word *hindrance* must be pronounced correctly. Although it may remind you of the verb *hinder* (to obstruct), you do not write it with an extra syllable: "hin der ance." It has just _____ syllables. What is the second syllable? _____

hindrance

**13.** The verb to hinder means to obstruct; the noun meaning an obstruction is _____.

remember

**14.** The noun *remembrance* has the same problem. It can remind you of what verb? _____

no

**15.** Pronounce the two words carefully: *remember, remembrance.* Is there a syllable in the noun that sounds like "ber"? _____

re mem brance

**16.** Divide the word into syllables. _____

remembrance

**17.** My grandmother gave me her gold watch as a re_____ _____.

3

**18.** Remembrance has only _____ syllables.

2

**19.** Two other words that must be pronounced correctly are *lightning* and *chimney.* Look at and then pronounce them. Both have _____ syllables.

2

**20.** If you pronounce *lightning* with an extra syllable (like light en ing), you will spell another word, *lightening,* which means becoming lighter. *Lightening* has three syllables. The word you want to spell, defined as an electrical discharge, has how many syllables? _____

lightning

**21.** Our electric power went out when _____
<sub></sub>

lightening, lightning

hit the transformer.

lightning

**22.** Sharp bolts of thunder accompanied the jagged streaks of _____.

chimney

**23.** Like *lightning,* the word *chimney* must not have an added syllable. It is not a "chim i ney," but a _____.

chimney

**24.** The passage through which smoke and gas escape from a furnace is called a smokestack or a _____.

2

**25.** The key to spelling *chimney* and *lightning* correctly is to pronounce only _____ syllables in each word.

### REVIEW

a. grievous
b. lightning
c. athlete
d. hindrance
e. mischievous
f. remembrance
g. chimney
h. athletics
i. disastrous
j. lightening

**26.** Now test your skill and fill in the missing letters. The definitions for the words are at the right.

a. griev_____          serious

b. light_____       electrical discharge

c. ath_____         competitor in sports

d. hin_____    obstruction

e. mis_____    playful

f. re_____     reminder or token

g. chim_____         passage for smoke

h. ath_____   competitive sports

i. dis_____    calamitous

j. light_____      becoming lighter

second (*a*)

**27.** The second group of words also demands proper pronunciation, but it differs from the first in that syllables are omitted, not added. For example, take *liable,* meaning responsible for, or likely. The word is li a ble, not "li ble." Which syllable is often omitted? _____

a

**28.** Which vowel is often left out of li__ble?

liable

**29.** The word which means responsible for or likely is _____.

liable

**30.** Who is _____ for the damages to the car?

| | |
|---|---|
| 3 | **31.** Two other words with the vowel *a* omitted are *finally* and *probably.* If you say them carelessly, you will hear only two syllables. Both words have how many syllables? ____ |
| *final*<br>*ly*<br>finally | **32.** The adverb *finally* has two parts: the root and the suffix. The root is _____ and the suffix is ____. Together they form the complete word _____. |
| finally | **33.** After six hours of debate, the legislature _____ came to a decision. |
| finally | **34.** The council _____ voted on the resolution. |
| *a* | **35.** The adverb *probably,* meaning most likely or presumably, also has three syllables, and again it is the vowel ____ that is often slighted. |
| *a*<br>*a* | **36.** Fill in the missing vowel: fin__lly and prob__bly. |
| probably | **37.** We will _____ hear about the strike to-<br>              most likely<br>morrow. |
| Probably | **38.** Whenever I ask, "Can we go on a picnic?" she replies, "P_____." |
| second (*er*) | **39.** Two common words that lose the vowel *e* when mispronounced are *federal* and *general.* Instead of saying "fed ral" and "gen ral" you should say "fed er al" and "gen er al." When carelessly pronounced, these two words lose a vowel in which syllable? _____ |
| 3 | **40.** How many syllables does each word have? ____ |
| fed  er  al<br>gen  er  al | **41.** Divide these words into syllables: federal _____ and general _____. |
| federal<br>generals | **42.** The f_____ government acknowledged the part that the three g_____s had played in the attack on the enemy. |
| generally | **43.** Their exploits are _____ly well known. |
| Generally<br>federal | **44.** _____ly speaking, most states would like to receive more money from the f_____ government. |

his to ry
mem o ry
fac to ry
soph o more
en vi ron ment

**45.** Now let us shift to the vowel *o*. Five words often mispronounced are *history, memory, factory, sophomore,* and *environment*. If you say them carelessly, you will not hear all the syllables. For example, we may say "his try," "mem ry," "fac try," "soph more," and "en virn ment," but in each case a syllable has been omitted. Divide each word into syllables and then underline the troublesome parts.

_____   _____
_____   _____

sophomore
history
factory

**46.** The college so_____ who was majoring in his_____ got a summer job at the fac_____.

memory

**47.** The ability to remember is known as mem_____.

environment

**48.** People are often affected by their en_____.

*o*

**49.** If you mispronounce any of these words, you will be leaving out the vowel _____.

### REVIEW

a. memory
b. sophomore
c. environment
d. disastrous

**50.** Find the misspelled word in each group and write it correctly.

a. hindrance, memry, finally, athlete

b. chimney, grievous, sophmore, history

c. mischievous, factory, general, envirnment

d. liable, federal, probably, disasterous

*n*

**51.** Not only are syllables omitted, but letters are also left out, and again mispronunciation or careless enunciation is the cause. *Government* is an excellent example. Pronounce the word by syllables: gov ern ment. Now say it quickly. What consonant in the second syllable can be passed over?
_____

ern

**52.** It is the second syllable that causes the misspelling: gov _____ment.

government

**53.** My cousin worked sixteen years for the federal _____

_____.

government

**54.** The professor then asked, "What form of _____

_____ would be best in this case?"

*r*

surprise
library

library

surprise

*t*

quantity

quantity

*ti* (second)

*f*

twelfth

twelfth

*f*

*a*
*a*
*e*

vowel

**55.** The next two words also lose a consonant if they are pronounced incorrectly: *library* and *surprise.* Say them quickly and then write the consonant that may be omitted: _____.

**56.** It was a s____prise to hear that Rudy has a job at the public li_____.

**57.** Dr. Hughes donated a collection of Sherlock Holmes mysteries to his hometown l_____.

**58.** We decided to give a _____ birthday party for Evelyn.

**59.** Every syllable in the noun *quantity* should be pronounced distinctly; otherwise, what letter in the second syllable can you easily omit? _____

**60.** A number or amount of anything is called a qu_____.

**61.** The overhead expenses are less when items are bought in _____.

**62.** The syllable in *quantity* that must be carefully pronounced is _____.

**63.** Say this title of one of Shakespeare's plays: *Twelfth Night.* If you pronounced the *f* in the first syllable, you were correct. If you did not, then you could misspell the word. In pronouncing this one-syllable word, remember to sound the _____.

**64.** Our anniversary is on the tw_____ of May.

**65.** We will be abroad between the first and the t_____ of October.

**66.** What consonant is often omitted in this word? _____

**67.** Over the years different pronunciations of words have developed, and occasionally they can cause spelling problems. Take, for example, *temperature, temperament,* and *vegetable.* There are only three syllables in each word, and it is the vowel in the third syllable of *temperament* and *temperature* and the vowel in the second syllable of *vegetable* that are frequently omitted: temper___ment, temper___ture, veg___table.

**68.** In each case you have a syllable in the middle of a word that consists of a single (vowel, consonant). _____

a. temperature
b. temperament
c. vegetable

**69.** Now complete these sentences:

a. The storm caused a severe drop in _____.

b. My cousin Mary Ann has a nervous _____.

c. I don't like a _____ with my meal.

a

**70.** *Boundary* is another word in this category. It is pronounced more often than not with just two syllables instead of three. What vowel would be omitted? _____

boundary

**71.** Something that indicates a limit or border is a _____ _____.

boundary

**72.** The two countries have warred for years over the north _____.

o

**73.** Now look at *chocolate.* It is usually pronounced in just two syllables (choc  lit). Which vowel is lost? _____

chocolate

**74.** Most people like ch_____ cake.

chocolate

**75.** My uncle Harry will eat a whole box of _____ _____ cookies at one sitting.

chocolate

**76.** The big jar is chock-full of _____ candy.

g

**77.** The last group of words is misspelled because of careless pronunciation. Take *background,* which consists of two words, *back* and *ground,* which through usage have become joined in solid form. Say the word quickly. Which consonant can be omitted? _____

background
background

**78.** The space behind closer areas is called back_____. Thus, in paintings the space farther back which provides relief for the principal objects portrayed is the _____.

background

**79.** A person's experience and training can also be called _____.

(a)

**80.** Now pronounce *hundred* by syllables: hun  dred. Which combination is at the beginning of the second syllable (a) two consonants, or (b) a consonant and a vowel? _____

dr

**81.** What consonants precede the *ed* in the second syllable? _____

hundred

**82.** The figure 100 stands for the word _____.

hundred

**83.** There were about a _____ counselors at the meeting.

*gra* (second)

**84.** The word *aggravate* is similar to hundred in that the consonants must precede the vowel to prevent the misspelling of the word. Pronounce it carefully: ag  gra  vate. Which syllable will cause the problem? _____ _____

*gr*

**85.** In the second syllable what two consonants precede the vowel *a*? _____

aggravate

**86.** To make worse or make more of a burden is the meaning of ag_____.

aggravate

**87.** In informal writing, to annoy or to vex can also be the meaning of _____.

*og*

**88.** If not correctly pronounced, the second syllable of *recognize* can be misspelled. Through carelessness it is easy to omit which letters? rec_____nize.

rec  og  nize

**89.** Write the three syllables of this word: _____ _____ _____.

recognize

**90.** If we acknowledge people on the street, we rec_____ _____ them.

recognize

**91.** Only after careful study will I _____ the validity of your argument.

a. 3
b. trag
prej
c. vowel

**92.** The last two words take careful pronunciation and distinction of syllables: *tragedy* and *prejudice*. Pronounce them slowly, then answer these questions:

a. How many syllables does each have? _____

b. Each has only four letters in the first syllable: _____ and _____.

c. Each has a single (vowel, consonant) in the second syllable. _____

trag  e  dy
prej  u  dice

**93.** Now syllabify each word: _____ _____.

tragedy
tragedy

**94.** A dramatic, disastrous event is called a tr_____. The terrible earthquake in Peru is a great _____.

prejudice

**95.** An adverse opinion or judgment made without sufficient knowledge is known as p_____.

prejudice

**96.** Mr. Doe has allowed his life to be ruled by _____.

## REVIEW

hundreds
government
librarians
surprise
background
aggravated
prejudice

**97.** Pick out the misspelled words in this passage and write them correctly.

My cousin Sue spent a whole week at the library checking hunderds of goverment documents and a quantity of bulletins on technology. The libarians expressed suprise that a girl with Sue's backround would be interested in science. This aggervated Sue considerably, and she chided them, saying that she could recognize predjuice when she heard it.

## POSTTEST

A. Pick out all the words incorrectly spelled and write them correctly.

1. The city officials condemned the factory for polluting the envirnment. The company president retorted that they were not libel for any damages, and that, in fact, a fedral agency had ruled that the plant was outside the boundry and could not be taken to court.

B. Fill in the troublesome spots in the words you have just studied.

| | | |
|---|---|---|
| 2. back___round | 8. quan_____ | 13. fin_____ly |
| 3. choc___late | 9. re_____nize | 14. hun_____ |
| 4. gover___ment | 10. tem_____ment | 15. ag_____ |
| 5. twel___th | 11. tem_____ture | 16. trag_____ |
| 6. s_____prise | 12. veg_____ble | 17. pr_____ice |
| 7. li_____ary | | |

C. The following words are often confused because at least one in each pair is pronounced incorrectly. Look up each pair of words in the second column, match the correct one with the definition, and write it in the blank.

| | | |
|---|---|---|
| 18. scene or setting | _____ | striped, stripped |
| 19. having one or more stripes | _____ | coral, corral |
| 20. logical basis | _____ | tortuous, torturous |
| 21. overcritical | _____ | alley, allay |
| 22. series of connected rooms for a living unit | _____ | solder, soldier |
| 23. join closely | _____ | deprecate, depreciate |
| 24. enclosure for livestock | _____ | local, locale |
| 25. metric unit of volume | _____ | hypocritical, hypercritical |
| 26. express disapproval of | _____ | rational, rationale |
| 27. twisting, wending | _____ | suit, suite |
| 28. unsophisticated | _____ | resume, résumé |
| 29. summary | _____ | nave, naive |
| 30. calm or pacify | _____ | liter, litter |

# CHAPTER FOUR
## THE UNSTRESSED VOWEL

Knowing where the proper stress (or accent) falls in words will help you not only to pronounce them correctly, but also to spell them correctly. Two simple marks indicate which syllable or syllables receive primary stress ( ´ ) and which have secondary stress ( ˘ ). Some words have just one primary stress (depict, cathédral); some have more than one (long-headed). Others have both primary and secondary stresses (galvanizé, declarátion, receívership). One-syllable words have no stress marks, as there can be no comparison between stress and unstressed (mud, bag, through).

Usually it is not the vowel in the stressed syllables that causes problems, it is the vowel in the unstressed. It can be heard in the beginning of a word (among), in the middle (remedy), in the end (media), or even in more than one syllable (elephant, banana). This unstressed vowel is called the schwa (the word was borrowed directly from the German and earlier from the Hebrew), and the reason it makes spelling difficult is that its sound is not represented by one particular vowel, as you can see from the examples above.

Inasmuch as research on categories of spelling errors indicates that vowels in the middle parts of words cause the greatest difficulties, most of the words you will study in this chapter have the schwa in syllables other than in the beginning or the end. Although there is no easy way for you to know which vowel appears as the schwa in a given word, the origin of that word will frequently show why it is one vowel and not another. If at any time you are unsure of the pronunciation of a word, check the dictionary. The symbol for the schwa is ə, so watch for it in the pronunciation guide which usually appears immediately after the word entry.

In this chapter then, you will (1) become aware of the problems that the schwa creates; (2) recognize the sound of the unstressed vowel and the syllable in which it appears; (3) spell a number of useful words in and out of context; (4)

from various contexts and definitions reproduce the correct words; and (5) apply what you learn to the spelling of other words with similar problems.

## PRETEST

Fill in the missing letter(s).

1. comp__tent
2. gramm__r
3. opt__mism
4. famil____r
5. hum__rous
6. compar__tive
7. elim__nate
8. sim__lar
9. dom__nant
10. warr__nt

11. cand__date
12. sent__nce
13. s__mester
14. dorm__tory
15. math__matics
16. sacr__fice
17. contr__versy
18. crit__cism
19. sep__rate
20. lin__n

21. calend__r
22. legit__mate
23 cat__gory
24. prob__bly
25. fasc__nate
26. partic__l__r
27. priv__lege
28. pecul_____
29. bull__tin
30. intell__gence

benefit
bulletin
ballot

**1.** The sound of the schwa (approximately the "uh" in conduct) varies little from word to word, but the vowel representing the sound does. The reason can often be found in the origin of the word.
Here are three origins and their English derivatives:

Latin *bene facere,* to do well
Old French *bullette* from bulle, a document
Italian *ballotta,* little ball

Study the spelling and meanings carefully and fill in the missing letters in the English words:

ben__fit, bull__tin, ball__t.

ballots

**2.** Before the advent of voting machines and printed forms, "little balls" were used to cast ball_____.

benefit

**3.** Something "well done" can become a ben_____.

bulletins
balloting

**4.** Both parties sent out bull_____s explaining the importance of _____ in the primaries.

ballot
benefit

**5.** The chairperson insisted on a secret _____, not a show of hands, because he said everyone would _____ from not knowing how each member voted.

bulletin

**6.** There are some excellent articles in the latest _____ _____ from the Department of Agriculture.

en   a
di
a

**7.** Here are the origins of three more English words:

Latin *calendarium* from *calendae,* the first days of the month on which accounts were due
Latin *candidus,* white, from *candere,* to shine
Latin *comparāre,* pair or match

After studying these origins, fill in the missing letters of the English derivatives:

cal__d__r            can____date            compar__tive

calendar

**8.** A system of reckoning time according to divisions of the year is known as a cal_____.

candidate

**9.** In ancient Rome a man campaigning for office was clothed in a white toga and was called a *candidātus.* From this origin we get our English word for a campaigner:
c_____.

comparative

**10.** The adjective pertaining to comparison, the "matching or pairing" is com_____ive.

Comparatively
candidates
calendars

**11.** Com_____ly speaking, the two can_____ have as many free days on their cal_____s as they have appointments.

no
*rant* (second)

**12.** Now pronounce *warrant.* Does the *a* sound the same in both syllables? _____ Which syllable has the schwa? _____

wArrAnt

**13.** You might remember the spelling of the vowel this way: wArr__nt.

warrant

**14.** A guarantee or written authorization is called a w_____.

warrant

**15.** The verb meaning to guarantee is _____.

second
a   i

**16.** Two common and useful words having the same problems are *grammar* and *similar.* First, look at the syllables: gram  mar, sim  i  lar. The unstressed vowel appears in which syllable in each word? _____ What is the vowel in each? _____ _____

a

**17.** The Latin origin *gramma,* meaning letter, tells you that the vowel representing the schwa is _____.

grammar

**18.** If one is not careful, one can certainly mar the gram _____.

*i*

**19.** To be related in appearance is to be sim__lar.

a. grammar
b. similar

**20.** Now fit these two words in the following contexts.

a. Depending upon the method of presentation, the study of _____ can be interesting.
b. The two plays have _____ plots.

last (third)
liar

**21.** *Familiar* and *peculiar* also have an unstressed vowel and a graphic similarity. Pronounce both of these words. In which syllable is the schwa? _____ What is the graphic similarity? _____

peculiar
familiar

**22.** To be unusual or strange is to be pe_____. Common, or well known, is the definition of famil_____.

a. familiar
b. peculiar

**23.** a. We are now on a _____ road.
b. He acts in a most _____ manner.

similar
familiar

**24.** Do not confuse these endings: simi_____ and fami _____.

*e*
no
last

**25.** Look at and then pronounce the word *sentence*. Both the first and last syllables have which vowel? _____ Do they have the same vowel sound? _____ Which syllable has the unstressed vowel (first, last)? _____

**REVIEW**

a. candidates
b. bulletin
benefit
calendar
c. grammar
warrant
d. similar
familiar
peculiar
e. comparative

**26.** Complete the word(s) in each sentence.

a. The can_____ denied that they bribed voters to stuff the ballot boxes.

b. Carol put this notice in Tuesday's bu_____: Don't forget to put the date of the ben_____ performance on your cal_____.

c. Not studying your lessons or gr_____ may war_____ my dismissing you from this English class.

d. Watch for the simi_____ endings in fami_____ and pe_____.

e. In this comparison—*late, later, latest*—*latest* is the superlative degree and *later* is the com_____ degree.

second

**27.** Look at, pronounce, and mentally syllabify these words: *definite* and *dominant.* In which syllable is the schwa (first, second, third)? _____

*i*

**28.** *Definite* is derived from the Latin *dēfinere,* to determine, and *dominant* from the Latin *domināns,* present participle from *domināri,* lord and master. These origins tell you to put which vowel in the second syllable to represent the schwa? _____

definite
dominant

**29.** To be specific is to be _____; to be outstanding or controlling is to be _____.

dominant

**30.** Now pronounce *dominant* once more and listen to the vowel sounds in both the second and third syllables. Here we have the schwa in two places. If you remember the origin of this word, you will place the right vowels in these syllables: dom__n__nt.

definite

**31.** She had a _____ reason for arriving late.
                                              specific

dominant

**32.** Of all the characteristics attributed to the one cause, the last one is _____.
                                   outstanding

*i  i  i*

**33.** Now pronounce these words distinctly: *sensitive, eliminate, sacrifice.* What is the unstressed vowel in each word? ___  ___  ___

each origin
has the *i*

**34.** What clue do the origins give you about the right vowel to use? _____

Latin *senus,* from *sentire,* faculty of feeling, mode of thought, meaning
Latin *ēlimināre,* to put outside the threshold
Latin *sacrificāre,* to make holy

sensitive

**35.** If a person is easily affected by criticism, that person is said to be sen_____.

eliminate

**36.** "To put outside the threshold" is to get rid of something, or to elim_____ it.

sacrifice
sacrifice

**37.** The ancient offering of a slaughtered animal at the altar was called a sac_____. Today, giving up something of value can be called a _____.

sacrifices

**38.** To accomplish a goal we must often make _____.

sensitive

**39.** Rosemary has very _____ skin.

eliminated

**40.** Because of increased expenses, the directors _____
                                                      removed

two positions in the sales department.

sacrifices

**41.** To attain my goal, I am willing to make many _____.

insensitive
eliminated

**42.** Because of his in_____tive attitude,
Bob Jones was e_____d from the contest.

second
second

**43.** Two words having similar endings can be presented
together: *optimism* and *criticism*. Pronounce them carefully,
listening to the stresses in each word.

Of the three syllables in *optimism,* which has the schwa?
_____

Which   syllable   has   the   stress   in   *criticism?*
_____

criticism
optimism

**44.** Complete the rest of each word:

crit_____          opt_____.

criticism
optimism

**45.** The act of making judgments is known as c_____;
tending to expect the best outcome is the definition of
o_____.

criticism

**46.** To learn to write well one must be open to _____.

optimism

**47.** At times there may be more people who express
pessimism than _____.

dormitory

**48.** The troublesome vowel in this next word is also in the
second syllable, but again the origin gives you a clue: Latin
*dormire,* to sleep. A place to sleep can be called a dor____
tory.

dormitory

**49.** A building to house a number of students is a _____.

dormitories

**50.** Because of increased enrollments last year, some
colleges had to build new _____tories.

o

**51.** Pronounce these words: *humorous* and *controversy.*
What vowel in the unstressed syllable do they have in
common? ____

humorous

**52.** Laughable or comical is the definition of hu_____.

controversy

**53.** A dispute, especially a lengthy one, is a con_____
versy.

a. humorous
b. controversy
c. controversy
   humorous

**54.** Supply the correct "o" word for these sentences.
a. On our travels we saw many _____ sights.
b. The new tax issue has started a _____
between the major political factions.
c. The _____ has become both serious and _____.

controversy
humorous

**55.** A long dispute is a _____; a
comical sight is a _____ one.

**REVIEW**

optimistically
eliminated
sacrifices

**56.** A Pick out all the misspellings and write the words
correctly.

Although the manager spoke optomistically, he cautioned
the staff that three or four positions could be elimanated,
and that everyone would have to make some sacrafices.

a. criticism
b. sensitive
c. definite
d. dominant
e. humorous
f. controversy

B. Choose the correct spelling in each group, and, from
memory, write each correctly.

a. critasim, critacism, criticism

b. sensetive, sensitive, sensative

c. definite, defenite, defanite

d. domanant, dominant, domanent

e. humerous, humerus, humorous

f. contraversy, contravercy, controversy

*a*

**57.** Now let us turn to these words with the troublesome
schwa: *salary* and *separate.* Pronounce them and identify
the vowel in the unstressed syllable: _____

separate

**58.** The word which can be a verb, adjective, or noun and
means "apart" is s_____.

sep  a  rate

**59.** The pronunciation of this word changes according to its
grammatical function, but the spelling remains the same. As
a verb, it is séparaté (note the long *a* sound in the last
syllable). As an adjective or noun, it can be pronounced in
either two or three syllables, but the last syllable has the
short sound of *i* (as in b*i*t): "sep  a  rit" or "sep  rit."
Regardless of the different pronunciation, however, the word
is always spelled sep __ _____.

separate

**60.** If you two do not stop talking, I will s_____
you.

separates

**61.** The combining of different jackets and skirts, or pants, is known as wearing _____.

separate

**62.** I prefer to go my _____ way.

salary

**63.** The second word in this pair is *salary,* a common word commonly misspelled. At one time during the days of the Roman Empire, the soldiers drew allowances for the purchase of salt as part of their pay. This allowance for "salt money" was called *salārium* (sāl = salt). This Latin word was borrowed into English as sal_____.

salary

**64.** The unstressed schwa in the word meaning fixed pay for regular work is sal__ry.

salary

**65.** The clerks demanded higher pay, but the supervisor said they had not earned an increase in their _____.

salary

**66.** Ancient "salt money" is known as _____.

second

**67.** Two more "a" words are *fundamental* and *freshman.* Say these words carefully. In which syllable does the schwa appear? _____

fundamental

**68.** The word meaning literally "to lay the bottom for" is fund _____.

fundamental

**69.** Having to do with a foundation is the definition of _____.

fundamental

**70.** Basic is a synonym for _____.

freshman

**71.** A student in the first year of high school or college is usually called a fresh_____.

freshmen

**72.** The spelling of this word is not to be confused with the word that means more than one first-year student: fresh _____.

freshman
Freshman

**73.** Each f_____ must take a course entitled F_____ Composition.

e

**74.** What is the common schwa in these words: *maintenance, category?* _____

category

**75.** A class or a specifically designated division is called a cat__gory.

categories

**76.** While observing people on a bus, I often mentally put them in c_____ies.

category

**77.** Should you put this item in _____ A or B?

te

**78.** For one simple reason, the word *maintenance* is one of the most frequently misspelled words in the English language: it is not pronounced correctly. The verb is *maintain,* but the noun is not "main   tain   ance" but main   te   nance. The schwa appears in the second syllable. How do you spell that syllable? _____

maintenance

**79.** The work of keeping something in order, like roads, is called main_____.

maintenance

**80.** The vigilantes said they were primarily interested in the _____ of peace.

category

**81.** The analyst took all the service jobs and put them in one _____.

i

**82.** What do the words *legitimate* and *privilege* have in common? It is the schwa _____.

It shows that the schwa is *i*.

**83.** Why is the origin (Latin *lēgitimus,* meaning legal or lawful) important? _____

legitimate

**84.** The word meaning lawful or reasonable is _____.

privilege

**85.** The English word which means a special benefit or advantage is derived from the Latin *prīvilēgium,* law affecting an individual. Using the origin as a guide, fill in the missing letters: priv__l_____.

d

**86.** Although the last syllable in *privilege* sounds like "lidge," there is no __ in this word.

privilege

**87.** The origin helps you to spell the unstressed vowel correctly; priv__lege.

privilege

**88.** A special advantage or benefit is a _____.

legitimate
privileges

**89.** Because the young ruler was not content with the _____ _____ he
                                     reasonable                    benefits
already had, he demanded rights he was not entitled to.

## REVIEW

a. freshman
b. legitimate
c. category
d. maintenance
e. fundamental
f. separate
g. privilege

**90.** For each definition, write the appropriate word.

a. a first-year student _____

b. lawful or reasonable _____

c. class or division _____

d. the keeping of something in order _____

e. basic _____

f. kept apart _____

g. a particular advantage _____

## POSTTEST

A. Ask someone to dictate the following exercise to test your skill in writing words with the unstressed vowel.

1. calendar      I bought next year's *calendar.*

2. peculiar      He acts in a *peculiar* manner.

3. bulletin      The spring *bulletin* has been published.

4. humorous      It was a *humorous* sight.

5. ballot      I cast my *ballot* today.

6. privileges      He has too many *privileges.*

7. sensitive      Mary is *sensitive* to her brother's moods.

8. warrant      His actions *warrant* suspension.

9. separate      Do not *separate* the items.

10. comparative      Brighter is the *comparative* of bright.

11. dormitory      One hundred students live in the *dormitory.*

12. category      According to seniority, he was placed in the lowest *category.*

13. freshman      John is a *freshman* in college.

14. benefit      The regulation will *benefit* no one.

15. maintenance      Joe has a job in the *maintenance* division.

B. Study the origins and definitions below and write the English derivatives.

16. _____ ic      G. *epi* (on, among) *demos* (people)
        contagious disease

17. _____      L. *murmur* (rumor, murmur)
        uttering indistinctly

18. _____  L. *offendere* (strike against)
    hurt someone's feelings

19. _____ ate  L. *tolerare* (to bear)
    put up with

20. _____  G. *apo* (defense) *logos* (speech, discourse)
    expression of regret

21. _____ ent  L. *per* (through) *manere* (to remain)
    changeless

22. _____ num  New L., earlier *alumium* (a metallic element)
    metallic element

23. _____ ary  L. *voluntarias,* free will
    acting on one's own
    initiative

24. _____ ion  L. *com* (together) *petere* (to seek, strive)
    vying with another

25. _____ ancy  L. *dis* (apart) *crepare* (to rattle, sound differ-
    divergence or disagreement      ent)

# CHAPTER FIVE
## "SILENT" LETTERS

If you have had words marked off because you left out a letter that was not sounded, usually called a "silent" letter, you may have wondered why it was there in the first place. In the Middle English period (the twelfth through the fifteenth centuries), some of the final e's and all the consonants were pronounced. For example, the *k* and *gh* in *knight* and the *k* in *know* were pronounced, and many words from the Greek had initial letters sounded, like the *p* in *psychology* and *pneumonia*. Gradually, the pronunciation of many words changed, some letters becoming "silent." The fact that they are silent does not mean they are to be omitted. On the contrary, they are here to stay until such time as the spelling is changed—not in the foreseeable future, however.

In this chapter, then, you will study the origins of a number of words having "silent letters" so that you will (1) recognize the relationship between the derivation and the present word; (2) spell a number of useful words in and out of context; and (3) reproduce words from definitions and origins.

### PRETEST

Fill in the missing letters. The definitions will help you to identify the words.

1. W_____day   a day of the week
2. d____t          something owed
3. cond_____     to express disapproval of
4. g_____ian   one who protects
5. ___ry           dryly humorous
6. _____ology  study of the mind
7. mor_____   contract or deed

8. num___          lacking feeling

9. debri___        ruins, rubble

10. s_____tle     capable of making fine distinctions

11. ___naw         to bite persistently

12. dou___t        to be uncertain, waver

13. ___erb         aromatic or medicinal plant

14. k___aki        brownish color, or material

15. je___pardy     danger, loss of risk

debt
doubt
undoubtedly
subtle

**1.** Four useful words have the same silent letter, having been derived from these Latin words: de*b*ere, meaning to owe; du*b*itare, meaning to waver; and su*b*tilis, meaning thin and fine.

If you owe something, you have a de___t.
If you waver, you dou___t; if there is no wavering, you will undou___tedly succeed.
If you can make fine distinctions, you are su___tle.

a. debt
b. doubt
c. undoubtedly
d. subtle

**2.** According to the context, write or complete these same words.

a. When you haven't paid a bill, you still have a _____.

b. If you are in _____, do nothing.

c. The word that means accepted without doubt is un

_____.

d. If a person can make a point so "fine" as to be elusive or abstruse, the person is said to be _____tle.

a. subtle
b. doubt
c. undoubtedly
d. debts

**3.** Now fit these four words into these contexts.

a. She has a reputation for being _____.

b. Why must they _____ everything I say?

c. He is _____ the most stubborn person I know.

d. Alex filed for bankruptcy because he had so many

_____.

*d*

**4.** *Wednesday* is pronounced differently than it is written, and because it is the spelling that bothers us, let us look at the origin for some help. The word is derived from the Old English *Wodnesdaeg*, or "Woden's Day"—as you may recall, Woden was the chief Teutonic god. Remembering the origin will enable you to put which consonant at the end of the first syllable: We___.

| | |
|---|---|
| Wed   nes   day | **5.** Divide the rest of this word: Wed_____  _____. |
| Wednesday | **6.** The day after Tuesday is _____. |
| Wednesday | **7.** Sometimes Christmas falls on a W_____. |
| h | **8.** Now pronounce the words *exhaust* and *rhythm* carefully. Which letter is not sounded? _____ |
| does | **9.** The words are derived from the Latin *exhaurīre* and *rhythmus.* Examine these words. The origin of the English words (does, does not) account for the "silent" letter. _____ |
| exhausts | **10.** *Exhaurīre* means to draw out, so if a long car ride draws the passengers out, it ex___austs them. |
| exhaust | **11.** To tire out is to ex_____. |
| exhaust | **12.** The legislator will soon _____ the listeners. |
| rhythm | **13.** The Latin word *rhythmus* means recurring motion or measure, so the English word meaning a regular beat in music is _____thm. |
| rhythm | **14.** The three basics of music are melody, harmony, and r_____. |
| rhythm | **15.** Some modern artists have an altogether new sense of _____. |
| rhythm  exhaust | **16.** The monotonous _____ of the windshield wiper will eventually annoy and _____ the elderly driver. |
| knowledge | **17.** *Know* means to learn and understand, and the understanding gained through experience and study is called _____ledge. |
| first | **18.** The silent letter in the word that means understanding or learning is at the beginning of which syllable? _____ |
| knowledge | **19.** He surprises me with his _____ of science. |
| knowledge | **20.** Despite all his _____, he is quite illogical at times. |

**REVIEW**

a. Wednesday
b. doubt
c. debts
d. rhythm
e. undoubtedly
f. exhaust
g. knowledge
h. subtle

**21.** Write the silent letter words for these sentences or questions.

a. What day precedes Thursday? _____

b. How long will you _____ his motives?
    hesitate over

c. You owe far too many _____.

d. The three essentials of music are melody, harmony, and
    _____.

e. He is _____ the finest jazz trombonist today.
    certainly

f. I am afraid that a long journey will _____ my grandfather.

g. Sometimes a little _____ is a handicap.
    learning

h. The distinction between the two is quite _____.
    fine

*n*

**22.** When you pronounce the verb *condemn,* which letter is not sounded? _____

Yes. (The original word has *n* it it.)

**23.** The word comes from the verb *condemnare.* Is the silent letter related to the original word? _____

condemns

**24.** The Latin word means to damage, so if one "damages" another, one expresses severe disapproval—in other words, one con_____ that person.

condemn

**25.** To censure or criticize severely is to _____.

condemned

**26.** Even before the trial, the defendant was called a _____ man.

end

**27.** Unlike the word *knowledge, condemn* has the silent letter at the _____ of the word.

*p*

**28.** Three words, *psychology, psychiatry,* and *psychopathy,* are derived from the Greek word *psukhe.* Each word has the silent letter _____.

psychology

**29.** *Psukhe* means life, breath, soul, and *ology* is an ending meaning study. From these two is produced the word meaning the study of the mind or mental processes _____ychology.

psychiatry

**30.** Since the ending *iatry* indicates medical treatment, the treatment of the mind is called _____iatry.

psychopathy

**31.** The ending *pathy* indicates disease. Disease of the mind, or mental disorder, can be called _____opathy.

psychology
psychiatry
psychopathy

**32.** The study of mental processes is _____;
the medical treatment of the mind is _____;
and a form of mental disorder is _____.

*u*

**33.** The words *guard* and *guardian* have a common derivation: Old French *garder* or *guarder,* from the Germanic. Here you find a shift in the spelling of the French verb, but the English words have retained the silent ____.

guard
guardian

**34.** To watch over is the meaning of the word _____;
one who watches over is a _____.

guard

**35.** To take precautions is also the meaning of the root word: The hospital tries to _____ against infection.

guardhouse
guardroom

**36.** The detention house for military personnel is called a _____house; the room in which prisoners are confined is a _____room.

*t*

**37.** To finance the purchase of a house, most people must pledge the property to a creditor as security against non-payment. That pledge is called a *mortgage.* Say the word and indicate which letter is not sounded. ____

death

**38.** Look at the origin for a moment: Old French *mortgage,* from the Latin *mort* (death) and *gage.* In case you are wondering what death has to do with a mortgage, the answer is simple. In this sense, death is the termination of the pledge. The money is paid or not paid—in either case the pledge "dies." Mortgage relates to the dea__h of a pledge.

mortgage

**39.** My parents have had to assume a second _____
gage on their house.

*t*
mortgage

**40.** "Death pledge" reminds you to put the __ in _____.

a. *pt* receipt
b. *n* column
c. *p* psalm
d. *h* rhinoceros
e. *c* victuals
f. *h* exhibit
g. *p* ptomaine
h. *cer* discern
i. *h* herb
j. *w* sword
k. *s* corps

**41.** Locate the origin of each English word and fill in the missing letters to make the word complete.

a. recei____        G. *psallein,* to pluck, sing to the harp

b. colum__          L. *recipere,* to take

c. __salm           Anglo-Saxon *sweord,* to cut, pierce

d. r__inoceros      L. *herba,* grass, green crops

e. vi__tuals        G. *rhin,* nose, + *keros,* horn

f.  ex___ibit      L. *ex*, out, + *habere,* to hold

g.  ___tomaine      L. *columna,* pillar

h.  dis_____n      L. *dis,* apart, + *cernere,* to sift, separate

i.  ___erb      G. *ptoma,* fallen body

j.  s___ord      L. *victus,* sustenance

k.  corp___      Fr. *corps d'armée,* army corps

## REVIEW

Fill in the missing letters or words for the sentences below.

mortgage

**42.** I cannot buy a new house unless I arrange for a _____.

psychology

**43.** Sandy is majoring in _____.

herbs

**44.** My son is growing _____ instead of flowers.

knowledge

**45.** Sometimes a little _____ can be dangerous.

exhibit

**46.** On Saturday we will ex_____ our jewelry at the show fair.

discerning

**47.** Jason is a very dis_____ing person.

condemn

**48.** We cannot con_____ her for what she did.

receipt

**49.** Always get a re_____ for your purchases.

## POSTTEST

Supply the missing letters or words.

1. To watch over is to _____.

2. It will _____ rain tomorrow.
   certainly

3. The day after Tuesday is _____.

4. A person clever enough to make fine distinctions is said to be _____.

5. To tire out is the meaning of _____.

6. The rain fell in a steady r_____.

7. Jan's parents must pay on two _____gages monthly.

8. The origin of this word, which means ruins or rubble, is the Latin prefix *de* and the root *brisier.* What is the unpronounced last letter of the English word debri__?

9. A large mammal having horns on its snout is called a _____.

10. A legal protector is usually called a _____.

11. Her fingers were num__ from the cold.

12. The woman bought so many articles on credit that she was always in _____.

13. To help prevent tooth decay, water is often treated with a certain compound. The origin of the English word that means this treatment, Latin *fluere* (to flow), shows you how to spell the first syllable: __ __ __oridation.

14. Blair's dog will __naw on bones for hours.

15. My aunt Sally baked six r__ubarb pies for the bazaar.

16. A word absorbed into the language years ago came from Persia (now called Iran). The original word *khak,* meaning "dust," tells us we must never omit which letter in k__aki?

17. The origin is Old English *andsware,* swearing back. In the modern English word ans__er, meaning reply, what letter has no sound?

18. The Latin verb *scire,* to know, will help you to spell s__ience.

19. The new magazine has four col_____ on each page.

20. One of the most beautiful shepherd songs is the Twenty-third __salm.

# CHAPTER SIX
## SOUND-ALIKE SUFFIXES

Is *able* correct, or is it *ible*? Should it be *ary* or *ery*? *ance* or *ence*? When suffix alternatives sound alike, how can you tell which one is right? As you know, questions like these arise daily, and without some forthcoming answers, it is difficult to spell words with these endings accurately. Although there are no strict rules to follow, there are guidelines that will help you to master many words with suffix problems.

In this chapter you will learn to (1) apply guidelines in the spelling of a number of words with these suffixes; (2) practice spelling these words in and out of context; (3) identify words that are exceptions to the guidelines; and (4) from stated definitions, recognize and write the required words. In addition, this chapter supplies a background needed to spell other words with troublesome suffixes, and attempts to stimulate your curiosity about language in general.

### PRETEST

Choose the correct ending for each of the following.

A. *able-ible*

1. permiss_____
2. accept_____
3. estim_____
4. change_____
5. admir_____
6. market_____
7. inevit_____
8. elig_____

9. consider_____
10. pass_____
11. poss_____
12. perish_____
13. defens_____
14. repress_____
15. reduc_____
16. educ_____

B. *ary-ery*

1. bound_____
2. station_____ (writing paper)
3. secret_____
4. libr_____

5. cemet_____
6. Febru_____
7. contempor_____
8. station_____ (fixed)

C. *ise-ize-yze*

1. adv_____
2. anal_____
3. critic_____
4. summar_____
5. surpr_____

6. emphas_____
7. paral_____
8. exerc_____
9. advert_____
10. real_____

D. *ance-ence (ant-ent)*

1. intellig_____ (ent, ant)
2. resist_____ (ance, ence)
3. equival_____ (ent, ant)
4. accid_____ (ant, ent)
5. defend_____ (ant, ent)
6. promin_____ (ance, ence)
7. exist_____ (ant, ent)
8. confid_____ (ence, ance)
9. sci_____ (ence, ance)
10. conseq_____ (ent, ant)
11. experi_____ (ence, ance)
12. magnific_____ (ence, ance)

13. mainten_____ (ance, ence)
14. excell_____ (ent, ant)
15. guid_____ (ance, ence)
16. influ_____ (ence, ance)
17. extravag_____ (ance, ence)
18. insist_____ (ent, ant)
19. attend_____ (ance, ence)
20. domin_____ (ant, ent)
21. preval_____ (ence, ance)
22. delinqu_____ (ant, ent)
23. brilli_____ (ance, ence)
24. signific_____ (ent, ant)

laughable
acceptable
lamentable
commendable

### ABLE–IBLE

**1.** *Able* and *ible* are suffixes (elements added to the ends of words) that form adjectives from verbs and nouns. When added to verbs, they mean capable of or worthy: *eat* + *able* = *eatable* (capable of being eaten). When added to nouns, they mean tending or liable to: *knowledgeable* (tending to have knowledge) or *perishable* (liable to perish). Generally, if the root is a full word, it will take *able: eat* + *able* = *eatable; drink* + *able* = *drinkable; read* + *able* = *readable.* Add the *able* ending to these full words: laugh, accept, lament, commend. _____ _____
_____ _____

a. adorable
b. desirable
c. valuable
d. deplorable
e. writable
f. excusable

**2.** For complete words ending in *e*, you generally drop the *e* before adding a suffix beginning with a vowel: *debate + able = debatable*. Apply this guideline to these "e" words.

a. adore _____     d. deplore _____

b. desire _____     e. write _____

c. value _____     f. excuse _____

a. justifiable
b. playable
c. rectifiable
d. employable
e. pitiable
f. enviable

**3.** For complete words ending in *y* preceded by a *vowel*, you simply add *able: enjoy + able = enjoyable*. But for those words ending in *y* preceded by a *consonant*, like *rely*, you drop the *y* and add *i* before adding *able: rely + able = reliable*. Now add *able* to these "y" words.

a. justify _____     d. employ _____

b. play _____     e. pity _____

c. rectify _____     f. envy _____

a. adaptable
b. receivable
c. correctable
d. blamable
e. fortifiable
f. endurable
g. compliable

**4.** Apply what you have learned so far by combining the *able* ending with these complete words.

a. adapt _____

b. receive _____

c. correct _____

d. blame _____

e. fortify _____

f. endure _____

g. comply _____

ible
s
ns
repressible
comprehensible
horrible
expressible

**5.** Look at these *ible* words carefully.

credible       admissible       defensible
terrible       permissible       sensible

Separating the *ible* ending from the rest of the word leaves just a base—or incomplete word:

cred (*ible*)       admiss (*ible*)       defens (*ible*)
terr (*ible*)       permiss (*ible*)       sens (*ible*)

A simple guideline results: if the root is *not* a full word, you generally add the (*able, ible*) ending, especially if the base ends in a double ___or n ___.

Complete words ending in *ss* also take the *ible* suffix. For example, the adjective which means capable of being repressed is repress_____. Now apply these guidelines to these words or bases:

comprehens_____; horr_____; express_____.

appreciable

**6.** However, if a base ends in *i*, it will probably take *able*. Combining *able* with *appreci* produces _____.

a. admissible
b. sociable
c. indivisible
d. susceptible
e. reversible
f. edible
g. impossible
h. feasible
i. appreciable
j. compatible

**7.** Add *able* or *ible* to these bases.

a. admiss _____    f. ed _____
b. soci _____    g. imposs _____
c. indivis _____    h. feas _____
d. suscept _____    i. appreci _____
e. revers _____    j. compat _____

inevitable

**8.** As you probably noticed, two bases in the preceding frame end in *t* to which *ible* was added: *compatible* and *susceptible*. Another base ending in *t*—*inevit*—does not, however; it takes *able*. Combine the base and suffix in this sentence: If circumstances are incapable of being avoided, they are said to be inevit_____.

a. receivable
b. marketable
c. admissible
d. variables
creditable
e. permissible
f. acceptable
g. taxable
h. justifiable
i. sensible
compatible

**9.** Apply what you have learned thus far by supplying the correct *able* or *ible* endings and spelling the complete words correctly.

a. Nell has difficulty in understanding the term "receive _____ goods."

b. Only the used television sets were market_____.

c. The evidence based on hearsay was not admiss_____ in court.

d. The experiment had too many vary_____s to be credit_____.

e. Free admittance to the Sunday concerts is not permiss _____.

f. Their explanation was not accept_____.

g. All of Larry's income is tax_____.

h. Occasionally Douglas's obnoxious behavior can be called justify_____.

i. Her ideas for reform were sens_____ as well as compat _____with existing practices.

*ation*
yes
*ion*

**10.** Another aid in choosing correctly between *able* and *ible* is to remember the related noun. Take a look at these two groups of words.

yes for 3 words
no for 2 words
no

A.
restoration
commendation
consideration
admiration
reformation

B.
permission
admission
repression
perfection
collection

What is the five-letter ending of each word in group A? _____ Is the part of each word before this ending complete? (Remember that final e words usually drop the e before a suffix beginning with a vowel.) _____ What is the three-letter ending of each word in group B? _____ Is the part before this ending complete? _____ Is the double s in incomplete words only? _____

complete
s

**11.** Even though there are only a few words in the above lists, we can point out some guidelines. The two nounal endings are important: *ation, ion.* The words in group A (ation) have (complete, incomplete) words within them. _____ Those in group B have either bases or complete words. The bases have what double letter? __

*able*
*ible*
*ible*

**12.** Here are the same nouns as well as the *able-ible* adjectives relating to them:

A.
restoration            restorable
commendation           commendable
consideration          considerable
admiration             admirable
reformation            reformable

B.
permission             permissible
admission              admissible
repression             repressible
perfection             perfectible
collection             collectible

Again, we can point out some guidelines.

If a noun is formed by adding *ation,* the adjective will probably be formed by adding (able, ible). _____
If *ion* is the ending of the noun, the ending for the adjective will undoubtedly be (able, ible). _____

The double s at the end of a base or a complete word will usually take (able, ible). _____

a. demonstrable
b. reputable
c. audible
d. incorrectly
e. adaptable
f. operable
g. irritable

**13.** From the following nouns, form the correct *able-ible* adjectives for each sentence.

a. Although Lou's new sales techniques sounded interesting, they were not _____.
<small>demonstration</small>

b. Mr. Benson was not as _____ a writer
<small>reputation</small>
as the community had first thought.

c. The singer's low notes were not _____ to the
<small>audition</small>
listeners in the balcony.

d. If you see this sign in a window, "Antiques and Collect-ables," you will immediately say that the last word in the sign is spelled (correctly, incorrectly). _____

e. Critics predict that Blain Cunningham's latest novel is not _____ to television.
<small>adaptation</small>

f. Susie's mother has an _____ cancer.
<small>operation</small>

g. Larry has been _____ all day.
<small>irritation</small>

a. S
b. S
c. S
d. H
e. H
f. H
g. S
h. S

**14.** The sound of *c* and *g* at the end of a complete word or a base can suggest the correct ending: *able, ible.*

The soft sound of *c* is like an *s* (city).
The hard sound of *c* is like a *k* (cat).
The soft sound of *g* is like the *g* in *gem.*
The hard sound of *g* is like the *g* in *go* or *get.*

Pronounce the words below and identify by S or H if the italicized portions are soft or hard sounds.

a. pea*c*e          e. for*g*ive

b. *c*hange       f. dedu*c*t

c. redu*c*e        g. eli*g*ible

d. edu*c*ate       h. la*c*e

soft
ce
able
able

g
hard
able

**15.** Look at and pronounce the following words:

serviceable          changeable
enforceable          legible

What sound of *c* or *g* do you have here? _____
Each word with the soft *c* has what two-letter ending before the suffix? _____
Each word with *ce* takes (*ible, able*)? _____
The word with *ge* at the end of the root takes (*able, ible*).

The word with the soft g and suffix *ible* has (g, ge) as its ending. _____

Now look at and pronounce these two words:

revocable          educable

What sound of c do you have here? _____
What ending does each word have? _____

able
ible
able
able

**16.** Using some of the words from the two groups above, let us develop some guidelines.

changeable          serviceable
legible              educable

Words having a soft g in *ge* at the end of a root word take (*ible, able*). _____

Those having a soft g at the end of a base take (*ible, able*). _____

Those having a soft c in *ce* at the end of the root word take (*able, ible*). _____

Those having a hard c take (*able, ible*). _____

a. serviceable
b. educable
c. eligible
d. enforceable
e. legible
f. revocable
g. changeable

**17.** Pronounce these *able-ible* words, look at the ending of the base or root word, then write the complete word.

a. service_____          e. leg_____

b. educ_____          f. revoc_____

c. elig_____          g. change_____

d. enforce_____

reducible

**18.** If something can be reduced, it is said to be reduc _____.

invincible

**19.** If a person is incapable of being conquered, that person is invinc_____.

**REVIEW**

a. peaceable
b. inevitable
c. noticeable
d. possible
e. unbelievable
f. indispensable
g. changeable
h. visible
i. legible
j. revocable
k. serviceable

**20.** Write the complete *able-ible* words for each sentence.

a. The factions came to a peace_____ solution.

b. It is inevit_____ that Congress will pass the housing bill.

c. Her negative attitude was extremely notice_____.

d. Is it poss_____ that the little boy stole his father's watch?

e. Her story is unbelieve_____.

l. eligible
m. enforceable
n. sociable
o. employable

f. The manager thinks he is indispens_____.

g. Mae's dress is made out of change_____ taffeta.

h. The smoke was vis_____ for miles.

i. The teacher's handwriting is not leg_____.

j. The new rule is not revoc_____.

k. My shoes are still service_____.

l. The twins are not elig_____ for skating tournaments.

m. I doubt that the law is enforce_____.

n. Lanny's mother is very soci_____.

o. The counselor said that Mary's uncle was no longer employ_____.

a. educable
b. exhaustible
c. imaginable
d. consolable
e. revocable
f. perceptible
g. impressionable

**21.** From these *ation* and *ion* nouns, form the correct *able* or *ible* adjectives.

a. education _____        e. revocation _____

b. exhaustion _____        f. perception _____

c. imagination _____        g. impression _____

d. consolation _____

### ARY–ERY

hatchery
creamery

**22.** If *ery* is added to a word, it usually forms a noun. Take *hatch* and *cream,* for instance. Adding *ery* to each produces these two nouns: _____ and _____.

creamery

**23.** An establishment where dairy products are prepared is a _____.

hatchery

**24.** An establishment where eggs are hatched is a _____.

a. machinery
b. distillery
c. imagery
d. foppery
e. bribery
f. cannery
g. bindery
h. snobbery

**25.** Form nouns from these words by adding the *ery* ending. (Remember that words ending in *e* usually drop the *e* before a suffix beginning with a vowel, and that one-syllable words ending in a single consonant preceded by a single vowel double the final consonant before adding a suffix beginning with a vowel.)

a. machine_____        e. bribe_____

b. distill_____        f. can_____

c. image_____        g. bind_____

d. fop_____        h. snob_____

fragmentary

**26.** If *ary* is added to a word or a base, it usually forms an adjective. Adding *ary* to *fragment* produces _____.

a. secondary
b. hereditary
c. sanitary
d. ordinary

**27.** Form adjectives by combining these roots and bases with *ary*.

a. second_____          c. sanit_____

b. heredit_____          d. ordin_____

stationery
stationary

**28.** Two words causing a spelling problem are derived from the same Latin word, but one takes *ery* and the other takes *ary*. Let us apply the previous guideline. One is a noun, so it would be written station_____. The second is an adjective and would be written station_____.

stationery
stationary

**29.** Association also helps. The word which means writing paper contains the last two letters of pap*er*, so the correct spelling is station_____. The other, which means not movable, is spelled station_____.

a. bravery
b. nursery
c. disciplinary
d. documentary
e. auxiliary
f. solitary

**30.** From the following words or bases, write the complete *ary-ery* words. Decide first whether they can be nouns only or adjectives.

a. brave_____          d. document_____

b. nurse_____          e. auxili_____

c. disciplin_____          f. solit_____

a. temporary
b. anniversary
c. cemetery
d. periphery
e. library
f. secretary
g. necessary
h. judiciary
i. infirmary
j. quandary

**31.** Guidelines are just that, and to properly spell every *ary-ery* word, you must study them carefully. Use the five-step method for these, writing each complete word from memory as your last step.

a. temporary      _____

b. anniversary    _____

c. cemetery       _____

d. periphery      _____

e. library        _____

f. secretary      _____

g. necessary      _____

h. judiciary      _____

i. infirmary      _____

j. quandary       _____

## REVIEW

stationary

**32.** A chair that is not movable is _____.

a. cemetery
b. millinery
c. February
d. secretary
e. contemporary
f. sanitary
g. necessary
h. tributary
i. stationery
j. extraordinary

**33.** Apply the guidelines whenever appropriate and select the correct spelling in each pair.

a. cemetary, cemetery

b. millinery, millinary

c. February, February

d. secretery, secretary

e. contemporery, contemporary

f. sanitery, sanitary

g. necessery, necessary

h. tributery, tributary

i. stationary, stationery (writing materials)

j. extraordinary, extrordinery

discovery
machinery
cannery
quandary
temporary
precautionary

**34.** Complete these *ary-ery* words.
Early Monday morning Max made the startling discov_____ that vandals had damaged all the machin_____ in his can _____. For a while he was in a quand_____, but he finally decided to put a tempor_____ hold on all the orders as a precaution_____ measure.

## ISE–IZE–YZE

surprise
exercise

**35.** It is not the purpose here to supply the derivations of verbs ending in *ise, ize,* and *yze.* Suffice it to say that they come from Old French or Latin, hence *ise,* or from the Greek, hence *ize* and *yze.* Because of their common origin, the *ise* words are grouped together, and because association helps you to remember, the words will be related, for the most part, in "association sentences." Here is the first: It should be no *surprise* that I *exercise* when I get up. There is one word with two syllables _____and one with three syllables _____.

sur    prise
ex    er    cise

**36.** Given the beginning syllables of each word, divide the remainder of sur_____ and ex_____.

surprise
exercise

**37.** To fill with wonder or disbelief is the meaning of s_____. To perform physical activities means to ex_____.

a. exercise
b. surprise
c. surprised
exercise
surprise
exercise

**38.** Read the sentences below and supply these two words.

a. Athletes must _____ every day to keep fit.

b. He will _____ us all some day.

c. My friends were not _____ when I started a vigorous diet and _____ schedule.

Now back to the original sentence: It should be no _____ _____ that I _____ when I get up.

advise
enterprise
supervise
advertise
merchandise

**39.** Let us put some *ise* words into a business setting: Investing in an *enterprise* may mean having to *advise* and *supervise* a number of employees, and to *advertise* the *merchandise*. The one word with two syllables is _____. The rest have three syllables each: _____, _____, _____, and _____.

a. merchandise
b. advise
c. enterprise
d. advertise
e. supervise

**40.** a. Goods or wares are known as _____.

b. To counsel is to ad_____.

c. A business venture is called an enter_____.

d. To make a public announcement is to adver_____.

e. To direct or inspect is to super_____.

enterprise
advise
supervise
advertise
merchandise

**41.** And here is the original sentence: Investing in an _____ may mean having to _____ and _____ a number of employees, and to _____ the _____.

analyze
paralyze

**42.** Now look at this group of words.

realize        criticize
emphasize      characterize
recognize      summarize
analyze        paralyze

Of the eight words, which two have the *yze* ending? _____and _____

analyze
paralyze

**43.** To separate a whole into its parts and examine them is the meaning of anal_____; to render ineffective, or to unnerve, is the meaning of paral_____.

analyze
paralyze

**44.** These two words are similar in another respect: an____ yze      par____yze

a. paralyze
b. analyze

**45.** Supply the correct *yze* word:

a. Some forms of polio will _____ a person.

b. To reach an effective solution you should first _____
_____ the problem.

advise
paralyzed

**46.** Should the doctor adv_____ Joe that he might become
para_____d?

a. patronize
b. theorize
c. penalize
d. liberalize
e. authorize
f. familiarize

**47.** It may help to know that far more words end in *ize* than
in *ise,* and many come from existing nouns and adjectives,
like civil ize, apolog(y) ize, or equal ize. Here are six
words from which you can form *ize* verbs:

a. patron_____      d. liberal_____

b. theor(y)_____      e. author_____

c. penal_____      f. familiar_____

re al ize
em pha size

**48.** Let us continue our "association sentences": Did you
*realize* that you didn't *emphasize* the right points in your
argument? The first syllables are *re* and *em.* You write the
rest of the syllables: re_____ and em_____.

realize
emphasize

**49.** To understand clearly, or to accomplish is to re_____.
To stress is to em_____.

a. realize
b. emphasized
c. realize

**50.** Choose the correct word for the context.

a. I do _____ what you are saying.

b. His boasting only _____d his lack of
knowledge.

c. Some day he may _____ his dreams.

realize
emphasize

**51.** To return to the original sentence: Did you _____
that you didn't _____ the right points in
your argument?

3
rec og nize
crit i cize

**52.** Now for another association: Even though you *recognize*
his faults, you don't need to *criticize* him publicly. Each word
has __ syllables. Complete them for each word: rec _____
_____and crit __ _____.

recognize
criticize

**53.** To take notice of is to r_____. To judge
or evaluate is to c_____.

criticize

**54.** Of these two words, which one often carries the idea of
simply finding fault? _____

recognize
criticize

summarize
characterize

characterize
summarize

a. characterize
b. summarized
c. characterize

a. paralyze
b. surprise
c. emphasize
d. criticize
e. brutalize
f. exercise
g. symbolize
h. analyze

a. apologize
b. disguise
c. pulverize
d. compromise
e. advise
f. formalize
g. hypnotize

*r*
vowel
second (last)

**55.** Back to the original sentence: Even though you _____ _____ his faults, you don't need to _____ _____ him publicly.

**56.** The last *ize* words are summar_____ and character _____.

**57.** To describe the qualities of or give character to is the definition of the verb _____.
To sum up or to restate briefly is to _____.

**58.** Write the correct one of these two words for each sentence.

a. His temper and his bad manners _____ _____ him as a boor.

b. The ideas in your paper are not well _____d.

c. How would you _____ Professor Jones?

## REVIEW

**59. A.** Choose the correctly spelled word in each pair.

a. paralyse, paralyze
b. surprize, surprise
c. emphasise, emphasize
d. criticize, criticise

e. brutalise, brutalize
f. exercize, exercise
g. symbolize, symbolise
h. analyse, analyze

B. Write the *ise, ize, yze* word that fits each definition.

a. ap_____ to make an excuse for a fault

b. disgu_____ a mask

c. pulver_____ to grind to a powder

d. comprom_____ to settle differences

e. adv_____ to counsel

f. for_____ to give formal endorsement to

g. hypnot_____ to fascinate, to put to sleep

## ANCE–ENCE

**60.** Unfortunately, there are no rules to follow in adding *ance-ence* endings to form nouns (or *ant-ent* endings to form adjectives and sometimes nouns). However, there are guidelines which can help in spelling quite a few words with these suffixes. Look closely at these two groups of words.

A.         B.

concur     refer

recur      defer

deter      confer

abhor     prefer

occur      infer

All are verbs ending in the consonant ___, which is preceded by a (vowel, consonant), and the accent in the word falls on the _____ syllable.

occurrence
occurrent

**61.** Every verb in the preceding frame takes the *ence (ent)* ending, but to prevent any other spelling errors, we will work first with those in column A. The doubling of the final consonant rule applies here: double if a word ends in a single consonant preceded by a single vowel and the accent falls on the last syllable. Pronounce *occur.* It fits the rule, so you would double the *r* and add *ence* (or *ent*). Write this noun _____ and the corresponding adjective _____.

concurrence,
concurrent
recurrence,
recurrent
deterrence,
deterrent
abhorrence,
abhorrent

**62.** The other five verbs in the column follow the same pattern. Write the nouns and adjectives for

concur (to approve)     _____    _____

recur (to occur again)     _____    _____

deter (to turn aside)     _____    _____

abhor (to hate)     _____    _____

concurrence
recurrences
deterrents

**63.** Complete these words with the appropriate ending. There was a general concur_____ that there would be no more recur_____s of the patient's violent behavior. The staff agreed that several deter_____ts were necessary.

deference
conference
preference
inference

**64.** The verbs in column B also fit the guideline, but in each case when the *ence* is added, the accent (or stress) shifts to the first syllable. You would not double the final consonant then. Take *refer* as an illustration. The accent is on refer´, but when you add *ence,* the accent shifts to reference— notice there is no double *r* in this word.

Now add *ence* to the rest of the words in the column:

defer_____        prefer_____

confer_____        infer_____

flu
qu

**65.** Here are four interesting words:

influence      delinquent

affluence      consequent

Certain letters at the end of the bases signal for the *ence (ent)* ending. In the first column we have three: _____; in the second column we have two: _____.

delinquent
influence
consequence or
consequent
affluence

**66.** A person who fails to do what law or obligation requires can be called delin_____.
A person who exercises power over someone or a course of events has in_____ence.
A logical conclusion is a conse_____.
Wealth is a synonym for af_____ence.

delinquent
influence
affluent
consequences

**67.** Complete the endings for these words.

Because the thief, already known to the police as a juvenile delin_____, had lots of in_____ over his buddies, he persuaded them to rob the homes of aff_____t people in the suburbs, regardless of the conse_____es.

conscience
obedience

**68.** Here is another guideline. If the root ends in *ci* ("sh" sound), or an *i* with an "e" sound, it will probably take *ence* or *ent*. Two roots will illustrate: *consci* ("sh" sound) and *obedi* ("e" sound). Adding *ence* to both produces con _____and obedi_____.

conscience

**69.** When I tell a lie, my con_____ bothers me.

obedience

**70.** Today many brides do not take the vow of o_____.

experience

**71.** Like the base in *obedience,* the base in this next word, meaning something a person lives through, ends in *i* with the sound of "e". It would be spelled experi_____.

experience
inexperienced

**72.** To get a job I need ex_____, but how do I get it when no one will hire inex_____d people?

efficiency
proficiency
sufficiency
deficiency
efficient
proficient
sufficient
deficient

**73.** Here are several roots ending in *ci* ("sh" sound). Supply the missing parts.

effici_____cy          effici_____t
profici_____cy         profici_____t
suffici_____cy         suffici_____t
defici_____cy          defici_____t

deficient
sufficient
efficient
proficient

**74.** Supply either *ence* or *ent.*

If Rudy's performance lacks a certain something, it can be said to be de_____; if it is adequate, it is suf_____. If his performance shows proven capability based on productiveness, Rudy can be called ef_____; if his performance shows expert correctness and facility, then he is pro_____.

## REVIEW

a. affluent
b. abhorrence
c. deficient
d. occurrence
e. preference
f. concurrence
g. existence
h. experience
i. consequence
j. recurrence
k. influence

**75.** Match the incomplete words with the correct definitions, add the appropriate *ence* or *ent* endings, and write the whole words.

a. wealthy         oc_____

b. hatred         pref_____

c. lacking         defi_____

d. event         inf_____

e. choice         ex_____

f. agreement         conc_____

g. state of continued being         re_____

h. knowledge from partici- pation in activities         ab_____

i. logical conclusion         af_____

j. return         exp_____

k. power         cons_____

*l*
*d*
*n*

**76.** These next words illustrate the tendency of certain consonants to take the *ence* endings:

equivalence      confidence      permanence

The consonant in each word that suggests this ending is _____, _____, and _____.

a. equivalence
b. permanence
c. confidence

**77. a.** Equality is a synonym for equiva_____.

**b.** The state of being changeless is the definition of per _____.

**c.** Trust in a person is known as con_____.

*ent*

**78.** If you remember these professionals—*lawyer, doctor,* and *nurse*—you will remember that roots ending in the consonants *l, d,* and *n* are likely to take (*ant, ent*).

a. excellent
b. prevalent
c. eminent
d. prominent
e. independent
f. imminent
g. antecedent
h. incident

**79.** Apply the guidelines and form adjectives from these:

a. excel_____      e. independ_____

b. preval_____      f. immin_____

c. emin_____      g. anteced_____

d. promin_____      h. incid_____

a. defendant
guidance

**80.** Study these words ending in *n* and *d* because they are exceptions:

maintenance
balance
dominant
b. abundance

balance                    abundance (*ant*)
dominance (*ant*)          attendance (*ant*)
maintenance                guidance
defendant

To better remember these exceptions, let us put them in contexts.

a. The defend_____ needs guid_____ for the mainten _____of bal_____ between fact and fiction, so that fiction is not domin_____.

b. A large crop suggests an abund_____ of potatoes.

abundant
defendant
eminent
dominant
independent
prevalent
dependence
guidance
balance
excellence
maintenance
imminence

**81.** Supply the correct endings for these "lawyer, doctor, and nurse" words and the exceptions.

| *ant* or *ent* | *ance* or *ence* |
|---|---|
| abund_____ | depend_____ |
| defend_____ | guid_____ |
| emin_____ | bal_____ |
| domin_____ | excel_____ |
| independ_____ | main_____ |
| preval_____ | immin_____ |

a. S
b. H
c. S
d. S
e. H
f. S

**82.** The sound of the *c* and *g* will govern which ending is correct. The hard sound of *c* (cat) and the hard sound of *g* (go) require *ance* (or *ant*). The soft sound of *c* (city) and the soft sound of *g* (gem) take *ence* (or *ent*).
Pronounce these words, then identify which sound each underlined consonant has. Use S (soft) and H (hard),
a. adolescent              d. magnificent
b. extravagance            e. significance
c. intelligence            f. emergence

*ance*   *ant*
*ence*   *ent*

a. significant
b. magnificent
c. intelligent
d. adolescence
e. extravagant
f. negligence

**83.** Words with a hard *c* or *g* take _____ or _____, whereas those with a soft *c* or *g* take _____ or _____.

**84.** a. The teacher made a signific_____ contribution to education.

b. The Grand Canyon is a magnific_____ sight.

c. Carolyn is highly intellig_____.

d. The period prior to adulthood is called adolesc_____.

e. The saleswoman made extravag_____ claims about her product.

f. The hit-and-run driver admitted his guilt and was charged with neglig_____.

complete
v

**85.** Generally, complete words and bases ending in *t* and *v* take *ance* or *ant. Accept* ends in *t* and is a (complete, incomplete) word. The base in *relevance* ends in _____.

annoy
allow
comply
v

**86.** How about *annoyance, allowance, compliance,* and *irrelevance? Annoyance* and *allowance* have complete words within them: _____ and _____. *Compliance* does also because the *i* replaced the *y* before the suffix was added. The smaller, complete word is _____. In *irrelevance* the consonant __ is at the end of the base.

noncompliance
annoyance

**87.** A loophole allowing noncom_____ with the clean-air regulation produced considerable annoy_____.

a. riddance
b. remittance
c. admittance
d. reliance
e. assurance
f. disturbance
g. resultant
h. important
i. discordant
j. descendant

**88.** Test your skill with these words. Remember the rules about doubling the final consonant and the final *e.*

*ance, ence*

a. rid_____

b. remit_____

c. admit_____

d. rely_____

e. assure_____

f. disturb_____

*ant, ent*

g. result_____

h. import_____

i. discord_____

j. descend_____

sense
license
expense
defense
pretense
suspense

**89.** Because the ending *ense* sounds just like *ence,* it is easy to spell words with this ending incorrectly.
Here are the most commonly misspelled *ense* words.

s_____

lic_____

exp_____

def_____

pret_____

susp_____

a. expense
license
sense
b. defense
suspense
pretense

**90.** Putting these words into context will help you to remember them.

a. The exp_____ of the lic_____ made Lucy realize that she must use more common s_____ in her money management.

b. The def_____ kept the court in susp_____ over the witness's pret_____ of having seen the armed robbery.

anse

**91.** There is one exception to these *ense* words: *expanse,* which means wide, open extent. The ending is not *ense,* but _____.

expanse

**92.** I was amazed at the exp_____ of Lake Vermillion.

## REVIEW

a. guidance
b. defense
c. inheritance
d. equivalent
e. eminent
f. maintenance
g. permanent
h. superintendent
i. defendant

**93.** Apply the guidelines to these words.

a. Simon is a guid_____ consultant in the public schools.

b. The boy had no def_____ for his actions.

c. Laurie received a large inherit_____.

d. Equal in substance or value is the meaning of equival_____t.

e. A renowned person is emi_____.

f. The state of keeping in proper condition is called main _____.

g. Lasting is the definition of perman_____.

h. I know the superin_____ well.

i. The judge berated the defend_____.

a. excellent
b. balance
c. attendance
d. sense
e. extravagant
f. confident
g. magnificence
h. dominant
i. expanse

**94.** Choose the correct endings and write the complete words.

a. excel_____ (*ant, ent*)_____

b. bal_____ (*ence, ance*)_____

c. attend_____ (*ance, ence*)_____

d. s_____ (*ence, ense*)_____

e. extravag_____ (*ent, ant*)_____

f. confid_____ (*ant, ent*)_____

g. magnific_____ (*ence, ance*)_____

h. domin_____ (*ant, ent*)_____

i. exp_____ (*ense, anse*)_____
wide extent

## POSTTEST

Complete the spelling of these words.

1. The subject is certainly debate_____(*ible, able*).

2. Mac's new toy seems to be indestruct_____(*able, ible*).

3. Tomorrow is my parents' twentieth annivers_____(*ery, ary*).

4. Susie would rather exer_____(*ize, ise*) in the gym than jog.

5. I was paral_____(*yzed, ized*) with fear.

6. His expensive presents surpr_____(*ised, ized*) me.

7. Sometimes Donny shows little common s_____(*ense, ence*).

8. Despite his excellent refer_____(*ances, ences*), Jack did not succeed in his new job.

9. Lately there have been several similar occur_____(*ences, ances*).

10. He expressed a prefer_____(*ance, ence*) for iced tea.

B. Pick out the misspelled word in each pair and write it correctly.

11. inoperable, inoperible          _____

12. collectables, collectibles       _____

13. analyse, analyze                 _____

14. superintendant, superintendent  _____

15. noticable, noticeable            _____

16. infirmery, infirmary             _____

17. equalise, equalize               _____

18. difference, differance           _____

19. permanant, permanent            _____

20. excellance, excellence           _____

21. prominant, prominent             _____

22. admitance, admittance            _____

23. desireable, desirable            _____

24. manageible, manageable          _____

25. impressionable, impressionible   _____

C. Find the 12 misspellings in this list of words and write them correctly.

26. eligible
27. marriagable
28. resistent
29. surprise
30. redeemable
31. primary
32. authorise
33. negligance
34. irritible

35. advisable
36. licence
37. defense
38. persistant
39. permissible
40. imaginary
41. insurable
42. generalise
43. deferrence

44. comprehensable
45. library
46. elementary
47. consistent
48. dominent
49. accessible
50. cemetary

# TEST
## PART TWO

A. Select the correct word in each sentence.

1. The politician's (critacism, critisism, criticism) was uncalled for. _____

2. The judge delivered a (contraversial, controversial, controversal) speech. _____

3. His business is certainly (legitimate, legetimate, ligitimate). _____

4. The comedian wasn't (humerus, humorus, humorous) at all. _____

5. The car needs a new (exaust, exhawst, exhaust) pipe. _____

6. The plaintiff's evidence is not (admisible, admissible, admissable) in court. _____

7. Damage to the store was (appreciable, apprecible, aprecible). _____

8. How much (experence, experiance, experience) do you have? _____

9. I went to Roselawn (Cematary, Cemetery, Cemetary) yesterday. _____

10. Ray is not (libel, lible, liable) for his wife's debts. _____

B. First, match the word with its origin; second, spell the complete word.

11. abu__ __ __nce

12. cong__ __ __ation

13. sa__ __ __ __ite

14. ac__um__late

15. ex__ __ __ __ __ate

16. im__ __ __ __ment

a. L. *ad* (to) *cumulare* (to pile up)

b. L. *de* (from) *rivus* (river, stream)

c. Nicholas Chauvin, a soldier who had an extreme enthusiasm for Napoleon

d. L. *villa* (country house)—the English word originally meant just a serf attached to a manor

e. L. *abundare* (to overflow, from *unda,* meaning wave)

f. L. *satellitem* (attendant or guard)

17. ch__ __ __ __ __ism

18. r__ __ __l

19. vi__ __ __in

20. der__ __ation

g. L. *gregis* (flock or herd)

h. L. *rivalis* (one living on opposite shore of stream, from *rivus*, stream or river)

i. L. *ex* (completely) *hilaris* (cheerful, from Gr. *hilaros*)

j. L. *impedire* (to entangle, fetter)

C. Fill in the missing letters.

21. mor__gage

22. __sychiatry

23. g_____rdian

24. predict_____ (*ible, able*)

25. station_____
        not movable

26. incid_____ (*ant, ent*)

27. prefer_____ (*ance, ence*)

28. prefer_____ (*ed*)

29. consci_____ (*ance, ence*)

30. elim_____nate

31. sal__ry

32. sep_____rate

33. __salm

34. quan_____ty

35. def__nite

36. condem__

37. solem__

38. warr__nt

39. __neumonia

40. __ymn

D. Combine the root word or base and the correct suffix.

41. emin_____ (*ant, ent*)

42. diffid_____ (*ent, ant*)

43. subsid_____ (*ize, ise*)

44. insurg_____ (*ance, ence*)

45. divis_____ (*able, ible*)

46. respons_____ (*able, ible*)

47. comment_____ (*ary, ery*)

48. vulcan_____ (*ize, ise*)

49. resist_____ (*able, ible*)

50. percept_____ (*ible, able*)

51. recogn_____ (*ize, ise*)

52. interfer_____ (*ence, ance*)

53. revers_____ (*ible, able*)

54. sens_____ (*able, ible*)

55. imagin_____ (*ery, ary*)

56. liter_____ (*ery, ary*)

57. anci_____ (*ant, ent*)

58. natural_____ (*ize, ise*)

59. endur_____ (*ible, able*)

60. legal_____ (*ize, ise*)

E. Have someone dictate these sentences so you can correctly spell each underlined word.

61. His age is a hindrance.

62. My Uncle owns a large factory.

63. Are you working at the library?

64. She has had one tragedy after another.

65. Today is the <u>twelfth</u> of December.
66. She has an extremely high <u>temperature</u>.
67. He works as a <u>chimney</u> sweep.
68. Little Joey is a <u>mischievous</u> child.
69. It will <u>probably</u> rain tomorrow.
70. I dislike <u>vegetables</u>.
71. He has a <u>cruel</u> streak.
72. I earned one <u>hundred</u> dollars.
73. Bill is a <u>sophomore</u> at the university.
74. The excessive heat makes me <u>perspire</u>.
75. I love <u>chocolate</u> ice cream.

F. Locate the misspelled words in this passage and write them correctly.

A writing system develops chiefly from attempts to standardise and innovate and from the political and educational movements rather than from the linguistic process itself. The English language has had an intresting development. It was intraduced in its earliest form from about the middle of the fifth century by the Angels, Saxons, and tribes from the northren part of Germany. These invaders eventually founded kingdoms of their own, and from the language of these Teutonic settlers developed the national tongue.

# PART THREE

## THREE

### MEANING AND SPELLING

# CHAPTER SEVEN
## PREFIXES

The building of words occurs in many ways. They can be combined to form new ones: *countdown, skyscraper, brain-wash, round-the-clock.* They can be contractions of words: *smoke + fog = smog; breakfast + lunch = brunch.* But one of the most basic ways is the adding of elements to a root word—these are called prefixes and suffixes. In this chapter we are concerned with prefixes, those elements added to the beginning of a root word, as in *re*peat, *mis*spell, *un*natural and *de*scribe. Prefixes have a meaning (or meanings) and can usually be traced to Latin or Greek; their function is to produce new words with different meanings. Take the root *scribe.* Add *de* and you have *describe* (to tell about something); add *pro* and you have *proscribe* (to denounce or condemn); add *pre* and you have *prescribe* (to set down a rule).

The objectives of this chapter are four: you will (1) pronounce carefully words that include prefixes such as *de, dis, pre,* and *pro;* (2) write the correct meanings for these and other prefixes; (3) choose the correct prefix for particular root words; and (4) write correctly a number of commonly misspelled words. In the course of this study you will also learn variant spellings which developed through assimilation or other linguistic change. For example, *ex* becomes *ef* before the root *fect* (*effect*), and *ad* becomes *at* before *tract* (*attract*).

Upon attaining these objectives, you will be better equipped to select and spell the correct prefix for many words in the English language. A handy reference list of prefixes that have variant spellings is included after the posttest.

## PRETEST

Choose the correct spelling in each pair. Definitions are given to help you.

1. to make familiar     acquaint, aquaint    _____

2. a group of people    comittee, committee    _____

3. to interrupt      disturb, desturb  ————————————

4. a skill or talent      abbility, ability  ————————————

5. lack of affectation      innocence, inocence  ————————————

6. needless      unecessary, unnecessary  ————————————

7. act of joining      connection, conection  ————————————

8. not rational      irrational, irational  ————————————

9. to speak to      adress, address  ————————————

10. to win over      pursuade, persuade  ————————————

11. a teacher      professor, proffessor  ————————————

12. remarkable      extraordinary, extrordinary  ————————————

13. to frustrate, thwart      disappoint, dissappoint  ————————————

14. accomplishment      sucess, success  ————————————

15. to leave out      accept, except  ————————————

B. From the list of prefixes, select the right one(s) for each root. In one case, two prefixes are added to one root. Definitions will help you to choose correctly.

| | |
|---|---|
| ab | in |
| ad (af) (at) | per |
| con | pro |
| de | re |
| dis | sub |
| ex (ef) | |

Root: *fect* (from Latin *facere,* to do)

16. ————fect      to contaminate

17. ————fect      to cleanse of contamination

18. ————fect      a failing

19. ————fect      flawless

20. ————fect      to change or alter

21. ————fect      a result

Root: *tract* (from Latin *trahere,* to pull)

22. ————tract      to turn aside, divert

23. ————tract      to extend forward

24. ————tract      to evoke interest in

25. ————tract      to reduce in size

26. ————stract      to remove

27. ————tract      to deduct

a. *dis*
b. *de*
c. *de*
d. *dis*
e. *de*
f. *dis*
g. *de*

**1.** In certain words the prefixes *dis* and *de* have so similar a pronunciation that it is easy to substitute one for the other. The sound of *i* in *dismiss* and *e* in *describe* is the same: the short sound of *i*. Because the sound is identical, the *s* following the *e* in describe provides the confusion: "dis cribe." The solution lies in the meaning of the prefix. *Dis* means apart. If one is dismissed, one is sent apart. The prefix also means not. To dislike someone is not to like him or her. The prefix *de* has two meanings. First, it means down. If you descend, you go down. Second, it means off (or away). To deduct a dollar is to take it off (or away).

Consider the meanings of *dis* and *de* and choose the correct prefix for each root or base below. For bases not easily identified the meanings are given.

a. _____approve          e. _____tour (turn)

b. _____tain (hold)       f. _____tend (stretch)

c. _____part (go)         g. _____cay (fall)

d. _____trust

a. apart
b. off
c. down
d. not

**2.** Now write the correct meaning for each prefix.

a. If you *dis*sect a frog, you cut it _____.

b. If you *de*cide, you cut _____ deliberation.

c. If you *de*grade something, you grade it _____.

d. If you *dis*trust people, you do _____ have confidence in them.

a. not   apart
b. down   off (away)

**3.** Supply two meanings for each prefix.

a. *dis*  _____   _____

b. *de*   _____   _____

a. *dis*
b. *de*
c. *dis*
d. *de*
e. *dis*
f. *de*

**4.** Read these sentences carefully for their meaning, then supply the missing prefix, *dis* or *de*.

a. Their actions _____ honored the family name.

b. The mountaineers had difficulty trying to _____scend.

c. The supervisor's easygoing manner _____pelled the clerk's fears.

d. You should rewrite your _____scription.

e. There is always a place in society for constructive \_\_\_\_\_ sent.

f. After a while Sue became _____*spondent*.

a. through
b. forward or forth
c. before

**5.** Confusing the prefixes *pre, per,* and *pro* usually results from similarities in pronunciation, from not knowing their meanings, and from not looking at them carefully. Since *you* can look at and pronounce these elements correctly, we are concerned here with their meanings:

*pre* before
*pro* forward or forth
*per* through

For the following sentences write the correct meaning of each prefix.

a. A performer is one who carries an act _____.

b. A proposal is a plan that is brought _____.

c. To precede is to go _____.

a. *per*
b. *pre*
c. *pro*
d. *per*

**6.** Now supply the correct missing prefix.

a. If you act or carry through you will _____form.

b. If you go before me you will _____cede me.

c. To place an idea forward is to _____pose it.

d. To see all the way through is to _____ceive it.

*pre* before
*pro* forward (forth)
*per* through

**7.** Write these three prefixes and their meanings.

_____ means _____

_____ means _____

_____ means _____

a. *per* through
b. *pre* before
c. *pro* forth
d. *per* through
e. *pro* forward
f. *pre* before

**8.** Read each sentence, then supply the correct prefix (*per, pre, pro*) and its meaning for each of these definitions.

a. To _____meate is to soak _____.

b. To _____cede is to go _____.

c. To _____claim is to cry _____.

d. To _____forate is to punch holes _____ something.

e. A _____cession is a movement of people going _____.

f. To _____cancel is to cancel a postage stamp _____ mailing.

# REVIEW

a. *pre*
b. *per*
c. *de*
d. *de*
e. *de*
f. *de*
g. *dis*
h. *per   per   pro*
i. *pro*
j. *pro*
k. through
l. forward
m. before

**9.** Test your skill in choosing the correct prefixes or their meanings.

a. When my cousin had a severe reaction to the new drug, the doctor _____scribed another drug.
  *per, pre*

b. To sweat or excrete a fluid through the pores of the skin is to _____spire.
  *pre, per*

c. How many times must I _____scribe her dress?
  *dis, de*

d. A severe earthquake will _____stroy even the well-constructed buildings.
  *dis, de*

e. The father of the little boy is filled with grief and _____spair.
  *de, dis*

f. Senator Fowler stated that he could easily _____spise all dishonest merchants.
  *dis, de*

g. The constant drumming of his fingertips on the table will surely _____turb the patients.
  *de, dis*

h. Instructors _____form duties _____taining to their
  *pre, per*                    *per, pre*
_____fessions.
  *per, pre, pro*

i. Even though I missed a month of school, the teachers decided to _____mote me.
  *pre, pro*

j. The high schools need a different _____cedure for
  *pro, pre*
registration.

k. Perform means to act _____.
  *through, before*

l. To propose is to place _____.
  *before, forward*

m. To precede is to go _____.
  *through, before*

a. dissimilar
b. off
c. defer
d. distorting
e. perceive
f. preventive
g. profusion

# REVIEW

**10.** a. To be different is to be _____similar.

b. To defend yourself you would ward _____ blows.

c. To postpone a decision is to ____fer it.

d. Twisting the truth is _____torting it.

e. From the Latin prefix meaning through and the root *capere* meaning to take comes the English word which means to take notice or _____ceive.

f. Warding off disease before it strikes is called _____ventive medicine.

g. A pouring forth is the definition of _____fusion.

again
back

**11.** The prefix *re* can mean again or back. For instance, to reenter is to enter _____; to recall some information is to call it _____.

back
again

**12.** Two commonly misspelled words are *recommend* and *recollect*. Each contains the prefix *re* and a root word. If we recollect, we recall or collect _____; if we recommend we commend _____.

collect
commend

recommend
recollect

**13.** These two words have the prefix *re* and a root word. What are the roots? _____ and _____

**14.** If employees do good work, they are often _____ _____ed for promotion.

I find it hard to _____ the exact details of the accident.

a. again
b. back
c. back
d. again

**15.** Now supply the correct meaning of *re* in each word below.

a. request: to seek _____

b. recall: to call _____

c. a reprieve: a taking _____

d. a reprint: a printing _____

a. misstep
b. disservice
c. unnumbered
d. mistake
e. misstate
f. unnerved
g. mistreat
h. uncertainty

**16.** Most of the spelling problems with the prefixes *mis, dis,* and *un* come from forgetting that the prefix and the root are two entities. For example, *mis* ends in *s* and *spell* begins with *s*. When you combine them, you must keep both *s*'s. The same is true when you add *un* to a word beginning with *n*. With this in mind, add the specified prefixes and the roots below.

i.  disrepair
j.  dissolve

a. mis   step    _____

b. dis   service    _____

c. un   numbered    _____

d. mis   take    _____

e. mis   state    _____

f. un   nerved    _____

g. mis   treat    _____

h. un   certainty    _____

i. dis   repair    _____

j. dis   solve    _____

a. c.

**17.** Some words are derived from a Latin root and the prefix *ad,* meaning to, toward, or near to, or used as an intensive. Take *adhere:* it comes from *ad* (toward) and *haērer* (stick). If you apply glue to a piece of paper it "sticks toward" or adheres. Another word is *acclaim: ad* (to) *clāmāre* (shout), to applaud. Note that the *d* from *ad* is absent.
If you pronounce *adhere* rapidly several times, the sound of the *d* does not change. If you pronounce *ad claim* in the same manner, the sound *does* change; it becomes muted and similar to the adjacent sound ("k" sound in claim). In other words, assimilation has taken place. To account for the *d,* the same sound ("k") is substituted—in this case the same letter: *ac claim.*
Pronounce the following combinations rapidly several times. In which ones is the *d not* assimilated? _____

a. ad   minister        c. ad   mire
b. ad   firm            d. ad   gression

a.
b.
d.
f.

**18.** Look at these words and their origins, then pronounce them rapidly. In which ones is the *d* assimilated? _____

a. ad ply (*ad plicāre*) to fold together

b. ad gregate (*ad gregāre*) to herd

c. ad monish (*ad monēre*) to remind

d. ad semble (*ad simul*) together

e. ad mit (*ad mittere*) to send in to

f. ad lure (*ad leurrer*) to lure

affirm

**19.** In assimilation the sound of the *d* in *ad* becomes similar to the sound of the beginning letter of the root. What is the correct spelling of *ad firm?* _____

a. apply
b. aggregate
c. assemble
d. allure

**20.** Write the correct spelling of the following:

a. ad ply         _____

b. ad gregate   _____

c. ad semble    _____

d. ad lure        _____

accurately

**21.** A common English word has this origin: *ad cūrāre,* to care for. If one "cares for" a job, one tries to do it _____ curately.

assist

**22.** Another common word has this origin: *ad sistere,* to stand near. If I stand near you, or help you, I _____sist you.

aggravation

**23.** In the combination *ad* and *gravāre,* the root means to burden and *ad* is an intensive (the burden is indeed heavy). Such a burden is an _____gravation.

The root has an
*a* (gravare).

**24.** How does the word origin signal that *aggrevation* is a misspelling? _____

_____

a. appear
b. aggression
c. applaud
d. attest

**25.** Decide if the *d* is assimilated, then complete the spelling of the modern English words.

a. *ad parēre* (to show)      _____pear
b. *ad gradī* (step toward)   _____gression
c. *ad plaudere* (to clap)   _____plaud
d. *ad testāri* (to be witness) _____test

correlation
community
difference
irrational
succumb
immediate

**26.** Assimilation can also occur in words that are derived from the Latin prefixes *con* (with, together), *dis* (apart, not), *in* (into, not), and *sub* (under, beneath). Here are roots to which you should attach the correctly spelled prefix, and then write the whole word.

_____relation     _____
*con*

_____munity      _____
*con*

_____ference     _____
*dis*

_____rational     _____
*in*

_____cumb       _____
*sub*

_____mediate    _____
*in*

correlation

**27.** Studies have shown that a positive relationship exists between good spellers and a systematic method for spelling. That relationship is called a _____relation.

succumbed

**28.** One who literally "lies under" has _____cumbed to great pressure.

irrational

**29.** To not be rational is to be _____rational.

irrigation

**30.** Supplying dry land with water is the process of _____ rigation.

difference

**31.** The condition of being dissimilar is called _____ ference.

hard

**32.** Assimilation also occurs in words like *acquaint* and *acquire.* Their derivations are *ad* (to) *quaerere* (seek, obtain) and *ad* (intensive) *cognōscere* (to know). In *acquaint* and *acquire,* we do not find the first letter of the root (*q*) doubled, but we do find the sound (*k*) doubled. In other words, the "k" sound of *quaint* and *quire* is the same as the _____ sound of the *c* in the prefix.
hard, soft

acquainted

**33.** If we "obtain" we acquire. If we "know" we become ___ quainted with something.

acquire
acquainted

**34.** When will Dan Williams _____ the chemical plant? I didn't know you were _____ with the governor.

## REVIEW

a. recommend
b. appalled
c. recall
d. collaborate
e. *sub* under
f. applause
g. recommendation
h. ally
i. unnatural
j. appease
k. appraise
l. unnecessary
m. 1st *g* and 1st *a*
n. replaces *d* in *ad*
o. misstated

**35.** Read the sentences carefully, then write the required word or phrase.

a. To commend again is to _____.

b. A modern English word is derived from the Latin *ad* and *palir* (to grow pale). If we see a situation and "grow pale" we are _____palled.

c. To call back information is to _____.

d. If two people work together they _____laborate.

e. To entreat or beg is the meaning of *supplicate.* This English word is derived from the Latin root *plicāre* (to fold) and the prefix _____, which means _____.

f. After the final curtain, the audience broke into thunderous _____plause.

g. Because of Lou's poor work record, I cannot write a letter of _____ation.

h. The Latin *ad* and *ligāre* mean to bind to. The person who becomes "bound to" another in a venture is an _____ly.

i. Their behavior is _____.
   un natural

j. The word meaning to placate or soothe comes from combining the Latin prefix *ad* and the root *pease*. Write the full word. _____

k. If you pronounce *ad* and *praise* (to evaluate) rapidly, the *d* is assimilated. Spell the word correctly. _____

l. Your explanation is _____.
   un necessary

m. What are the critical spots in aggravate? _____

n. Why is *c* present in *acquire* and *acquaint*? _____

o. He has _____ the facts.
   mis stated

## POSTTEST

A. Combine the following prefixes and roots. Remember that one letter of the prefix may change. Check your dictionary if you are unsure of the meaning of any word.

1. in          regular        _____
2. contra      diction        _____
3. in          oculate        _____
4. ex          fect           _____
5. per         ception        _____
6. dis         satisfaction   _____
7. dis         appearance     _____
8. post        graduate       _____
9. trans       lation         _____
10. extra      ordinary       _____
11. pre        caution        _____
12. re         organize       _____
13. ex         cavate         _____

14. un      natural      _____

15. super   natural      _____

16. intra   venous       _____

17. circum  stances      _____

18. in      modest       _____

19. ab      sent         _____

20. pro     clamation    _____

21. de      parture      _____

22. in      eligible     _____

23. ex      planation    _____

24. ad      sembly       _____

B. Test your knowledge of prefixes by answering these questions or filling in the blanks.

25. What is the Latin prefix in *appear* and *attest?* _____

26. A star's dynamic personality can _____tract many followers.

27. A distraction is something that draws you _____.

28. A person who is not reputable is _____reputable.

29. To set above in favor is the meaning of _____fer.
    pro, per, pre

30. The state of being perplexed is to be literally "entwined" all the way _____.

31. Combine the prefix *ad* and the root *quit* into a modern English word. _____
_____

32. A person's death or demise is a going _____.

33. To sweat means to _____spire.
    pre, per

34. Mr. Roe finally _____suaded the visitor to leave.
    pre, per

35. Frieda is just a casual _____ance.

## COMMON PREFIXES WITH VARIANT SPELLINGS

| PREFIX | MEANING | SAMPLE WORDS | |
| --- | --- | --- | --- |
| *ad* | to, toward, for | adhere | assume |
| | | appear | aggressive |
| | | attract | affiliate |
| | | accept | |

## COMMON PREFIXES WITH VARIANT SPELLINGS (cont)

| PREFIX | MEANING | SAMPLE WORDS | |
|---|---|---|---|
| *com (cum)* | with, together | *com*bine | *con*sist |
| | | *col*lect | *con*tent |
| | | *cor*relate | *co*alesce |
| | | *con*cave | *co*erce |
| | | *con*gress | *co*incide |
| | | *con*jugal | *co*operate |
| | | *con*nect | *co*unite |
| | | *con*quer | *co*here |
| *dis* | apart, away, not | *dis*like | *dif*ference |
| | | *dis*pel | *di*vergence |
| *ex* | out, out of | *ex*hale | *e*nunciate |
| | | *e*laborate | *e*rect |
| | | *e*ducate | *e*ject |
| | | *e*gress | *e*vade |
| | | *e*mit | |
| *in* | in, into, on | *in*ject | *im*bibe |
| | | *il*luminate | *ir*rigate |
| *in* | not | *in*hospitable | *ir*relevant |
| | | *im*mature | *il*legal |
| *sub* | under, below | *sub*merge | *sup*press |
| | | *suc*ceed | *sur*reptitious |
| | | *suf*fice | *sus*tain |
| *trans* | across, beyond, over | *trans*late | *tra*verse |

# CHAPTER EIGHT

## THE "SEED" ROOTS

Because the roots *sede, cede,* and *ceed* are pronounced alike ("seed"), they must be distinguished by another means, their meaning. And so in this chapter you will concentrate on the meaning of these roots as well as on the meaning of various prefixes to be attached to these roots, and practice spelling a number of useful words. By the end of the chapter you will combine the right prefix with the right root and understand the reasons for your choice. Also, by learning the meanings of the prefixes included in this chapter you will be able to choose the correct prefix for other words.

### PRETEST

A. Fill in the blanks with the appropriate ending:

*ceed, sede, cede*

1. ac_____
2. pro_____
3. con_____
4. se_____

5. ex_____
6. suc_____
7. ante_____
8. re_____

9. super_____
10. inter_____

B. Fill in the appropriate prefix.

11. To replace is to _____sede.

12. To yield consent is to _____cede.

13. To advance is to _____ceed.

14. To go before is to _____cede.

15. To follow after in time or order is to _____ceed.

16. To settle differences is to __cede.

17. To go beyond is to _____ ceed.

18. To withdraw from a political group is to _____cede.

19. To yield strongly or to admit is to _____cede.

20. To go back is to _____cede.

a. *cede*
b. *ceed*
c. *cede*
d. *ceed*
e. *cede*
f. *ceed*
g. *cede*
h. *sede*

**1.** Word endings that sound like "seed" are easy to learn as there are only three: *sede, cede, ceed*. The sede ending has only one prefix combined with it: *super.* The *ceed* ending has only three: *pro, ex, suc.* The *cede* ending takes other prefixes.
For the following prefixes attach the correct root.

a. con_____          e. ac_____

b. pro_____          f. ex_____

c. pre_____          g. inter_____

d. suc_____          h. super_____

supersede

**2.** *Super* means over or above. Combining this prefix with the root that comes from the Latin *sedere,* meaning to sit, produces the word meaning that which sits above or over, in other words, replaces it. That word is _____.

It has sede in it.

**3.** How does this Latin verb *sedere* govern the spelling of the English derivative? _____.

supersede

**4.** The word that means to "sit over or above" or to replace is _____.

pro
ex
suc
suc

**5.** Three words have a different ending—*ceed*—which comes from the Latin *cede*re, meaning to go. The prefix *pro* means forward, and *ex* means beyond.

If you go forward, you _____ceed.
If you go beyond, you _____ceed.

The prefix *suc* is a variant of *sub,* which means under, next, or following after.

If you go next (follow after in order), you _____ceed.

Succeed also means to attain a desired end.

If you get to your goal, you _____ceed.

a. proceed
b. exceed
c. succeeds
d. exceed
e. proceed
f. succeed

**6.** Read the sentences for their meaning, then write the correct "seed" word for each.

a. Why can't the meeting _____?

b. Drew realized he was going to _____ the speed limit.

c. At the next meeting club members will decide who _____ Joe Casey as president.

d. The demand for strawberries will _____ the supply.

e. Now you can _____ with the next part of the examination.

f. You must work diligently if you want to _____.

exceed
proceed
succeed

**7.** What three words end in ceed?

_____ _____ _____

supersede

**8.** Name the only word ending in *sede.*

_____

cede

**9.** The rest of the "seed" words must end in (*sede, cede, ceed*). _____

cede

**10.** The third ending which also comes from the Latin *cedere,* meaning to go or to withdraw, constitutes a complete word, meaning to surrender possession formally, usually rights or territory. If a country formally gives up some of its possessions, it is said to _____ them.

cede

**11.** Some countries have been forced to _____ parts of their territories.

precede

**12.** Prefixes can be combined with this root to form quite a few words. For instance, adding *pre,* which means before, gives you the word _____.

before

**13.** If Henry precedes Jack, he goes _____ him.
 before, after

precede

**14.** If you tell an anecdote before you begin your main speech, this anecdote will _____ the speech.

recede

**15.** Let us try another with the same root. The prefix *re* means back. To go back would be to _____.

recede

**16.** The tidal waters will _____ in about an hour.

precede
recede

**17.** To go before is to _____; to go back is to _____.

a. accede
b. concede

**18.** The prefix *ac* (a variant of *ad*) means to, so with this root it forms *accede,* meaning to go to, or to agree, assent. *Con* in *concede* is an intensive, so this word has a strong meaning of yielding (for example, a privilege or a right) or of admitting.
Write the appropriate word in each sentence.

a. The members of the minority party will eventually _____ to the wishes of the majority.

b. After a bitter conflict, the senator agreed to _____ to the committee's demands.

concede

a. accede
b. concede

a. 4
b. 2
c. 3
d. 5
e. 1

a. *cede*
b. *ceed*
c. *sede*
d. *ceed*
e. *cede*
f. *cede*
g. *ceed*
h. *cede*

intercede

antecedes

antecedes

intercede

recede

between

a. *ante*
b. *inter*
c. *pro*
d. *ex*

**19.** Which word has the stronger sense of yielding: *accede, concede?* _____

**20.** Read the sentences first to decide which has the stronger sense of yielding, then write the correct word.

a. Joe urged his brother to _____ to his supervisor's wishes.

b. I doubt that Don Hardy will ever _____ his voting rights.

**21.** Now match these words with their definitions.

a. cede          1. to go before          _____

b. accede        2. to agree              _____

c. recede        3. to go back            _____

d. concede       4. to surrender          _____

e. precede       5. to yield a right      _____

**22.** Complete these words.

a. ac_____          e. con_____

b. ex_____          f. pre_____

c. super_____       g. suc_____

d. pro_____         h. re_____

**23.** *Inter* means between or among. If you go between two persons, say to settle a quarrel, you inter_____.

**24.** *Ante* means to precede in time or space. An event that goes before another in time _____ it.

**25.** The First World War _____ the Second World War.

**26.** To act between parties to settle differences is to _____.

**27.** The weather bureau predicted that the river would reach its crest and then would start to _____.

**28.** To intercede is to go _____.

**29.** Read the sentences for their meaning, then choose the correct prefix for each root: *ac pre ante inter pro ex con*

a. A person's ancestors are called _____cedents.

b. Since the members have reached a deadlock, I hope that an arbitration board will _____cede soon.

c. Let us _____ceed with the meeting.

d. The supply will _____ceed the demand.

## REVIEW

a. succeed
b. proceed
c. recede
d. accede
e. precede
f. supersede
g. exceed
h. intercede
i. concede
j. succeed
k. procedure
l. cede

**30.** Read the sentences carefully, then write the correct "seed" words for each.

a. The eldest son will _____ his father as president.

b. When the road is cleared, the parade will _____ up the street.

c. The water will _____ by tomorrow.

d. Larry will _____ to the desires of his uncle.

e. If Amy stands in front of Eric in the ticket line, she will _____ him.

f. As the age of automation continues, new methods of production and management will _____ the old.

g. If you are not careful, you will _____ the limit.

h. The workers asked for a mediator to _____ in the dispute.

i. To strongly yield is the definition of the word _____.

j. You must work diligently if you want to _____.

k. I must find a new _____ure for posting in the two ledgers.

l. Some countries have been forced to _____ part of their territory to other countries.

proceed
succeed
exceed

**31.** What words end in *ceed*?

_____  _____  _____

a. ceed
b. cede
c. sede
d. ceed
e. cede
f. cede
g. cede
h. ceed
i. cede
j. cede

**32.** Finish the spelling of the following words:

a. suc_____     f. con_____

b. inter_____    g. pre_____

c. super_____    h. pro_____

d. ex_____       i. retro_____

e. ac_____       j. ante_____

secede

**33.** The Latin *se,* meaning away or apart, can be combined with the root that comes from the Latin *cedere,* meaning to go. If a state would "go away" from the Union, it would _____ from the Union.

a. away (apart)
b. back
c. beyond
d. before
e. forward
f. next
g. above
h. between

**34.** Supply the correct prefix meanings.

a. To secede is to go _____.

b. To recede is to go _____.

c. To exceed is to go _____.

d. To precede is to go _____.

e. To proceed is to go _____.

f. To succeed is to come _____ in order.

g. To supersede means to sit over or _____.

h. To intercede is to act _____.

proceed
precede

**35.** The word meaning to go forward is _____.

The word meaning to go before, or in front of, is _____.

a. precede
b. proceed
c. supersede

**36.** The following words are misspelled. Write the words correctly.

a. preceed _____

b. procede _____

c. supercede _____

## POSTTEST

Read this short paragraph, locate any misspelled "seed" words and write them correctly.

On Monday the sales manager assembled his staff to describe a new procedure. He stated that the new regulations would supercede the old ones and that every employee would procede from Step No. 1. No exceptions would be made; in fact, he made it quite clear that he would never accede to anyone's request for exemption from any of the rules. He also stressed that no employee would be allowed to interceed for another employee, no matter how slight or grievous the infraction of the rule or rules might be. He then closed the meeting with these words: "There is no room for failure. I expect everyone to succede, and everyone should excede his or her quota."

# CHAPTER NINE

## HOMONYMS

Homonyms are words that sound exactly alike but differ in spelling and meaning. A spelling error occurs when one homonym is substituted for another. For instance, if you use *principle* meaning a rule or law, for *principal,* meaning a head of a group, you will puzzle your readers, and undoubtedly irk them as well. The homonyms included in this chapter are those that cause a great deal of difficulty. But by the time you finish the chapter, you will have no difficulty with them. The main objective of this chapter is to provide you with sufficient material concerning the meanings and the parts of speech of these homonyms so that you can readily choose between them, not only according to their definitions but also in the context of sentences. Also, by working diligently with these homonyms, you can form a basis for learning other pairs (or sets) of words identical in sound.

### PRETEST

Choose the correct homonyms for these sentences.

1. The president of the firm paid me a high _____.
   complement, compliment

2. I placed the book _____.
   they're, their, there

3. We are _____ too late.
   all ready, already

4. The puppy kept scratching _____ ears.
   its, it's

5. Burlap is a _____ material.
   course, coarse

6. What is your _____ reason?
   principal, principle

7. The recommendation was made by members of the _____.
                                                      council, counsel

8. He is _____ correct.
            all together, altogether

9. Did you buy any _____?
                stationary, stationery

10. I am meeting Judge Doe in his office at the state _____.
                                                   capital, capitol

11. For your report you must _____ two references.
                                  cite, site, sight

12. He _____ directly in front of us.
          past, passed

13. Mary wants to go _____.
               to, too

14. The well is on _____ property.
              their, there

15. How far is the _____ for the new hospital from here?
                 sight, site

16. It was a _____ performance.
              capital, capitol

17. A _____ of people surrounded the speaker.
          hoard, horde

18. An avalanche stopped the _____ of the climbers.
                      assent, ascent

19. Proudly he _____ the troops into the conquered city.
              lead, led

20. Ned couldn't find a _____ to complete his Dracula costume.
                mantel, mantle

---

a. already
b. all ready

**1.** Two expressions that are used interchangeably when they should not be are *all ready* and *already*. Besides being different in the number of words, they have different meanings. *All ready* is an adjective phrase meaning quite or completely ready. *Already* is an adverb meaning at or by this time.
Write the appropriate expression.

a. The best tickets were _____ sold.

b. We are _____ to go to the lake.

all ready
already

**2.** The expression meaning quite or completely ready is _____; the one meaning at or by this time is _____.

a. all ready
b. already

**3.** Choose the correct homonym: *all ready, already.*

a. By noon the soldiers were _____ to move to the front.

b. By the time we arrived, John had _____ gone.

2  2

**4.** The expression meaning completely or quite ready has how many words _____ and how many *l's* _____?

1  1

**5.** The expression meaning at or by this time has how many words _____ and how many *l's* _____?

all together
altogether

**6.** *All together* and *altogether* are another pair. The two-word expression concentrates on the *all*—everyone in a group—whereas the single word has meanings of completely, on the whole, or thoroughly. Which expression is correct for each sentence? After the storm the farmer found the animals huddled _____. I am _____ certain that he lied.

everyone in a group
on the whole,
completely,
thoroughly

**7.** Write the correct meaning(s) for each expression.

all together _____

altogether _____

a. altogether
b. altogether
c. all together

**8.** Choose the correct expression: *all together, altogether.*

a. The assumption is _____ false.

b. The critics said the performance was _____ entertaining.

c. To win a lasting peace, nations must work _____.

2

**9.** Here is a controversial pair: *all right* and *alright.* For some time the one-word expression has been considered (and still is by some) a misspelling of the two words, meaning satisfactory or correct. Today *alright* is accepted as an alternative form, but usually in informal writing only. The one way you can always be right is to spell this expression as _____ word(s).

informal

**10.** Alright is accepted by some but only in (formal, informal) writing. _____

all right

**11.** Which form is always correct? _____

all right

**12.** Choose the expression that is correct in all styles of writing:
His responses to the panel's inquiries were _____.

alright, all right

building

**13.** Although *capital* and *capitol* are easily confused, they are just as easy to use correctly. *Capitol* (with an *o*) is the building in which a state legislature meets, a building that usually has a dome on top. *Capitol* (with a capital *C*) refers to the building in Washington, D.C., where Congress meets. *Capital* (with an *a*) is used in contexts which demand other meanings than the _____ where a legislature assembles.

capitol
Capitol

**14.** The state legislature assembles at the _____ and the Congress of the U.S. occupies the _____ in Washington, D.C.

capital

**15.** If you remember that *capitol* relates to a building, then it is easy to use *capital* correctly for other meanings. For example, the major city or town of a state is called a _____.

capital

**16.** Lima is the _____ of Peru.

capital

**17.** This word also has the meaning of first-rate or excellent: It was a _____ performance.

capital

**18.** It can also mean a stock of wealth. To buy the franchise, the grocer needed a great deal of _____.

a. Capitol
capital
b. capitol
Capitol
capital

**19.** Choose the correct one: *capital, Capitol, capitol.*

a. To finance my trip to the _____ in Washington, D.C. I need more _____.

b. When referring to the building where a state legislature meets you write _____; to the building where Congress meets _____; and to the major city of a state _____.

a. principal
b. principal
c. principles
d. principal

**20.** The nouns *principle* and *principal* are easy to distinguish. *Principle* is a noun only and refers to basic truths, laws, or rules. *Principal* can be either an adjective meaning chief or main, or a noun referring to a leader, or a sum of money. Choose the correct homonym.

a. The head of a school is a _____.

b. He cited three _____ reasons.

c. The community recognized the governor as a person of high _____s.

d. A sum of money on which interest is calculated is _____.

noun
wrong (incorrect)

**21.** The word principle is not correct in this phrase "a principle reason" because it can be used only as a _____, not as an adjective. Also the meaning is _____ for this context.

principle

**22.** The noun referring to basic truths, laws, or rules is _____.

a. principle
b. principal
principal
principles
c. principal

**23.** Choose the correct homonym: *principal, principle.*

a. Some people live only according to the _____ of self-preservation.

b. The _____ reason Mr. Brown was appointed _____ of Stock High School is that he has high _____.

c. Lindsay's account totaled $1,000, of which approximately $900 was the _____.

a. stationary
b. stationery

**24.** *Stationery* and *stationary* are another good pair to learn. *Stationery* is a noun, meaning either the paper you write on or the establishment that sells it and related items. *Stationary* is an adjective meaning fixed, not movable. Write the appropriate word.

a. The group remained _____.

b. My mother bought me some _____.

stationary
stationery

**25.** The adjective meaning fixed is _____; the noun meaning writing paper is _____.

stationery

**26.** The last syllable of the word *paper* contains *er,* and so do the last syllables of the word for writing paper: _____.

noun

**27.** In this sentence—The architect suggested putting in stationary seats—the word *stationery* cannot be substituted because the sentence needs the adjective to modify seats, and *stationery* is always a _____.

stationery

**28.** Mavis wrote to me on her best _____.

stationary

**29.** The rows of seats in the auditorium are _____.

a. coarse
b. course
c. coarse
d. course
e. course

**30.** The adjective *coarse* cannot be substituted for the noun *course.* *Coarse,* meaning inferior in quality, crude, or harsh, is always an adjective. *Course,* on the other hand, can be used as a noun or verb, but never as an adjective. As a noun, it means a direction, route, or onward movement; as a verb it means to follow a direction.

Supply the correct word.

a. Burlap is a ＿＿＿＿＿＿ material.

b. He follows a definite ＿＿＿＿＿＿.

c. The clerk has ＿＿＿＿＿＿ manners.

d. We followed the ＿＿＿＿＿＿ of the stream.

e. Rivers ＿＿＿＿＿＿.

coarse

**31.** Although his manners were ＿＿＿＿＿＿, he had an engaging personality.

course

**32.** Fads usually run their ＿＿＿＿＿＿ in a short time.

course, coarse

coarse
course
verb

**33.** Whereas ＿＿＿＿＿＿ is always an adjective, ＿＿＿＿＿＿ is either a noun or a ＿＿＿＿＿＿.

a. site
b. sight
c. cite
d. sight
e. sight

**34.** *Site, cite,* and *sight* are homonyms to watch out for. *Site* is always a noun and means a place of location or an event. *Cite* is always a verb, meaning to mention or quote as an authority. *Sight* can be used as a noun or a verb. As a noun it can mean one's vision, a field of vision, or a spectacle; as a verb, it means to aim.
Choose the correct homonym.

a. Orchard Gardens is the ＿＿＿＿＿＿ for a new development project.

b. Soon the sailor will ＿＿＿＿＿＿ land.

c. The politician will ＿＿＿＿＿＿ many authorities to refute the argument.

d. He should ＿＿＿＿＿＿ his target at any minute.

e. Suddenly it came into ＿＿＿＿＿＿.

site
noun
cite
verb
noun
sight

**35.** The word meaning a place of location ＿＿＿＿＿＿ is always a ＿＿＿＿＿＿.

noun, verb

The word meaning to mention or quote an authority ＿＿＿＿＿＿ is always a ＿＿＿＿＿＿.
The third homonym can mean to take aim, as a verb, or a view or spectacle as a ＿＿＿＿＿＿. This word is ＿＿＿＿＿＿.

a. cite
b. sight
c. site
d. sighted

**36.** Choose one for these sentences: *cite site sight.*

a. Did you ＿＿＿＿＿＿ Forster's theory?

b. The Grand Canyon is a breathtaking ＿＿＿＿＿＿.

c. We came around the curve and then saw the _____ for the plant.

d. He raised his rifle and carefully _____ his target.

## REVIEW

a. capitol
b. course
c. all ready
d. stationery
e. principal
f. cite
g. altogether
h. already
i. site
j. coarse

**37.** Now test your skill by writing the correct homonyms.

a. I drove to the _____ in twenty minutes.
state legislature building

b. Richard has decided on a definite _____ of
coarse, course
action.

c. When the whistle blew, the workers were _____ to leave.
already, all ready

d. Jane received two boxes of _____.
stationary, stationery

e. The speaker emphasized the _____
principal, principle
points strongly.

f. He did not _____ sufficient evidence to win.
site, cite, sight

g. Her behavior is _____ proper.
altogether, all together

h. By the time Joe arrived, his brother had _____ left.
all ready, already

i. My uncle picked a _____ in the country for his new
sight, site
house.

j. Shoppers often choose a _____ material for
course, coarse
drapes.

| | | | |
|---|---|---|---|
| a. | P | e. | P |
| b. | C | f. | C |
| c. | P | g. | P |
| d. | C | h. | C |

**38.** Contractions are not to be mistaken for possessives. Contractions are identified by an apostrophe which stands for an omitted letter. For example, the ' in *it's* stands for the omitted *i* in the verb: it *is*. The possessive *its* never has an apostrophe. Identify by P or C whether these words are possessives or contractions.

a. their _____    e. whose _____

b. who's _____    f. it's _____

c. its _____    g. your _____

d. you're _____    h. they're _____

who *is*
it *is*
you *are*
they *are*

a. who's
b. you're
c. its
d. their

**39.** In the contractions the apostrophe stands for the beginning letter of a verb. What is it in *who's?* _____ in *its?* _____ in *you're?* _____ in *they're?* _____

**40.** Choose the correct words.

a. Do you know _____ going to the dance?
who's, whose

b. Tell me when _____ ready.
your, you're

c. We watched the mother bird feed _____ young.
it's, its

d. They did not like _____ seats downstairs.
they're, their

They're
there
their

**41.** A word sounding exactly like *their* and *they're* is *there.* It is an adverb meaning in or at that place: I placed the package over *there.* Write the correct word—*there, their, they're,* in these related sentences.

Nancy shouted, "_____ here."
"Where?" I replied. "Over _____," she said, "waving _____ hands."

a. too
b. two
c. to
d. to
e. too

**42.** These words also sound alike but differ in meaning and spelling: *to too two.* The word *two* pertains to the number 2. *To* (with one *o*) can be a preposition, as in *to the store,* or it can help to form an infinitive, as in *to go* home. *Too* (with two *o's*) is an adverb meaning also or more than enough: I want to go *too,* or It is *too* much.
Fill in the correct homonyms below.

a. Do you want a cone _____?

b. I received a _____ dollar raise.

c. Mary went downtown _____ buy a robe.

d. Don't bother about giving a present _____ me.

e. There is _____ much noise.

two
too
to

**43.** The numeral is _____; the adverb is _____; the preposition or part of an infinitive is _____.

a. too
b. two
c. to
d. too

**44.** Choose the correct homonym: *to, too, two.*

a. I, _____, was offered a job there.

b. The typist gets _____ dollars an hour.

c. Don't give it _____ her.

d. We had _____ many problems to worry about Jim's ball game.

verb

**45.** You need never confuse *know* and *no* because *know* is a verb meaning to perceive, or to be certain of, and *no* is either an adjective "no bananas are left," or an adverb, "he is no better than I."

In this sentence—How do you know he is over 20?—you cannot use *no* because it is an adverb or an adjective, and the sentence requires a _____.

a. know
b. no
c. no
d. know

**46.** Write *know* or *no* below.

a. I don't _____ the instructor.

b. He is _____ better than he appears to be.

c. I looked, but there were _____ strawberries on the counter.

d. How do you _____ the speaker is right?

no   know

**47.** The word that means none as an adjective and not as an adverb is _____. The word that sounds like it but is a verb is _____.

passed—sentence
needs a verb

**48.** *Passed* and *past* should present no problem as *passed* is simply the past tense (*ed*) of the verb *pass:* He passed in front of me. *Past* can be either a noun: a distinguished *past;* an adjective: in *past years;* or an adverb: walked *past* the store. In this sentence—He _____ me on the street—which homonym is correct and why?

_____

past

**49.** Of the two, *passed* and *past,* which one can be either a noun, adjective, or adverb? _____

a. passed
b. past
c. past
passed

**50.** Write *passed* or *past* for these sentences.

a. The train _____ within 20 feet.

b. He thanked us for _____ favors.

c. In the _____ the Johnsons have _____ us on the street without any sign of recognition.

a. yes
b. The meaning is
wrong—need verb
meaning praise.

**51.** Although both *compliment* and *complement* are nouns and verbs, they have such different meanings that they should never be confused. A *compliment* is an expression of praise, and to *compliment* is to praise someone. A *complement* is something that completes and to *complement* is to complete.

a. Is the homonym used correctly in this sentence: The new complement of soldiers arrived today. _____

b. Why won't *complement* fit this sentence: He continued to compliment me for my fine work. _____

_____

**52.** Write in *complement* or *compliment*.

a. I waited for him to _____ me, but when the _____ came, it dripped with sarcasm.

b. In finishing the design, Mrs. White _____ the rows of red figures with a row of blue ones.

c. When the fresh _____ of soldiers arrived, the general _____ them on their appearance.

**53.** The last group is *council, counsel,* and *consul.* All three are nouns. A *council* is a deliberative body (like a city council, for example). *Counsel* means either a lawyer or a group of lawyers giving advice, or the advice itself. *Consul* refers to an officer in the foreign service of his country. *Counsel* can also be a verb, to give advice or to recommend.

a. In this sentence—He tried to _____ me about going to college—*council* would be incorrect. State two reasons why. _____

b. Is the correct homonym used here? He offered his counsel. _____

c. *Council* and *consul* are nouns only, but _____ can be either a noun or a verb.

**54.** Choose the correct word: *counsel, council, consul.*

a. A deliberative assembly is a _____; a lawyer who conducts a case in court is called _____; and an officer in the foreign service is a _____.

b. The student _____ sought _____ from the French _____.

**55.** Which word can be a noun or a verb? _____

**56.** When is a boarder not a boarder? The answer: when it is a border. A *border* is a boundary or a rim of something; a *boarder* is one who pays an owner for room and food. Fill in the blanks with the correct choice of these two words: The owner asked the _____ to plant petunias near the north _____ of the lot.

**57.** The artist painted tiny roses along the _____ of the plate.

**58.** When Mrs. Allen decided to sell her house, she told her _____s they would have to move.

borders

**59.** In some areas of the world barbed wire fences separate the _____s between countries.

altering

**60.** Look at these Latin roots: *alter,* meaning other, and *altāre,* originally meaning "material for burning sacrificial offerings." A pair of homonyms is derived from these words. Read the sentence carefully, check the origins, and write the correct English word: *alter, altar.* In changing the basic style of a garment, the seamstress is making it other than it is, or _____ing it.

verb
noun

**61.** These words have a different grammatical function. *Alter* is a verb (I alter my plans). *Altar* is a noun (The altar is made of marble). In these sentences—"I alter my plans" and "The altar is made of marble"—the word *alter* is a _____ and *altar* is a _____.

altered
altar

**62.** Jim could not make the Friday rehearsal, so we _____ our plans. Because Mary had not eaten all day, she collapsed halfway to the _____.

led
lead

**63.** If you forget that *led* is the past tense of the verb to *lead,* then you could easily write *lead* (a metallic element) because the noun and the past tense of *lead* are pronounced exactly alike. The easiest way to remember the difference is to conjugate the verb: Today I lead the way. (present) Yesterday I _____ the way. (past) Tomorrow I will _____ the way. (future)

led

**64.** The general dejectedly _____ his troops into the valley.
past tense

led

**65.** The actions of the committee at yesterday's meeting _____ me to resign as treasurer.

led

**66.** Don Russell said he would continue to lead the group in the same manner as Ray Brown, who had _____ them in past years.

**REVIEW**

a. complement
b. passed
c. know no
d. You're
e. too
f. Who's
g. compliments

**67.** Test your skill in choosing the correct homonym.

a. The new _____ of soldiers saved the
compliment, complement
fortress.

b. As we neared the reviewing stand, Mike _____
past, passed
us on the left.

c. Many inhabitants _____ _____ other way of life.
<br>know, no　　　know, no

d. Jim gasped, "_____ going."
<br>Your, You're

e. I want to go _____.
<br>two, to, too

f. _____ driving to school?
<br>Whose, Who's

g. Lorraine received many _____ for her
<br>compliments, complements

fine portrayal of Anna.

## POSTTEST

A. Write the correct homonym for each sentence.

1. Do you plan to take a specific _____?
<br>course, coarse

2. They huddled _____ in the barn.
<br>all together, altogether

3. Ned decided not to run for office on the city _____.
<br>council, counsel

4. It was a thrilling _____.
<br>site, sight, cite

5. The auditorium seats are _____.
<br>stationery, stationary

6. My uncle works at the _____ in Washington, D.C.
<br>capital, capitol, Capitol

7. I received _____ free tickets.
<br>too, two

8. By the time we arrived he had _____ gone.
<br>all ready, already

9. Dan _____ us yesterday; I want Joe to _____ us today.
<br>lead, led　　　　　　　　　　　　　　lead, led

10. The student is a person of high _____.
<br>principals, principles

11. Please don't _____ your plans.
<br>alter, altar

12. The mother bird fed _____ young.
<br>its, it's

B. If some of the homonyms given in the sentences below are unfamiliar, look up their meanings (and pronunciation) in the dictionary. Choose the appropriate word or words for each sentence, then check the dictionary again to see if you did them correctly.

13. Two of the commissioners gave verbal _____ to the proposal.
    assent, ascent

14. The high official was so angry he _____ed his teeth.
    grate, great

15. The emperor was _____ up the side of the mountain by six servants.
    born, borne

16. Each chapter in the new text is supposed to be _____.
    discrete, discreet

17. It is only _____ that the _____ be increased ten cents.
    fair, fare      fair, fare

18. The facts did not _____ with what the witness had said.
    gibe, jibe

19. It is _____ stupidity to _____ the flock at this time of the year.
    sheer, shear      sheer, shear

20. If you omit a word in your sentence, use a _____ to show the insertion.
    caret, carat

21. On the last day of school Michael fell _____ down a flight of stairs.
    forward, foreword

22. To make room for the new civic center, the city has to _____ two blocks
    raise, raze
    of old buildings.

23. Rachel said the _____ was so tough she couldn't drive a _____
    stake, steak      stake, steak
    through it.

24. _____ Amy quietly _____ away a Sunday afternoon, Sue tried with
    Wile, While      whiled, wiled
    all her _____ to capture the attention of Amy's boyfriend.
    wiles, whiles

25. The chef's project is perfecting his _____ pudding.
    current, currant

# CHAPTER TEN
## SIMILAR WORDS

Words that are similar in appearance or sound can frequently be confused. For example, the pairs *accept-except* and *affect-effect* are used interchangeably when they should not be. By noting differences in spelling, sound, and particularly meaning, you can quickly eliminate any hesitation in choosing the right word of such a pair, or set, as the case may be.

The objectives of this chapter are these: you will (1) distinguish between alternatives by their meaning and spelling; (2) practice spelling and using a number of these similar words; and (3) establish a method for spelling other confusing words.

## PRETEST

A. Choose the correct word for each sentence.

1. This has been _____ a day.
   <br>quiet, quite

2. Do you have _____ to the storeroom?
   <br>access, excess

3. I'm afraid I will _____ my place in line.
   <br>lose, loose

4. His greeting was certainly _____.
   <br>causal, casual

5. Can you _____ what will happen?
   <br>prophecy, prophesy

6. Please _____ my apology.
   <br>except, accept

7. She is taller _____ I.
   <br>than, then

8. Do you expect any bad _____ from the new drug?
   <br>effects, affects

9. Please do a _____ job.
   through, thorough

10. Can you _____ the storm?
    weather, whether

11. I listened patiently to the complaints of the _____.
    personal, personnel

12. He cannot _____ me.
    advice, advise

13. Perry tripped on the _____ board.
    lose, loose

B. Match each word with the correct definition.

14. moral           _____        a. scorn

15. conscience      _____        b. pieces of fabric

16. ingenuous       _____        c. clever

17. instants        _____        d. earlier

18. angle           _____        e. second of two things mentioned

19. formally        _____        f. pertaining to the good

20. cloths          _____        g. moments

21. flaunt          _____        h. migrant coming in to settle

22. later           _____        i. wearing apparel

23. immigrant       _____        j. example

24. morale          _____        k. supernatural being

25. formerly        _____        l. migrant leaving native land

26. latter          _____        m. aware

27. ingenious       _____        n. naive

28. flout           _____        o. show off

29. conscious _____ p. corner, point of view

30. emigrant _____ q. in a regular manner

31. angel _____ r. comparative degree of late

32. instance _____ s. well-being

33. clothes _____ t. voice within

a. noun
b. result or outcome
c. verb form
d. bring about
e. verb
f. changed or altered

**1.** Both *affect* and *effect* come from the same Latin root: *facere* (to make, do). What makes them distinguishable are the prefixes (elements added to the beginning of a word). *Af* (meaning to, toward) is a variant of *ad* through assimilation. *Affect* is to do something to someone or something—to change or alter. *Ef* is a variant of *ex* (meaning out of) or a bringing about something—a result, for example. Another way to distinguish between them is their function in a sentence. *Affect* is always a verb, never a noun. *Effect* is a noun and can be a verb. Now answer the questions pertaining to the three sentences below.

(1) What will be the *effect*?

(2) How do the legislators expect to *effect* the changes in the new law?

(3) His fall from the roof has *affected* John's hearing.

a. Is *effect* in (1) a noun or a verb? _____

b. According to the definition, substitute a word for *effect* in (1). _____

c. Is *effect* in (2) a noun or a verb form? _____

d. Substitute a phrase for *effect* in (2). _____

e. Is *affected* in (3) a noun or verb? _____

f. Substitute one word for *affected* in (3). _____

a. affect
b. effects
c. effect

**2.** Choose the correct word: *affect, effect.*

a. The new housing bill will _____ many people.

b. What major _____s do you expect?

c. Can the school system _____ the changes without more money?

verb
change
result
bring about (a result)
a. accepted
b. except

**3.** *Affect* is always a _____ and means to _____.
*Effect* as a noun means _____; as a verb it means
_____.

**4.** *Accept* and *except* are another pair whose origin is the same Latin root: *capere* (to take). *Ac* is a variant of *ad* (to, toward), and *ex* means out. If I accept something, I literally take it *to* me, or receive it. If I except something, I take it *out,* or exclude it. In these illustrations, *accept* and *except* are verbs. *Except,* however, is more often used as a preposition: All the boxes, *except* one, were smashed; or as a conjunction: I would take a cruise, *except* that it's too expensive.

Read these sentences, then choose the correct word for the context.

a. Mac Lewis humbly _____ed the medal.

b. All eighth-grade students, _____Sandy Smith, will attend the concert.

accept
exception
except

**5.** When I take a present, I _____ it.
                          accept, except

When I "take myself out of" going to the fair, I become the _____ion.

Every student, _____Mary Jo, graduated.

exclude   receive

**6.** *Except* means _____. *Accept* means _____.

a. except
b. exceptions
c. accept
d. except
accept

**7.** Choose the correct word (*accept, except*):

a. When I moved, all my hat boxes, _____ one, were lost.

b. The teacher emphatically stated that there would be no _____ ions.

c. How can I _____ this money for a trip to Bermuda?

d. Everyone, _____ Jack Daniel, will _____ the citations.

No. Causal pertains to
a cause. Sentence
needs "unconcerned."

**8.** In the two adjectives *casual* and *causal,* watch the placement of the *s* and *u.* The word that means aimless, unconcerned, or occurring by chance, is *casual.* Read the following sentence: He has a <u>causal</u> appearance.

Is the underlined word used correctly? _____ If not, why not? _____

causal

a. casual
b. causal
c. casual

aimless,
unconcerned
pertains to
a cause

advise

advise
advice

advise
advice

advise

Loose is an adjective,
not a verb and has
wrong meaning.

a. loose
b. lose
c. lose
d. lose

adjective
free, not
fastened tight
verb
mislay

**9.** The adjective that refers to a cause is _____.

**10.** Choose the correct word: *casual, causal.*

a. He has a _____ manner.

b. To prove his argument he must show more _____
relationships.

c. Because he had no time for preparation, he could offer
only some _____ remarks.

**11.** Define casual: _____

and causal: _____.

**12.** *Advise* (s has the "z" sound) is a verb meaning to
counsel; *advice* (c has the "s" sound) is a noun meaning
the counsel given. Which word is appropriate here: What
did he (advice, advise) you to do? _____

**13.** The counselor offered to _____the students,
but he knew they would not accept his _____.

**14.** The verb meaning to counsel is _____; the
noun meaning the counsel given is _____.

**15.** In which word is there a "z" sound? _____

**16.** *Lose* and *loose* differ in three ways. *Lose* is a verb;
*loose* is an adjective. *Lose* means to mislay, to be deprived
of; *loose* means free, not fastened down tight. *Lose* has one
o; *loose* has two.

Name two reasons why *loose* cannot be used in this
sentence: I always loose my gloves. _____
_____

**17.** Select the correct word: *lose, loose.*

a. The bolt on the door is _____.

b. If Tim is not careful, he will _____his privileges.

c. Don't _____your balance.

d. So that you will not _____any more time, take the
bus downtown.

**18.** Loose is an _____, meaning _____
_____. Lose is a _____, meaning _____.

quite quiet

**19.** Here are two interesting words which are derived from the same Latin root but which differ in spelling, meaning, and pronunciation. The root is *quiētus* meaning free, clear. *Quiet* is to be free from noise or disturbance; *quite,* which means entirely or rather, somewhat, is clear of any "disturbance." If I am *quite* satisfied, I can be entirely satisfied. If I am *quiet,* I do not make any noise or disturbance.

Combine these two words in a phrase meaning entirely (or rather) still: _____ _____

a. It is not an adjective and has wrong meaning.
b. It is an adverb modifying proud and meaning is correct.

**20.** Two other differences should be remembered. First, pronounce these words carefully: *quite* has one syllable; *quiet* has two syllables. Second, *quite* is an adverb; *quiet* is an adjective.

a. Why would *quite* be inaccurate in this phrase?
a quite day _____

b. Why would *quite* be accurate here? We are quite proud of your promotion to superintendent. _____

quiet

**21.** After twelve o'clock, the park is _____.

quite

**22.** Today is _____ hot for June.

cold

**23.** Since *quite* is an adverb, it modifies what word in this sentence? It is quite cold. _____

adjective
still
adverb
entirely
rather, somewhat

**24.** Quiet is an _____ and means _____.
Quite is an _____ and means _____
or _____.

a. advice
b. affect
c. causal
d. effects
e. quiet
f. affected
g. accepted
h. lose
i. quite
j. except
k. affect
effects
effect

## REVIEW

**25.** Test your skill by selecting the correct words.

a. Whose _____ will you take?
      advice, advise

b. Bob's actions will _____ all of us.
      effect, affect

c. He lost his argument by stating false _____
      casual, causal
relationships.

d. Don't expect too many worthwhile _____ from
      effects, affects
the new tax law.

e. There is a _____ zone around the hospital.
quite, quiet

f. I am not _____ by her flattery.
affected, effected

g. Her defeat was _____ good-naturedly.
excepted, accepted

h. If you say yes, you may _____ your rights.
lose, loose

i. Carol was _____ disappointed with the outcome.
quiet, quite

j. No one, _____ Randy Duncan, voted for the
accept, except
newcomer.

k. Choose between *affect* and *effect* for each blank:
I expect the new ordinance will adversely_____
many citizens in the southern part of the city. However, it
will have some positive _____, including one
which will _____ a reconciliation between the
mayor and the city council.

**a. than**
**b. then**

**26.** *Then* means at that time in the past: I was six *then;* or
next in time or space: First I will go to the store, *then* I will
go downtown. *Than* relates to a statement showing comparison: Mary is more agile *than* Betty; or a preference: I
would rather dance *than* eat.
Write the correct word for each sentence:

a. He is younger _____ I am.

b. He was younger _____.

Then refers to time or
space; a word indicating
preference is needed.

**27.** In this sentence—I would rather play tennis than golf—
why would *then* be incorrect?_____
_____
_____

time or space
comparison or
preference

**28.** The adverb *then* refers to _____. The
conjunction *than* refers to a _____ or a
_____.

**a. than**
**b. then**
**c. than**

**29.** Choose the correct word: *then, than.*

a. He writes better _____ I do.

b. If she practices hard for the next hour, _____ she
can play outdoors.

c. I would prefer exercising on the machine rather _____
jogging for ten minutes.

a. through
b. thorough
c. through

**30.** *Through* and *thorough* are like *quite* and *quiet* in that one word has only one syllable and the other has two. *Through,* the one-syllable word, is a preposition which means by way of, to the end, to finish successfully. *Thorough,* the two-syllable word, is an adjective meaning complete, or painstakingly accurate.
Write the correct word for each sentence.

a. I got my information _____ Jane.

b. He did a _____ job.

c. I saw the performance _____.

thorough
through

**31.** The adjective meaning finished and accurate is _____ _____. The preposition meaning by way of, to the end, finish successfully is _____.

a. to the end
b. by way of
c. finished
successfully

**32.** What is the meaning of *through* in these sentences?

a. The critic saw the opera through. _____

b. It was through Larry that we found out the truth. _____

c. I got through the examination. _____

a. painstakingly
accurate
b. complete

**33.** What does *thorough* mean in these sentences?

a. Josie is a thorough worker. _____

b. He listened with thorough enjoyment. _____.

personnel

**34.** Now take *personal* and *personnel*. *Personal* is an adjective and pertains to something done to or for a person. *Personnel* is a noun referring to a body of persons employed by or active in an organization. Which word is correct here?

The supervisor spoke to the _____.

personal
personnel

**35.** The adjective referring to a person is _____; the noun referring to people employed in an office is

_____.

a. personal
b. personnel
c. personal
d. personnel

**36.** Choose the correct word: *personal, personnel*.

a. He resigned for _____ reasons.

b. The factory _____ want a representative to discuss their needs.

c. After hearing the case, the judge said that most of the complaints were _____.

d. The adjective *personal* cannot be substituted for the noun _____.

a person
a body of people

a. weather
b. whether
c. weather

whether

verb

whether
weather

immigrants
emigrants

immigration

emigrants

emigrate
immigrant

imminent
eminent

**37.** *Personal* refers to _____.
*Personnel* refers to _____.

**38.** Although *weather* and *whether* sound almost alike, they differ in all other respects. *Weather* is a noun that means atmospheric conditions, or a verb that means to expose to those conditions or to pass through an ordeal safely. *Whether* is a conjunction which introduces the first of two or more alternatives. Choose the correct word for each sentence.

a. We will have cold _____ soon.

b. It does not matter _____ we sit or stand.

c. I cannot _____ many more snowstorms.

**39.** The word that introduces an alternative is (whether, weather). _____

**40.** *Whether* is a conjunction, but *weather* serves either as a noun or as a _____.

**41.** The result of the debate matters not; what is important is _____ Tony can _____ the long and
        weather, whether                weather, whether
tiring ordeal.

**42.** If you know the meaning of the prefix in these next two words—*immigrant* and *emigrant*—you will not confuse them. *Im* is a variant form of *in* (to, toward) and *e* is a variant of *ex* (away). When people come from another country to settle in the United States, we call them _____migrants. If these people come from England, for example, the British would call them _____migrants because they went away from England to settle in another country.

**43.** Because so many people want to enter the United States, _____migration laws are necessary.

**44.** Some countries are worried about the number of _____ leaving their native land.

**45.** To leave one's homeland is to _____grate. A person who settles in another country is an _____.

**46.** Another pair of words with the same prefixes are the adjectives *imminent* and *eminent*. Both come from the Latin root *minēre*, to stand or project. Remembering that *im* means to or toward and *e* means away (or out), you can figure out the literal meaning. To project toward is to near something— in other words, if an event is about to occur (or near occurring) it is _____minent. To stand or project out is to be ___minent.

eminent

**47.** The IDS Tower in Minneapolis is _____ among the other downtown buildings.

imminent

**48.** From all the excitement in the courtyard, we knew that the court's decision was _____.

eminent
imminent

**49.** Two _____ economists cautioned that a recession was _____.

latter

**50.** The last three pairs of words look something alike, but if pronounced properly, they cannot be confused. The first is *later* (long a sound) and *latter* (short a sound). *Later* is simply the comparative form of the adverb *late:* I will go later. *Latter* (2 t's) is the second of two things mentioned: If I must choose between cake and ice cream, I'll take ice cream, or the _____.

latter

**51.** The small cafe serves only lemon pie and chocolate cake for dessert. If I go after five-thirty, I will get only the

_____.

later, latter

later
latter

**52.** I was late, but Robin was _____.
Mark and I like meat balls and meat loaf, but if we have to choose, he will take the former and I the _____.

moral
moral
morale

**53.** The next pair—*moral* (accent on the first syllable) and *morale* (accent on the second syllable)—are easy to distinguish. *Morale* is a noun meaning spirit of well-being; *moral* is an adjective meaning ethical, or a noun meaning a lesson or principle. Read these sentences carefully and write the appropriate word for each.

Every fable has a _____.
A citizen has a _____ obligation to vote.
The officer complimented her staff on their high _____.

a. moral
b. moral
c. moral
d. morale

**54.** Fill in the blanks with either *moral* or *morale*.

a. In the insurance business, a risk resulting from uncertainty about the insured's honesty is called a _____ risk.

b. He ends every speech with a _____.

c. She felt that everyone had his or her own _____ code.

d. After his inspection of the plant, the superintendent complained about the low _____ of the employees.

ingenious
ingenuous

**55.** The last pair is *ingenious,* meaning clever, and *ingenuous,* meaning frank or naive. If you are unsure of the pronunciation, take time to check the dictionary. Now look carefully at the origins:

ingenious: Latin *ingenium* (inborn talent)
ingenuous: Latin *ingenuus* (honest, frank)

Since you have already noticed the important vowel in the middle of each word, fill in the vowels here: ingen___ous (clever) and ingen___ous (naive).

ingenious
ingenuousness

**56.** Although his suggestions for improvement were exciting and in_____ous, he showed a certain in_____

naivete

ness about their implementation.

ingenious

**57.** David is clever, so we may say he is _____.

ingenuous

**58.** Frank is childlike in his directness and simplicity, so we can say he is _____.

## REVIEW

a.  eminent
b.  later
c.  moral
d.  immigrants
e.  ingenuous

**59.** Select the correct word in each sentence.

a. If the pianist is famous, would you call him (imminent or eminent)? _____

b. I cannot make the two o'clock appointment, so I will go (latter, later). _____

c. What is the (moral, morale) of the story? _____

d. Congress is concerned about the number of (immigrants, emigrants) settling in the United States. _____

e. If one is naive, he could be called (ingenious, ingenuous). _____

## POSTTEST

A. Write the full word to fit each context.

1. Kim insisted on wearing c_____ clothes to the opera.

2. If my m_____ was any lower, it would drag on the floor.

3. Not all inventors are as in_____ as Tom.

4. Dan does every job in a systematic and th_____ manner.

5. Since Pat lost fifty pounds, her dresses are so l_____ they look like tents.

6. No one can ad_____ you; you must decide for yourself.

7. The issue does not concern all the personnel; it is strictly a p_____ matter between Carrie and Sue.

8. Of the two proposals, only the l_____ is practical.

B. These words often can be confused, so try matching the definition with the correct word in each pair. If some words are unfamiliar, check the dictionary. Write the word in the blank.

9. a supernatural being  _____   angle, angel

10. inhale and exhale  _____   breathe, breath

11. pay out  _____   disperse, disburse

12. example  _____   instants, instance

13. earlier  _____   formerly, formally

14. draw out, evoke  _____   illicit, elicit

15. false belief from self-deception  _____   illusion, delusion

16. wearing apparel  _____   cloths, clothes

17. show off  _____   flout, flaunt

18. aware  _____   conscience, conscious

19. point of view  _____   perspective, prospective

20. pertaining to a climax  _____   climatic, climactic

# TEST
## PART THREE

A. Fill in the correct form of the missing prefix (*per, pre, pro, in, de, dis, con, ad*). Be sure to check the meanings of the words in the right-hand column.

1. Sandra recently received a _____motion.                                    advancement

2. Several government documents have been _____classified          downgraded
from "secret" to "confidential."

3. The store owner _____credits the thieves' story.                          cast doubt

4. She _____formed without a rehearsal.                                            act

5. His attitude _____palled me.                                                          dismay

6. Two of the children have a contagious _____ease.                         illness

7. The weather bureau's _____dictions came true.                            foretelling

8. A student should always read the _____face of a book.               introduction

9. I put a dollar in the _____lection box.                                           accumulation

10. The recital _____mences at eight o'clock.                                    begin

11. The rule was _____revocable.                                                       incapable of
                                                                                                                  being revoked

12. Her actions are _____testable.                                                     hateful

13. New techniques show the _____gress in science.                      forward course

14. The group engaged in _____legal activities.                               not legal

15. The zoo charges a five dollar _____mittance fee.                       entrance

B. Select the correct homonym or similar word for each sentence.

16. What (affect, effect) will Jerry's absence from class have on his grade? _____

17. Yesterday three members of the (council, counsel) resigned. _____

18. I have no time to (alter, altar) the hemline. _____

19. Abby needs more (capital, capitol) to start her gift shop. _____

20. We watched the (immigrants, emigrants) arriving in New York. _____

21. Don Brown was unwilling to (accept, except) his superior's advice. _____
22. Pamela is coming (latter, later). _____
23. Forest Hills is a beautiful (site, sight) for a ranch. _____
24. The (lose, loose) board fell on Lee's arm. _____
25. The boy (lead, led) the donkey across the road. _____
26. Is Roy Adams a school superintendent or a (principle, principal)? _____
27. (You're, Your) going to the fair will create much excitement. _____
28. The board will hold Jack's (passed, past) actions against him. _____
29. The green and yellow draperies (complemented, complimented) the dark brown carpeting. _____
30. Mrs. Higgins has six (boarders, borders) staying in her big house on the hill. _____

C. Have someone dictate these sentences so you can write the underlined word from memory.

31. It was a quaint description.
32. I offered my proposal today.
33. The novelist is highly acclaimed by most critics.
34. The boy turned around immediately.
35. I see no difference.
36. The questions were unnumbered.
37. I hope Helen will intercede for me.
38. How many math courses are you taking?
39. Will you bring back some stationery from the store?
40. It is quiet on the border tonight.
41. She insisted on presenting irrelevant evidence.
42. Let's eat at the new French restaurant.
43. Is Jodie an acquaintance of yours?
44. Please don't embarrass me.
45. There is no time for an explanation.
46. She expressed her dissatisfaction.
47. We have a new procedure to follow.
48. Her accomplishments are many.
49. It is simply a matter of convenience.
50. Peggy is often overcome with loneliness.

# PART FOUR

# FOUR

## RULES AND SPELLING

# CHAPTER ELEVEN
## *IE–EI*

If you have been plagued by the *i* and *e* combination, you need not worry any longer. Sound plays an important part in deciding which combination to use; in this chapter, therefore, you will (1) identify the various vowel sounds represented by *ie* or *ei;* (2) apply the rules for combining *e* and *i;* (3) recognize and spell correctly the exceptions; and (4) spell a number of useful words in and out of context. The chapter will also give you a basis for spelling other *i* and *e* words.

## PRETEST

Fill in the correct combination: *ei* or *ie.*

1. To ease means to rel____ve.
2. Vanity is another name for conc____t.
3. To get is to rec____ve.
4. The doctors were able to control his s____zures.
5. To be lacking in something is to be defic____nt.
6. The postman w____ghed my packages.
7. The head of a tribe is usually called a ch____f.
8. Please give me a p____ce of cake.
9. Strange is a synonym for w____rd.
10. Another word for forgery is counterf____t.
11. What is your h____ght and w____ght?
12. To accomplish means to ach____ve.
13. The role I must play is entirely for____gn to my nature.
14. We live in a blighted n____ghborhood.
15. How much l____sure time do you have?

yes

**1.** Even though the old rhyme will not work for all *i* and *e* words, it is a good place to begin:

*I* before *e*
   Except after *c*
      Or when sounded as *a*
         As in *neighbor* and *weigh*

Look carefully at the two columns of words below and say them aloud, stressing the underlined part.

piece        conceit
chief        receive
niece        deceive
siege        receipt

Do both columns of words have the long *e* sound? _____

*e*
*ie*
*c*

**2.** The combination of *i* and *e* is not the same in both columns, however. In the first column, all the words have *ie;* in the second, they have *ei.* The first two lines of the rhyme give you the clue: if *i* and *e* sound like a long _____, write _____, unless the preceding consonant is _____.

The consonant
preceding *i* and
*e* is *l*, not *c.*

**3.** Why would you not spell *relieve* with the *ei* combination?
_____

a.  yield
b.  receipt
c.  siege
d.  chief
e.  conceit
f.  believed
g.  deceiving

**4.** Each word below has the long *e* sound. Write in the correct combination: *ei, ie.*

a. y_____ld        e. conc_____t

b. rec_____pt      f. bel_____ved

c. s_____ge        g. dec_____ving

d. ch_____f

a.  *ei*
b.  *ie*
c.  *ie*
d.  *ie*
e.  *ei*
f.  *ie*
g.  *ei*

**5.** Complete the words in these sentences with *ie* or *ei.*

a. She has no cause to dec_____ve.

b. Betsy has only one n_____ce.

c. The army ended its long s_____ge.

d. His statement is hard for me to bel_____ve.

e. My aunt has many cash rec_____pts.

f.  Please give me a p_____ce of paper.

g. Lou is more conc_____ted than Ted.

a. receive
b. siege
c. achieve
d. relieve
e. deceive

**6.** At the left is a panel of words requiring *ie* or *ei*. Read each sentence carefully for its meaning, choose the word from the panel, and write the complete word.

dec____ve     a. The principal said I would _____
s____ge        a prize.
ach____ve
rec____ve      b. The fortress withstood the _____
rel____ve      for a full month.

c. I worry that I may not _____ my goal.
                               accomplish

d. Many new drugs help to _____ discomfort.

e. Someone who will mislead another will _____ that person.

*ie*
*ei*

**7.** The usual spelling of *i* and *e* with the long *e* sound is _____ except after *c;* then it is _____.

yes
receive
*c*

**8.** Now let us take these words. Look at them closely and pronounce them.

weird          seize          either
leisure        seizure        neither

Do they have the same sound as *belief* and *receive?* _____
Is the combination of *i* and *e* written as in *belief* or *receive?*
_____

To best remember them you can link them with those words with the long *e* sound coming after which consonant? _____

neither
seizure
leisure
weird

**9.** You can also associate them in some way. For example, two have similar sounds: *either* and n_____.
Another two go together: the verb seize and its noun s_____ure. Another rhymes with *seizure:* l_____.
The one that stands alone is w____rd, meaning strange.

a. either
b. neither
c. seize
d. seizure
e. leisure
f. weird

**10.** Finish spelling the exceptions:

a. One or another is the definition of e_____.

b. Not one or the other is the meaning of n_____.

c. To grasp is to s_____.

d. The act of grasping is s_____.

e. Free time is called l_____.

f. To be strange is to be w_____.

either
neither
seize
seizure
leisure
weird

no

a.  Neither
b.  conceited
c.  leisure
d.  seized
e.  either
f.  tiers
g.  pier
h.  yield

c.  bay

weighty
reign
reindeer
sleigh

*ei*

**11.** Write the six exceptions to the long *e* sound of *i* and *e*.

_____  _____  _____  _____  _____  _____

## REVIEW

**12.** Look at this group of words. Are there any *i*'s and *e*'s out of order? \_\_\_\_\_

| | | |
|---|---|---|
| conceive | conceit | receipt |
| achieve | receive | thief |
| relief | believe | belief |

**13.** Supply the missing *ie* or *ei*.

a. John said, "N\_\_\_\_ther Jane nor I will admit that what we saw in the sky was a UFO."

b. Joseph is terribly conc\_\_\_\_ted.

c. Mary Beth has too much l\_\_\_\_sure time.

d. The police s\_\_\_\_zed the phony salesman.

e. I should buy \_\_\_\_ther a new table or a chair.

f. In the new orchestra hall there are three t\_\_\_\_rs of seats in the balcony.

g. The boat is docked at the p\_\_\_\_r.

h. She will not y\_\_\_\_ld to his demands.

**14.** Check which sound in the underlined portion of the following words matches the sound of the *i* and *e* in the words to the right.

a. b<u>i</u>t          neighbor

b. b<u>ee</u>f          freight

c. b<u>ay</u>          weigh

d. b<u>i</u>te

**15.** All the words below have the *ei* combination. Pick out those with the long *a* sound as in *bay*.

| | |
|---|---|
| either | reign |
| weird | reindeer |
| weighty | seize |
| leisure | sleigh |

**16.** Like the six exceptions to the long *e* sound, the words with the long *a* sound have which combination (*ie*, *ei*)? \_\_\_\_

Yes—all are
spelled *ei*.

**17.** Does the long *a* rule apply to the underlined words?

_____

a. During the <u>Reign</u> of Terror thousands of people were executed.

b. Joe hopped on a <u>freight</u> car.

c. One controls a horse with <u>reins</u>.

d. My mother is <u>overweight</u>.

e. <u>Reindeer</u> Lake is in Manitoba.

a. long *a*
b. long *e*
c. long *e*
d. long *a*
e. long *e*
f. long *e*
g. long *a*

**18.** Now indicate which sound each *i* and *e* combination has.

a. weight _____    e. leisure _____

b. weird _____    f. neither _____

c. seizure _____    g. neighbor _____

d. freight _____

b.

**19.** In the preceding frame, the words having the long *e* sound:

a. follow the rule for long *e*.
b. are exceptions to this rule.

a. *ei*
b. *ei*
c. *ei*
d. *ei*

**20.** Read the sentences first, then fill in the missing *i* and *e* combinations.

a. Some women like v_____ls on their hats.

b. A pleasurable sport in the winter is a sl_____gh ride.

c. A vessel that carries blood back to the heart is a v_____n.

d. How much do you w_____gh?

*ie*
*ei*
*ei*

**21.** Generally, the long *e* sound of *i* and *e* is written _____ except after *c* when it is written _____; the long sound of *a* is written _____.

b.

**22.** Now pronounce the word *height*. The *ei* corresponds to which underlined sound below? _____

a. b<u>e</u>d    b. b<u>i</u>te    c. b<u>ee</u>f    d. b<u>i</u>t    e. b<u>ay</u>

*ei*

**23.** Both the long *a* and long *i* sounds are written (*ie* or *ei*)?

_____

*ei*

**24.** When one measures how tall he is, he measures his h_____ght.

height

**25.** The word meaning tallness is often misspelled not only because of the *ei*, but because of the ending: Johnny is nearly the h____gh__ of his father.

a. *ei   ei*
b. *ei*
c. *ei*
d. *ei*
e. *ei*

**26.** Read each sentence first, then write the correct combination(s) of *i* and *e*.

a. What is your w____ght and h____ght?

b. The troops numbered ____ghty thousand.

c. I wonder how long this king will r____gn.

d. After dark Tim sneaked down to hop on a fr____ght.

e. If you want to control your horse, tighten the r____ns.

d.

**27.** Now look at these words closely and pronounce them:

foreign          counterfeit

The sound of the *ei* corresponds to which underlined sound below:

a. bay     b. bite     c. beef     d. bit

*ei   ei*

**28.** The short *i* sound is in the words *counterf____t* and *for____gn*.

*feit*

**29.** An imitation or forgery is the definition of the noun *counter____*.

*eign*

**30.** To be alien to one's nature is to be for____ to it.

*ei*
*ei*
*ei*

**31.** The short *i* is also apparent in three other words:

*forf____t      surf____t      sover____gn*

*feit*
*feit*

**32.** To surrender a privilege for committing an offense is to for____; to feed to excess or to overindulge is to sur____.

*ei*

**33.** A king or queen can also be called a sover____gn.

counterfeit
surfeit
forfeit

**34.** Three words having the same short *i* sound of *i* and *e* are ____feit, ____feit, and ____feit.

foreign
sovereign

**35.** Two words having the same ending with the short *i* sound of *i* and *e* are ____gn and ____ gn.

a. foreign
short *i*

b. weighty
long *a*

c. height
long *i*

d. counterfeit
short *i*

e. reign
long *a*

f. forfeit
short *i*

g. reindeer
long *a*

**REVIEW**

**36.** Fill in the missing *i* and *e* combination and identify the vowel sound for each word.

Vowel sound

a. for____gn            _____

b. w____ghty          _____

c. h____ght            _____

d. counterf____t       _____

e. r____gn             _____

f. forf____t            _____

g. r____deer           _____

a. sovereign
b. surfeit
c. skein
d. stein
e. kaleidoscope
f. sleigh
g. seismograph

**37.** Pick out the misspelled word in each pair and write it correctly. Definitions will help you identify the words.

a. sovereign,        ruling monarch

soveriegn                              _____

b. surfeit, surfiet   oversupply      _____

c. skein, skien      coil of yarn     _____

d. stein, stien      mug             _____

e. kaliedoscope     constantly changing

kaleidoscope        set of colors    _____

f. sliegh, sleigh    vehicle on runners  _____

g. seismograph,     instrument for

siesmograph         detecting earth

                    movements        _____

a. foreigner
b. forfeit
c. weigh
eight
d. height
e. counterfeit

**38.** Complete these *ei-ie* words.

a. Nancy married a for____gner.

b. John must forf____t a day's pay.

c. Only five girls in the class w____gh over ninety-____ght pounds.

d. Mary's h____ght prevents her from playing basketball.

e. Sam was convicted of printing counterf____t bills.

shent

**39.** Now let us take *efficient* and divide it first into syllables: ef  fi  cient. Pronounce them. The last has which sound ("sent," "shent")? _____

the "sh"

**40.** Because we are interested in the *i* and *e*, what part of the "shent" sound in *cient* does the *cie* have? _____

*cie*

**41.** This "sh" sound then is represented by the letters _____.

yes

**42.** Do these adjectives also have the "sh" sound of *cie*? _____

*proficient     sufficient     deficient*

second and third
(*fi   cient*)

**43.** Let us look at the four words again: *proficient, sufficient, deficient, efficient.* Which two syllables are spelled the same? _____

*ef   suf*
*pro*
*de*

**44.** Only the first syllable differs. To be effective is to be _____ficient; to be enough, or to suffice, is to be _____ ficient. The prefix *pro* means forward and *de* means away or down. If one is skilled in a trade (gone forward, in other words) he is said to be _____ficient; if he has gone down or is lacking in some way he is _____ficient.

a. sufficient
b. efficient
c. deficient
d. proficient

**45.** Write the correct "shent" words for each sentence.

a. There will be _____ food for the picnic.
                              enough

b. This is the most _____ way to operate the machine.
                           effective

c. Despite their education, they are _____ in their
                                                   wanting
knowledge of the English language.

d. In her layout work at the printshop she is _____.
                                                         skilled

*t*
*cy*

**46.** The state of being efficient is *efficiency.* In spelling the noun you drop the _____ from the adjective and add _____.

a. sufficiency
b. deficiency
c. proficiency

**47.** How would you spell these nouns?

a. the state of being enough_____

b. the state of being wanting_____

c. the state of being skilled_____

**REVIEW**

patient
ancient

**48.** How would you spell these words with the "shent" sound: pat_____ and anc_____?

a. deficient
b. sufficient
c. efficient
d. proficient
e. efficiency

**49.** Supply the "cie" word to fit each definition.

a. to be wanting _____

b. to be enough _____

c. to be effective _____

d. to be skilled _____

e. the state of being effective _____

# POSTTEST

Supply the correct combination, *ie* or *ei,* and write the complete word.

1. I cannot bel_____ve your story.

2. The Army finally ended its long s_____ge.

3. He thinks he has a sover_____gn right to do that.

4. Where is the fr_____ght office?

5. I expect to rec_____ve four presents.

6. He must forf_____t all his privileges.

7. Have you seen any r_____ndeer on the trail?

8. Sandy Black is very effic_____nt.

9. Don't y_____ld to their demands.

10. As he comes around the corner, s_____ze him.

11. How much do you w_____gh?

12. To be lacking is to be defic_____t.

13. I am working so hard I have no l_____sure time.

14. The child told a w_____rd story.

15. He has a reputation as a th_____f.

16. Murder is a h_____nous crime. (long a)

17. The *i* and *e* have the short sound of *e:* fr_____nd.

18. The *i* and *e* in this word also has the short *e* sound but is spelled differently: a young cow is a h_____fer.

19. The police kept the couple under surv_____llance for almost a month.

20. Although this word has the same sound as the word meaning forgery, it does not have the same spelling: s_____ve.

# CHAPTER TWELVE

## DOUBLING THE FINAL CONSONANT

Knowing when to double the final consonant and when not to will help you to spell many words correctly. In this chapter you will not only learn several rules about doubling in words of one or more syllables, but you will also apply them to many words. Also you will learn to immediately recognize words that do not follow the doubling rule, words that do and do not double depending on the shift in stress when a suffix is added, and a few exceptions to the rules. By the end of the chapter you will not be misspelling *occurrence*, *transferring*, or other words requiring the final consonant to be doubled, nor will you be misspelling words that do not double the final consonant.

### PRETEST

Add the specified suffixes to the following words.

| | | | | | |
|---|---|---|---|---|---|
| 1. plan | *er* | _____ | 14. gossip | *y* | _____ |
| 2. wit | *y* | _____ | 15. instill | *ing* | _____ |
| 3. streak | *ed* | _____ | 16. equip | *ed* | _____ |
| 4. plug | *er* | _____ | 17. omit | *ed* | _____ |
| 5. tax | *ing* | _____ | 18. dim | *er* | _____ |
| 6. exploit | *er* | _____ | 19. excel | *ent* | _____ |
| 7. drop | *ed* | _____ | 20. confer | *ence* | _____ |
| 8. begin | *ing* | _____ | 21. benefit | *ed* | _____ |
| 9. occur | *ence* | _____ | 22. chagrin | *ed* | _____ |
| 10. dim | *ly* | _____ | 23. vex | *ing* | _____ |
| 11. repeal | *ed* | _____ | 24. delight | *ful* | _____ |
| 12. transfer | *ing* | _____ | 25. traffic | *er* | _____ |
| 13. propel | *ant* | _____ | | | |

c.  d.  f.  g.  h.
· · · · · · · · · · · · ·
b.  c.  e.  f.  h.

**1.** One-syllable words ending in a single consonant preceded by a single vowel double the final consonant before adding a suffix beginning with a vowel (or the suffix *y*). For instance, the word *cup* ends in a single consonant (*p*) preceded by a single vowel (*u*). If you add the suffix *ed* (which begins with the vowel *e*) you double the consonant: *cupped.* But if you add the suffix *ful* (which begins with the consonant *f*) you do not double the *p: cupful.* Let us look at the words *link* and *peel. Link* ends in two consonants (*nk*) and *peel* in a consonant preceded by two vowels (*eel*), so these words do not meet the requirements.

One consonant cannot be doubled even though it is preceded by a vowel. This consonant—*x*—has a *ks* sound and is treated as two consonants. Take the word *tax* as an example; pronounce it slowly and you will hear the *ks* sound. If you add *ed* to *tax* you would spell it: *taxed.*

In the one-syllable words below identify those that end in a single consonant preceded by a single vowel.

| | | |
|---|---|---|
| a. hail | d. club | g. bug |
| b. drill | e. pack | h. rip |
| c. mop | f. tap | |

· · · · · · · · · · · · · · · · · · · · · · · · · · · · · · · · · ·

Identify the suffixes that would require doubling.

| | | |
|---|---|---|
| a. *ment* | d. *ly* | g. *ful* |
| b. *ing* | e. *y* | h. *ance* |
| c. *er* | f. *ed* | |

a.  chatty
e.  dimmed
f.  clammy
g.  fretting

**2.** Pick out each combination of a word and a suffix to which this doubling rule applies, add the specified suffix, and write the complete word. If the rule does not apply to a combination, leave the space blank.

a. chat     *y*     _____

b. streak   *ed*    _____

c. farm     *er*    _____

d. tax      *ing*   _____

e. dim      *ed*    _____

f. clam     *y*     _____

g. fret     *ing*   _____

h. burn     *er*    _____

b.  stooped
d.  fretful
e.  taxed

**3.** If a particular word or suffix does not meet the requirements of this rule, you can assume that the final consonant is not doubled before the suffix. Choose the combinations below

f. pealing
h. grimly

to which this rule does *not* apply, add the specified suffix, and write the complete words.

a. bar     *ed*    _____

b. stoop    *ed*    _____

c. stop     *ed*    _____

d. fret     *ful*    _____

e. tax     *ed*    _____

f. peal     *ing*    _____

g. chub     *y*    _____

h. grim     *ly*    _____

a. planner
b. droplet
c. restful
d. clubs
e. dimmer
f. speared
g. shrieking
h. plugged
i. skinny
j. dimly
k. vexing
l. dropped

**4.** Now test your skill by writing complete words for all the combinations.

a. plan     *er*    _____

b. drop     *let*    _____

c. rest     *ful*    _____

d. club     *s*    _____

e. dim     *er*    _____

f. spear     *ed*    _____

g. shriek     *ing*    _____

h. plug     *ed*    _____

i. skin     *y*    _____

j. dim     *ly*    _____

k. vex     *ing*    _____

l. drop     *ed*    _____

## REVIEW

c.   d.   f.

**5.** Which factors must be considered in the doubling of the final consonant in a one-syllable word?

a. It must end in a single vowel.

b. It must end in a single consonant preceded by a single consonant.

c. It must end in a single consonant preceded by a single vowel.

d. It must not end in the consonant *x*.

e. The suffix begins with a consonant.

f. The suffix begins with a vowel or is the suffix *y*.

The last *f* is preceded by another *f* (consonant).

**6.** Why don't you double the final consonant in *puff?*

_____

The *k* is preceded by two vowels (*oa*).

**7.** In adding the suffix *ed* to *soak,* the *k* is not doubled. Why not?_____

The suffix *ly* begins with a consonant (*l*).

**8.** Even though *dim* ends in a single consonant preceded by a single vowel, you do not double the *m* before *ly.* Why not? _____

a. cupful
b. stopper
c. shrouded
d. mopped
e. witty
f. taxing
g. primly
h. pouter
i. tags
j. deepest
k. pithy
l. kindness

**9.** Test your skill by adding the suffixes to these one-syllable words.

a. cup  *ful*  _____

b. stop  *er*  _____

c. shroud  *ed*  _____

d. mop  *ed*  _____

e. wit  *y*  _____

f. tax  *ing*  _____

g. prim  *ly*  _____

h. pout  *er*  _____

i. tag  *s*  _____

j. deep  *est*  _____

k. pith  *y*  _____

l. kind  *ness*  _____

a.  d.  f.
• • • • • • • • • • • •
a. 4
b. 1
c. 2
d. 2
e. 1
f. 4
g. 3

**10.** Words of more than one syllable must also have a single consonant preceded by a single vowel to be doubled. Also, the stress (or accent) must be on the *last* syllable. Take the word *compel.* It ends in *l* preceded by *e,* and the stress is on the last syllable. Because it meets all the requirements, the *l* is doubled before a suffix beginning with a vowel: *compel* + *ed* = *compelled.*

If a word does not meet these requirements, then the final consonant is not doubled. Take the verbs *instill* and *exploit.* Although the accent is on the last syllable in each, the *l* is preceded by another *l* and the *t* is preceded by two vowels. The final consonant *x* is the exception here as well, as the *x* (pronounced like *ks*) counts as two consonants. Even though the word *relax* meets the requirements, the *x* is not doubled.

Now identify those words that have the stress on the last syllable:

a. recur          d. prefer

b. offer          e. enter

c. differ         f. propel

· · · · · · · · · · · · · · · · · · · · · · · · · · · · · · · · · · · ·

Look at and pronounce each word, then match it with the correct explanation for doubling or not doubling.

a. enchant   _____        e. compel    _____

b. occur     _____        f. repeal    _____

c. benefit   _____        g. determine _____

d. enlighten _____

1. doubles: accent and ending correct
2. does not double: ending correct, but accent is wrong
3. does not double: accent and ending are wrong
4. does not double: accent correct but ending is wrong

a. referred
b. visitor
c. benefited
d. repellent
e. rebuttal
f. repealing
g. occurrence
h. gossipy

**11.** Applying the doubling rule when appropriate, add the specified suffixes to the following words.

a. refer     *ed*    _____

b. visit     *or*    _____

c. benefit   *ed*    _____

d. repel     *ent*   _____

e. rebut     *al*    _____

f. repeal    *ing*   _____

g. occur     *ence*  _____

h. gossip    *y*     _____

a.   c.

**12.** *Equip* ends in a single consonant preceded by two vowels *u* and *i*. However, only the *i* counts as a vowel because a *u* combined with a *q* makes a *kw* sound (e kwip). *Equip* then meets the requirements of this rule.
There is one suffix before which you do *not* double the *p:* *age.*
Choose the suffixes before which you would double the *p* in *equip.*

a. *ing*          c. *ed*

b. *ment*         d. *age*

equipped  equipage
equipment
equipping

**13.** Add the following suffixes to equip:

*ed*   _____        *age*  _____

*ment* _____        *ing*  _____

transferring
transferred

**14.** Modern usage permits two pronunciations of *transfer:* tranśfer or transfeŕ. In spelling the word, however, you follow the doubling rule. Add *ing* and *ed* to this word.

_____     _____

a. controlling
b. occurred
c. equipped
d. difference
e. beginning
f. transferred
g. happened
h. revealed
i. appearance
j. benefited
k. recurring
l. patrolling
m. relaxing

**15.** Now combine the root word and suffix for each sentence.

a. The nurse had a difficult time _____ the patient.
control   *ing*

b. This same situation has _____ many times.
occur   *ed*

c. The kitchen was _____ with the latest appliances.
equip   *ed*

d. Many cannot see the _____ between the two
differ   *ence*
items.

e. Since I lost my place, I will have to start reading from the
_____.
begin   *ing*

f. My father has been _____ to Detroit.
transfer   *ed*

g. What has _____ to the Olsons?
happen   *ed*

h. A thorough study of the project _____ several
reveal   *ed*
statistical errors.

i. The prima donna has made only one concert _____ this year.
appear   *ance*

j. Many peasants have _____ from the agrarian reform
benefit   *ed*
program.

k. The invalid was plagued by a _____ fever.
recur   *ing*

l. The municipal police department does a good job of _____ the area.
patrol   *ing*

m. Fishing can be a _____ sport.
relax   *ing*

The *l* was doubled before the suffix, so the extra *l* must be taken off to form the original word.

**16.** Sometimes the word that requires doubling is misspelled. Take *rebellion,* for example. The word is made up of two parts, the root and the suffix. Take away the suffix *ion* and you have "rebell." This is the wrong spelling of the root. Why? _____

a. control
b. excel
c. repel
d. compel

**17.** Now reduce these words to their roots.

a. controlled  _____

b. excellent  _____

c. repelling  _____

d. compeller  _____

chagrined

**18.** The word *chagrin,* which means mental distress, ends in a single consonant preceded by a single vowel and the stress is on the last syllable. But it is an exception to the doubling rule. Add the suffix *ed* to this word. _____

chagrin

**19.** The word which means mental distress is an exception to the doubling rule. That word is _____.

chagrined

**20.** If a person is suffering from embarrassment or distress caused by failure, that person is _____.

last
first
second *r*

**21.** If the addition of a suffix causes the stress to be shifted to an earlier syllable, then the final consonant is not doubled. Let us add *ed* and then *ence* to *occur: occurred* and *occurrence.* There has been no shift in accent, as it is still on *cur.* Now add *ed* and *ence* to *refer.* On what syllable is the stress in *referred* (first, last)? _____ in *reference* (first, last)? _____ What letter is missing in the second word? _____

yes

**22.** In your mind add *ence* to these words: *prefer, confer, infer, defer.* Are these examples of words in which the accent shifts to an earlier syllable? _____

excellent  excellence

**23.** Now pronounce these words:
*excelled      excelling      excellent      excellence*

The root word is *excel,* which has the stress on the last syllable. In which of the above words, if any, does the accent shift? _____

no

**24.** Do *excellent* and *excellence* follow the same spelling pattern as *reference?* _____

double

**25.** *Excel* is then an exception. Regardless of the shift in stress to an earlier syllable, you still _____ the final *l.*

excel

**26.** What is the root of *excellent* or *excelling?* _____

a. deferment
b. preferred
c. preferable
d. deference
e. reference
f. interment
g. excelled
h. occurrence
i. deferred
j. conferring

**27.** Pronounce the following complete words carefully, noticing where the accent falls. Then write them.

a. defer      *ment*      _____

b. prefer     *ed*        _____

c. prefer     *able*      _____

d. defer      *ence*      _____

e. refer      *ence*      _____

f. inter      *ment*      _____

g. excel      *ed*        _____

h. occur      *ence*      _____

i. defer      *ed*        _____

j. confer     *ing*       _____

yes
yes
no

**28.** The last few words to be studied also end in a single consonant preceded by a single vowel (*ic*). But the stress is not on the last syllable, so the final *c* is not doubled. There is a pronunciation problem, however, and these words must be treated for it. Take the word *picnic*. The final *c* has a hard sound (as in cat), not a soft sound (as in city), and to preserve this hard sound you must add a *k* before a suffix beginning with a vowel (or the suffix *y*). You do not need the *k* if the suffix begins with a consonant, like *ry* or *some*.

Pronounce these words:

*traffic      panic      colic      mimic*

Does the final *c* have a hard sound? _____

Is the *k* necessary before a vowel suffix? _____

Is the *k* necessary before a consonant suffix? _____

a. panicked
b. trafficker
c. frolicsome
d. colicky
e. mimicry
f. mimicking

**29.** Add the specified suffixes to these "ic" words.

a. panic     ed         _____

b. traffic   er         _____

c. frolic    some       _____

d. colic     y          _____

e. mimic     ry         _____

f. mimic     ing        _____

a.
e.
g.
h.

## REVIEW

**30.** In general, which of the following factors must be present to double the final consonant of a word having more than one syllable?

a. The suffix begins with a vowel (or is the suffix *y*).

b. The suffix begins with a consonant.

c. The final consonant is preceded by one or more vowels.

d. The final consonant is preceded by one or more consonants.

e. The final consonant is preceded by a single vowel.

f. The accent can be on any syllable.

g. The accent is on the last syllable.

h. The consonant *x* is not doubled.

a. shifts
b. excel
c. chagrin

**31.** The exceptions to this rule are:

a. You do not double if the accent _____ back to an earlier syllable.

b. One word doubles regardless of a shift in stress—it is _____.

c. The word meaning mental distress does not double—it is _____.

a. occurrence
b. difference
c. equipped
d. controlling
e. benefited
f. beginning
g. existence
h. equipment
i. equipage
j. transferred
k. reference
l. preferred
m. excellent
n. relaxed
o. picnicking

**32.** Now test your skill in adding the specified suffixes to these words, applying the doubling rules when appropriate.

a. occur      *ence*    _____

b. differ      *ence*    _____

c. equip       *ed*      _____

d. control    *ing*     _____

e. benefit     *ed*      _____

f. begin       *ing*     _____

g. exist        *ence*    _____

h. equip      *ment*    _____

i. equip       *age*     _____

j. transfer    *ed*      _____

k. refer        *ence*    _____

l. prefer       *ed*      _____

m. excel       *ent*     _____

n. relax        *ed*      _____

o. picnic      *ing*     _____

a. propel
b. control
c. rebel
d. excel
e. compel
f. deter

**33.** Write the root words from these combined forms.

a. propeller  _____

b. controlled  _____

c. rebellion  _____

d. excelling  _____

e. compelled  _____

f. deterred  _____

## POSTTEST

A. Combine the root word and the suffix.

| | | | | | | |
|---|---|---|---|---|---|---|
| 1. acquit | al | _____ | 11. develop | ment | _____ |
| 2. propel | er | _____ | 12. sum | ary | _____ |
| 3. traffic | ing | _____ | 13. woman | ish | _____ |
| 4. allot | ment | _____ | 14. allot | ed | _____ |
| 5. depend | able | _____ | 15. equip | ment | _____ |
| 6. exceed | ing | _____ | 16. mimic | ry | _____ |
| 7. ballot | ing | _____ | 17. differ | ent | _____ |
| 8. admit | ance | _____ | 18. relax | ing | _____ |
| 9. repel | ent | _____ | 19. stop | age | _____ |
| 10. gossip | y | _____ | 20. man | ish | _____ |

B. From this list select the 14 words to which the doubling rule can apply, add the specified suffix, and write the whole word.

| | | | | | |
|---|---|---|---|---|---|
| begin | er | _____ | instill | ed | _____ |
| conduct | ing | _____ | picnic | ing | _____ |
| omit | ing | _____ | sneak | er | _____ |
| gallop | ing | _____ | swim | er | _____ |
| panic | ed | _____ | repeat | ed | _____ |
| exist | ence | _____ | point | ed | _____ |
| defer | ment | _____ | excel | ent | _____ |
| compel | ed | _____ | beg | ar | _____ |
| prefer | ence | _____ | propel | er | _____ |
| chagrin | ed | _____ | plan | ing | _____ |
| frolic | ing | _____ | plane | ing | _____ |
| conceal | er | _____ | cramp | ed | _____ |

| bag | ing | _____ | drum | er | _____ |
| shriek | ed | _____ | design | er | _____ |
| blot | er | _____ | regret | able | _____ |
| drop | ing | _____ | rebel | ion | _____ |

C. Add the appropriate suffixes to these root words.

ed   er   ing   ence   ar   age

35. equip  _____    41. occur  _____

36. defer  _____    42. omit  _____

37. skim  _____    43. prefer  _____

38. bag  _____    44. transfer  _____

39. blot  _____    45. refer  _____

40. beg  _____    46. stop  _____

# CHAPTER THIRTEEN
## THE FINAL *E*

When adding a suffix do you drop the final *e* of a word or do you keep it? That question is answered in this chapter, and by working carefully through the frames you will learn the rules for dropping or retaining the final *e* and you will apply the rules to a number of useful words. At the same time you will learn to spell them quickly and unhesitatingly and use them in various contexts. Also you will identify the exceptions to the rules and write them correctly in and out of context.

## PRETEST

Add the specified suffixes and write the complete words.

| | | | | | |
|---|---|---|---|---|---|
| 1. desire | *ing* | _____ | 14. lose | *ing* | _____ |
| 2. use | *less* | _____ | 15. rare | *ity* | _____ |
| 3. service | *able* | _____ | 16. singe | *ing* | _____ |
| 4. due | *ly* | _____ | 17. argue | *ing* | _____ |
| 5. dense | *ity* | _____ | 18. adventure | *ous* | _____ |
| 6. nine | *th* | _____ | 19. dine | *er* | _____ |
| 7. come | *ing* | _____ | 20. canoe | *ist* | _____ |
| 8. receive | *ed* | _____ | 21. enforce | *ing* | _____ |
| 9. argue | *ment* | _____ | 22. whole | *ly* | _____ |
| 10. write | *ing* | _____ | 23. indispense | *able* | _____ |
| 11. true | *ly* | _____ | 24. nine | *ty* | _____ |
| 12. whole | *some* | _____ | 25. accurate | *ly* | _____ |
| 13. advertise | *ment* | _____ | | | |

a. b. d. e.
· · · · · · · · · · · · · ·
b. d. f.
· · · · · · · · · · · · · ·
a. c. d.

**1.** When you add a suffix beginning with a *vowel* to a word ending in a silent *e* you usually drop the *e* before adding the suffix. Words like *come, write,* or *desire* end in a silent *e*—the last sound you hear is the consonant preceding the *e: come,* write, desire. Words like *thee, devotee,* or *Jeanie* sound the *e* so they are not words with the silent *e*. Notice, too, that the last three end in a double vowel, not a consonant followed by the silent *e*. Let us look at *come* and the suffix *ing.* Both meet the requirements of the rule, so you would drop the *e: coming.*

Check the words below that end in a silent *e*.

a. use             d. dine

b. surprise      e. relate

c. devotee       f. Swanee

· · · · · · · · · · · · · · · · · · · · · · · · · · · · · · ·

Pick out the suffixes that can require the silent *e* to be dropped.

a. *ly*      c. *ment*      e. *some*

b. *ing*     d. *able*      f. *ity*

· · · · · · · · · · · · · · · · · · · · · · · · · · · · · · ·

Choose the combinations of words and suffixes to which this rule applies.

a. write     *ing*           d. advance     *ed*

b. advise   *ment*         e. adventure   *some*

c. desire    *ous*          f. vile          *ness*

a. dining
b. receivable
c. writing
d. useless
e. desirous
f. advertising
g. rudeness

**2.** Write the complete words, applying the rule as appropriate.

a. dine       *ing*         _____

b. receive   *able*      _____

c. write      *ing*         _____

d. use        *less*       _____

e. desire     *ous*        _____

f. advertise   *ing*       _____

g. rude      *ness*      _____

lose
silent
vowel
drop

**3.** Now take the word *losing.* It is spelled correctly because:
The root word is (*lose, los*).
The root ends in a (silent, pronounced) *e*
The suffix begins with a (vowel, consonant).
Before adding this suffix you (keep, drop) the *e*.

a. desire
b. write
c. conceive
d. suppose
e. hope
f. use

**4.** The words below have also been formed from roots ending in a silent *e*. So that you will always recognize the parts of such combinations, write the root words.

a. desirous _____

b. writing _____

c. conceivable _____

d. supposed _____

e. hoping _____

f. using _____

a. accuse accusing
b. receive received
c. surprise surprising
d. guide guidance
e. dine dinette
f. value valued

**5.** Now perform two steps: (1) Write the root word from these combinations and then (2) add the specified suffix to it.

| Root | | Suffix | Complete word |
|---|---|---|---|
| a. accuser | _____ | *ing* | _____ |
| b. receivable | _____ | *ed* | _____ |
| c. surprised | _____ | *ing* | _____ |
| d. guiding | _____ | *ance* | _____ |
| e. dining | _____ | *ette* | _____ |
| f. valuable | _____ | *ed* | _____ |

a. writing
b. coming
c. dining
d. pleasurable
e. receivable
f. dividing
g. receiving
h. using
i. density
j. argued
k. indispensable

**6.** Combine the word and suffixes and write the complete word for each sentence.

a. My cousin is _____ a novel.
  write  *ing*

b. Do you know if Marty is _____?
  come  *ing*

c. When we walked into the cafe we saw Miss Nash _____ with her niece.
  dine  *ing*

d. Sleigh riding is a _____ winter activity.
  pleasure  *able*

e. The student had difficulty understanding the term "_____ goods."
  receive  *able*

f. Uncle Joe is _____ his money between
  divide  *ing*
his daughter and his niece.

g. For several weeks Mr. Green has been _____
  receive  *ing*

_____ mysterious calls.

h. How many books are you _____?

                        use   *ing*

i. We could not see the dome of the Capitol because of the _____ of the fog.

       dense   *ity*

j. Sam and his sister _____ for hours.

             argue   *ed*

k. Logical thinking is _____to good writing.

              indispense   *able*

soft
drop
keep

**7.** Some "silent *e*" words with the soft sound of *g* retain the *ge* before certain suffixes, like *able* and *ous*. Take *change,* for instance. The *g* is soft (as in *gem*), not hard (as in *go*). Before suffixes like *ing, er,* or *ed* you follow the rule and drop the *e: changing, changer, changed*. But before the suffix *able* you must keep the *e* to preserve the soft sound of *g: changeable*.
Pronounce the words *manage* and *advantage*.

Do they have the (hard, soft) sound of *g*? _____
Do you (keep, drop) the *e* before *ing* or *ed*? _____
Do you (keep, drop) the *e* before *able* or *ous*? _____

a. managing
b. changeable
c. advantageous
d. manageable
e. disadvantaged
f. changer

**8.** Combine these words and suffixes.

a. manage        *ing*   _____

b. change         *able*   _____

c. advantage    *ous*   _____

d. manage        *able*   _____

e. disadvantage  *ed*   _____

f. change         *er*   _____

soft
drop
keep
· · · · · · · · · · · · ·
a. noticing
b. serviceable
c. enforced
d. servicing
e. noticeable
f. enforceable

**9.** Some "silent *e*" words with the soft sound of *c* retain the *ce* before the suffix *able*. The *c* in *notice*, for example, has the soft sound (as in *city*) not the hard sound (as in *cat*). For suffixes like *ing, er, ed,* you follow the general rule and drop the *e*, but for the suffix *able* you keep the *e: noticing—noticeable*.
Now pronounce the words *service* and *enforce*.

Do they have the (soft, hard) sound of *c*? _____
Do you (drop, keep) the *e* before *ing* or *er*? _____
Do you (keep, drop) the *e* before *able*? _____

· · · · · · · · · · · · · · · · · · · · · · · · · · · · · · · · · · · · · · ·

Combine the words and suffixes below.

a. notice    *ing*   _____

b. service  *able*  _____

c. enforce  *ed*  _____

d. service  *ing*  _____

e. notice  *able*  _____

f. enforce  *able*  _____

c.
d.

**10.** Pick out the suffixes that require the *e* after a soft *c* or *g* to be kept.

a. *ed*          b. *ing*          c. *able*          d. *ous*          f. *er*

a. advantageous
b. noticing
changeable
c. manageable
managing
d. enforceable
e. disadvantaged
f. pronounceable

**11.**   Write the complete word for each.

a. The proposal is _____ to both factions.
<br>advantage  *ous*

b. I kept _____ John's _____ attitude.
<br>notice  *ing*          change  *able*

c. Although her child is not _____ Mrs. Brown is
<br>manage  *able*
_____ to put up with the temper tantrums.
<br>manage  *ing*

d. That law is not _____.
<br>enforce  *able*

e. The minority members will be _____
<br>disadvantage  *ed*
by the new rules.

f. The words are not _____.
<br>pronounce  *able*

c.   e.
a.   b.   d.   f.

**12.** You have been adding suffixes beginning with a vowel to words ending in a silent *e*. Now let us turn to suffixes beginning with a consonant. Generally, the *e* is retained before such endings. The word *use* is a good example. Before *ing, er,* and *ed* you drop the *e: using, user, used.* But before *ful* you keep the *e: useful.* Here is a list of suffixes:

a. *ness*          c. *ing*          e. *able*
b. *s*          d. *ly*          f. *ment*

Before which suffixes will you drop the *e?* _____
Before which will you keep the *e?* _____

a. using
b. user
c. useless
d. uses
e. useful
f. used
g. usage

**13.** Now add these suffixes to the root word *use.*

a. *ing*  _____          e. *ful*  _____

b. *er*  _____          f. *ed*  _____

c. *less*  _____          g. *age*  _____

d. *s*  _____

a. advertises
b. advertising
c. advertisement
d. advertiser

**14.** Using *advertise* as the root, add these suffixes to it.

a. *s* _____   c. *ment* _____

b. *ing* _____   d. *er* _____

a. arrangement
b. sincerely
   sincerity
c. accurately
d. ninety

**15.** Write the complete word(s) for each sentence.

a. What kind of _____ does Sue
                          arrange   ment
have for babysitting?

b. Although Tom acts _____ toward his sister,
                              sincere  ly
his _____ can sometimes be questioned.
       sincere   ity

c. The students computed every example _____.
                                              accurate   ly

d. In our college over _____ percent of the professors
                          nine   ty
are fifty years or older.

ninety
ninth

**16.** In the preceding frame you simply added *ty* to *nine*
because the *ty* begins with a consonant. Adding *th* to *nine*,
however, constitutes an exception. So *nine* + *ty* = _____
_____, but *nine* + *th* = _____.

ninety
ninth

**17.** Out of a class of one hundred and _____, Henry
                                              nine   ty
Bowen was _____ from the top.
              nine   th

drop

**18.** Another exception is the combination of *argue* and *ment*.
Even though *ment* begins with a consonant, it is treated like
a suffix beginning with a vowel. So you would (drop, keep)
the *e* in *argue*. _____

a. argument
b. argued
c. arguing
d. arguable

**19.** Add these suffixes to *argue*.

a. *ment* _____   c. *ing* _____

b. *ed* _____   d. *able* _____

arguing
argument

**20.** Although the different factions have been _____
                                                    argue  ing
for an hour, the _____ has not been an emotional
                    argue   ment
exchange of words.

# REVIEW

a. rarity
b. accommodating
c. agreeable
d. alleging
e. interference
f. reconcilable
g. usable
h. responsible
i. writing
j. ninth
k. choosing
l. believable
m. noticeable
n. issuing
o. peaceable
p. scarcity
q. ninety

**21.** Combine the root word and suffix.

a. Art experts consider the painting Jean Smith donated to the museum a _____.
   rare + *ty*

b. The hotel staff has been very _____.
   accommodate + *ing*

c. There is no question about their being _____
   agree + *able*
to the merger.

d. The lawyer is _____ that his client lied
   allege + *ing*
on the witness stand.

e. We do not need any _____ from the coach.
   interfere + *ence*

f. The differences are not _____.
   reconcile + *able*

g. The shop can accept only _____ items of clothing.
   use + *able*

h. I cannot be _____ for another's actions.
   response + *ible*

i. An art that is not easy to master is the art of
_____.
   write + *ing*

j. Marie was the _____ entry in the contest.
   nine + *th*

k. What color will you be _____ for your walls?
   choose + *ing*

l. His story is not _____.
   believe + *able*

m. Their attitude toward all the neighbors is quite
_____.
   notice + *able*

n. The company is now _____ new stock certificates.
   issue + *ing*

o. We hope you can find a _____ solution.
   peace + *able*

p. The heavy rains caused a _____ of berries.
   scarce + *ty*

q. There were _____ cans of fruit on hand.
   nine + *ty*

a. canoed
b. hoes
c. shoer
d. canoeing
e. hoer
f. shoeing
g. canoeist
h. shoes

**22.** Words ending in *oe*, like *canoe*, also follow the general rules for keeping the *e* before a suffix beginning with a vowel. The one exception is a suffix beginning with *i*—here you must keep the *e*.

a. *canoe ed* _____

b. *hoe s* _____

c. *shoe er* _____

d. *canoe ing* _____

e. *hoe er* _____

f. *shoe ing* _____

g. *canoe ist* _____

h. *shoe s* _____

shoeing

**23.** Ted is spending his summer _____ his uncle's
shoe *ing*
horses.

canoed
canoeing
canoeist

**24.** Although Joan _____ for five hours yesterday, she
canoe *ed*
will go _____ tomorrow because she wants to become
canoe *ing*
an expert _____.
canoe *ist*

hoed

**25.** I've never _____ so much in my life.
hoe *ed*

a. dying
dyeing
b. singing
singeing

**26.** To avoid confusion, the silent *e* at the end of two words, *singe* and *dye*, must be retained before *ing*. *Singeing* means scorching or burning; *dyeing* means coloring. If you drop the *e* before the *ing* you will write two different words: *singing* and *dying*. Choose the appropriate words for each sentence below.

a. Although Mary's mother was slowly _____ from cancer, she spent an hour yesterday _____ Mary's coat.

b. The cooks concentrated so much on their _____ that they didn't do a good job of _____ the hair from the chickens.

a. dyed
b. singes
c. dyer
d. singeing
e. dyes
f. dyeing

**27.** If the suffix *ing* is the only exception for the words *singe* and *dye*, you follow the general rules for either dropping or keeping the final *e*. Add the specified suffixes to these two words.

a. *dye ed* _____

g. singed

b. singe    *s* _____

c. dye    *er* _____

d. singe    *ing* _____

e. dye    *s* _____

f. dye    *ing* _____

g. singe    *ed* _____

drop
duly
truly
wholly

**28.** The last three words to be studied, *due, true, whole,* follow the general rule for the silent e before a suffix beginning with a consonant except for *ly.* So before *ly* you would (drop, keep) the e in these words. _____ Now add *ly* and write the complete words. _____ _____ _____

a. truly
b. dues
c. wholesome
d. trues
e. duly
f. trueness
g. wholly
h. wholeness

**29.** Write the complete words for all these "silent e" words.

a. true    *ly* _____

b. due    *s* _____

c. whole    *some* _____

d. true    *s* _____

e. due    *ly* _____

f. true    *ness* _____

g. whole    *ly* _____

h. whole    *ness* _____

due
true
whole

**30.** Name the three words that drop the final e before *ly.*

_____ _____ _____

a. wholly
b. hoeing
canoeing
c. dyeing
d. truly
e. singeing
f. shoed
g. duly
h. wholesome

**REVIEW**

**31.** Add the words and suffixes and write the complete words.

a. His actions were _____unforgivable.
                            whole  *ly*

b. While some teenagers spent the afternoon _____,
                                            hoe  *ing*
others went _____.
                      canoe  *ing*

c. The process of putting coloring permanently into fibers of cotton or wool is called _____.
                                    dye  *ing*

d. I am _____ sorry for my rudeness.
true   *ly*

e. Becky keeps _____ her hair with the hot
singe   *ing*
curling iron.

f. The blacksmith _____ all the horses yesterday.
shoe   *ed*

g. The newly elected commissioner will begin his reform program within a _____ specified time.
due   *ly*

h. Her two nephews are _____ youngsters.
whole   *some*

## POSTTEST

A. Combine the roots and suffixes and write the complete words.

| | | | | | | |
|---|---|---|---|---|---|---|
| 1. lose | *ing* | _____ | 10. pleasure | *able* | _____ |
| 2. manage | *able* | _____ | 11. desire | *ous* | _____ |
| 3. issue | *able* | _____ | 12. true | *ly* | _____ |
| 4. pursue | *ing* | _____ | 13. advantage | *ous* | _____ |
| 5. sincere | *ly* | _____ | 14. hope | *ful* | _____ |
| 6. argue | *ing* | _____ | 15. ache | *ing* | _____ |
| 7. remote | *ness* | _____ | 16. canoe | *ing* | _____ |
| 8. judge | *ing* | _____ | 17. whole | *ly* | _____ |
| 9. disburse | *ment* | _____ | 18. argue | *ment* | _____ |

B. Add the appropriate suffixes to each verb.

*ed*   *er*   *ing*   *able*   *ment*

| | | | | |
|---|---|---|---|---|
| 19. challenge | _____ | 25. advise | _____ |
| 20. pronounce | _____ | 26. trace | _____ |
| 21. accuse | _____ | 27. amuse | _____ |
| 22. believe | _____ | 28. oppose | _____ |
| 23. acknowledge | _____ | 29. arrange | _____ |
| 24. dye (to color) | _____ | 30. dine | _____ |

# CHAPTER FOURTEEN
## THE FINAL Y

Have you had words like *studying, angrily,* or *tries* under-scored and marked with "sp" in the margin? Even if this has only happened occasionally, this chapter will be worthwhile for you to read, because by the end of it you will know when to keep the *y* or when to change it to *i* before a suffix. By learning and applying the rules and spelling a number of common and useful "final y" words, both in and out of context, you will master the techniques needed to distinguish between those words that follow the rules and those that do not, and to recognize the exceptions immediately. In the case of plurals of words ending in *y,* you will spell them accurately as well as reduce them to their singular form, ensuring the spelling of both forms correctly at all times.

## PRETEST
Combine the root and suffix and write the complete word.

| | | | | | | |
|---|---|---|---|---|---|---|
| 1. accompany | *ing* | _____ | 8. beauty | *ful* | _____ |
| 2. hurry | *es* | _____ | 9. happy | *ness* | _____ |
| 3. occupy | *ing* | _____ | 10. disobey | *ing* | _____ |
| 4. study | *es* | _____ | 11. identify | *able* | _____ |
| 5. employ | *ment* | _____ | 12. duty | *ful* | _____ |
| 6. county | *es* | _____ | 13. luxury | *ous* | _____ |
| 7. bury | *al* | _____ | 14. tragedy | *es* | _____ |

| | | | | | | |
|---|---|---|---|---|---|---|
| 15. busy | *ness* | _____ | 23. employ | *able* | _____ |
| 16. day | *ly* | _____ | 24. try | *al* | _____ |
| 17. pity | *ful* | _____ | 25. pity | *ing* | _____ |
| 18. pray | *er* | _____ | 26. copy | *ist* | _____ |
| 19. story | *es* | _____ | 27. pay | *ee* | _____ |
| 20. shiny | *er* | _____ | 28. rely | *able* | _____ |
| 21. deny | *al* | _____ | 29. company | *es* | _____ |
| 22. lively | *est* | _____ | 30. study | *ing* | _____ |

displays
displayed
displaying

**1.** Adding suffixes to words ending in *y* is really quite simple. Only two rules govern keeping or dropping the *y* and only a few exceptions must be remembered.
The first rule is: If the word ends in *y* preceded by a *vowel, keep* the *y. Defray* is an example. Add the verb endings and the words look like this:

He defrays the expenses.          defray + s = *defrays*
He is defraying the expenses.  defray + ing = *defraying*
He defrayed the expenses.       defray + ed = *defrayed*

Now take *display,* which also fits the rule. Add the specified suffixes and write the full words:

*s* (third person verb form or plural form)  _____
*ed* (past tense)                                         _____
*ing* (participle ending)                              _____

baby
duty
beauty
ferry

**2.** The rule cannot apply to four of the following words. Which are they? _____

medley          chimney
baby             beauty
duty             ferry
relay            destroy

consonant
*i*
*i*
keep

**3.** Each of the four exceptions ends in *y,* but the *y* is preceded by a consonant; therefore, the *y* must be changed to *i* before adding the suffix: baby + es = *babies;* duty + es = *duties;* beauty + es = *beauties;* ferry + es = *ferries*. If we change the *y* to *i* and then try to add *ing,* however, we have a problem: babiing. Not only does the word look awkward, but it is almost impossible to pronounce, so we *keep* the *y* before *ing: babying*. The second rule can be stated this way: when adding a suffix to a final *y* which is preceded by a _____, change the *y* to __ before adding a suffix, except before __; then you must _____ the *y.*

a. medleys
b. buyers
c. employment
d. enjoyable
e. carrying
f. babies
g. portrayal
h. replies

**4.** Write the complete word for each sentence.

a. The symphony played several _____ in last night's concert.
*medley + s*

b. How many fashion _____ does the store have?
*buy + ers*

c. Cindi is looking for different _____.
*employ + ment*

d. Their trip to Peru was _____.
*enjoy + able*

e. Yesterday Dan carried two heavy trunks to the attic, but today he is _____ small cartons up there.
*carry + ing*

f. Researchers have found a new feeding formula for _____.
*baby + es*

g. I was amused by his _____ of the music teacher.
*portray + al*

h. How many _____ to the questionnaire did you get?
*reply + es*

a. paid
b. laid
c. daily
d. said
e. payer
paid
payee

**5.** *Day, lay, say,* and *pay* require special handling, so let us see why. Adding the plural *s* to *day,* or adding the third person singular ending to *lay, say,* and *pay* present no problem: *days, lays, says, pays.* But adding *ly* to *day* does— you must change the *y* to *i: daily.* And if you add the past tense (*ed*) to *lay, say,* and *pay,* you must change the *y* to *i* and drop the *e: laid, said, paid.*
Using only these four words, write the one(s) that fit(s) the context of each sentence.

a. Jack _____ a hundred dollars for his recorder.

b. Today I lay the book on the chest; yesterday I _____ it there.

c. Most newspapers in large cities are published _____.

d. What he _____ in anger last Monday should not stand against him.

e. The person who pays the money is the _____; the
*pay er*
person to whom the money is _____ is the _____.
*pay ed*      *pay ee*

accompanied
accompanying
accompaniment

**6.** Use *accompany* as the root word and add these suffixes to it: *ed  ing  ment.*

_____  _____  _____

**REVIEW**

**7.** Test your skill by writing the full words for each blank.

a. varying
b. enemies
c. angrily
d. wealthiest
e. clumsily
f. pitying
g. reliable
h. pennies
i. studying
j. burial
k. merciful
l. lobbyist

a. vary — ing — _____
b. enemy — es — _____
c. angry — ly — _____
d. wealthy — est — _____
e. clumsy — ly — _____
f. pity — ing — _____
g. rely — able — _____
h. penny — es — _____
i. study — ing — _____
j. bury — al — _____
k. mercy — ful — _____
l. lobby — ist — _____

day
society

**8.** To avoid misspelling some root words, let us reverse the procedure of adding elements. With suffixes being added to a word ending in *y* preceded by a vowel, you simply add the suffix, so in subtracting the suffix you just take it off: toys − s = toy. For a word ending in *y* preceded by a consonant, you change the *y* to *i* and add the suffix, so in subtracting the suffix you take off the suffix, replace the *i* with *y:* relies − es = reli (*y*) = rely.

What is the singular form of days? _____

What is the singular form of societies? _____

company

**9.** The word *companies* means several establishments. Just one establishment would be a _____.

lobbies
lobby

**10.** The hotel has several _____. Just one
lobby es
would be a _____.

**POSTTEST**

A. Supply the correct form for each sentence.

*convey*

1. I am _____ing the message now.

2. Every day last week Bob _____ed the messages.

3. They are _____ers of the messages.

4. A broken-down bus is the only available _____ance.

*rely*

5. Mark has _____ on you for many years.

6. Mark still _____ on you for advice.

7. Mark puts too much _____ance on friends.

8. Mark shows he is not as _____able as we think he should be.

B. Locate the misspellings and write the words correctly.

Renee's attorney was dissatisfyed with the discrepancys in the replys prepared by the opposition. He said that their theories were controversyal and unjustifyable. He further stated that his client should not have been Xraid so often because it constituted a threat to her health; in fact, she has payed dearly for the treatments.

# CHAPTER FIFTEEN
## LY AND OUS

Do you often wonder whether to add *ly* or *ally,* and whether to change the ending of a word before adding *ous?* You need not wonder any longer, because Chapter 15 will present a few easy rules for you to follow. In this chapter you will (1) distinguish between words that take *ly* or *ally;* (2) recognize those words whose last letter must be kept, dropped, or changed before *ly* or *ous;* (3) recognize the exceptions to these rules; (4) state the reasons why pronunciation can be important in adding *ly* or *ous;* and (5) spell correctly a number of useful words in and out of context. By the end of the chapter you will be spelling such words as *publicly, truly, angrily, mischievous,* and *advantageous* correctly and confidently.

## PRETEST

Choose the correct ending and write the complete word.

A. *ly-ally*

1. basic_____
2. moral_____
3. true_____
4. frequent_____
5. continuous_____
6. public_____
7. accidental_____
8. angry_____
9. chief_____
10. due_____

11. final_____
12. accurate_____
13. vague_____
14. whole_____
15. easy_____
16. coy_____
17. dry_____
18. safe_____
19. simple_____
20. sly_____

Add the suffix and write the complete word.

B. *ous*

21. vary_____
22. peril_____
23. advantage_____
24. mischief_____
25. libel_____
26. pity_____

27. mountain_____
28. adventure_____
29. trouble_____
30. grief_____
31. victory_____
32. space_____

## LY-ALLY

finally

**1.** The general rule about forming an adverb with the suffix *ly* is to simply add *ly* after the root word. For example, *month + ly = monthly*.
Combine the root final and *ly:* _____.

a. frequently
b. morally
c. really
d. certainly
e. cruelly
f. accidentally
g. continuously
h. chiefly

**2.** Apply the rule to these roots.

a. frequent _____
b. moral _____
c. real _____
d. certain _____

e. cruel _____
f. accidental _____
g. continuous _____
h. chief _____

No—you were right not to drop it.

**3.** Several of the above adjectives end in the consonant *l*. Before adding *ly* did you drop the *l* at the end of the root? _____

a. scarcely
b. duly
c. sparsely
d. truly
e. wholly
f. genuinely
g. crudely
h. simply

**4.** Some adjectives end in a silent *e* (an *e* that is not pronounced). Take the word *accurate* (the last sound is *t*). In adding *ly* you keep the *e: accurately*. There are four silent *e* words that do not keep the *e: due, true, whole,* and *simple*. Now add the suffix *ly* to the eight words below.

a. scarce _____
b. due _____
c. sparse _____
d. true _____

e. whole _____
f. genuine _____
g. crude _____
h. simple _____

whole
due
simple
true

**5.** From this list choose the words that drop the *e* before *ly*.

large      vague      simple
whole      like       true
safe       due        nice

duly
wholly
simply
truly

**6.** Add *ly* to the four exceptions and write the complete words.

_____          _____

_____          _____

a. b. d. f.
· · · · · · · · · · · · ·
easily
hungrily
temporarily
trickily
· · · · · · · · · · · · ·
coyly   slyly

**7.** Some words ending in *y* keep the *y* before *ly* and some do not. Pronounce the word *happy*. The *y* here has a long *e* sound (hap   pee). Now pronounce the word *coy*. Here you do not have a long *e* sound, but a diphthong, *oy*. If a word ending in *y* has the long *e* sound, you drop the *y* and change it to *i* before adding *ly: happy* + *ly* = *happily.* If not, then you keep the *y: coy* + *ly* = *coyly.*
Identify which words have the long *e* sound of *y:*

a. easy          _____

b. hungry        _____

c. sly           _____

d. temporary     _____

e. coy           _____

f. tricky        _____
· · · · · · · · · · · · · · · · · · · · · · · · · · · · · ·
Write the *ly* adverbs for easy _____, hungry _____, temporary _____, tricky _____.
· · · · · · · · · · · · · · · · · · · · · · · · · · · · · ·
Write the *ly* adverbs for *coy* and *sly.* _____ _____

dryly or drily
shyly or shily

**8.** According to the rule *dry* and *shy* do not drop the *y* (they do not have the long sound of *e*). Modern usage, however, permits an alternative spelling; in other words, you could change the *y* to *i* before adding *ly.*
Write the two correct spellings of both words: _____
_____   _____   _____.

dry
shy

**9.** Name the two words that can be written with *y* or *i* before the *ly:* _____   _____

The *y* in each word has a long *e* sound. The *y* in both words has a long *i* sound, not a long *e* sound.

**10.** The words *hungry* and *angry* change the *y* to *i* before the *ly.* Why? _____
The words *wry* and *sly* retain the *y* before the *ly.* Why? _____

## REVIEW

**11.** Test your skill in forming *ly* adverbs.

a. tastily
b. finally
c. extremely
d. slyly
e. wholly
f. equally
g. coyly
h. duly
i. unusually
j. dryly or drily
k. truly
l. entirely
m. morally
n. gorgeously
o. simply
p. easily

a. tasty  _____

b. final  _____

c. extreme  _____

d. sly  _____

e. whole  _____

f. equal  _____

g. coy  _____

h. due  _____

i. unusual  _____

j. dry  _____

k. true  _____

l. entire  _____

m. moral  _____

n. gorgeous  _____

o. simple  _____

p. easy  _____

comfortably
conceivably
profitably

**12.** Adjectives ending in *ble* (like *considerable*) already have the *l* in the last syllable. To form the adverb, just change the *e* to *y*. Considerable becomes considerably. What would be the adverbs for these "ble" words?

comfortable  _____

conceivable  _____

profitable  _____

laughably
perceptibly

**13.** These adjectives also end in *ble: laughable* and *perceptible*. What are the *ly* adverbs? _____

change the *e* to *y*

**14.** To form the *ly* adverb from an adjective ending in *ble*, what do you do? _____

ally   ally
ally   ly

**15.** To most adjectives ending in *ic* you must add *ally* instead of *ly*. To form the adverb from the adjective *basic* you add *ally: basically*. The *one* exception is the word *public*—it takes *ly*.

What is the correct suffix for each of these words (*ly, ally*)?

academic  _____    genetic  _____

automatic  _____    public  _____

a. critically
b. automatically
c. specifically
d. drastically
e. publicly

**16.** Now form the adverbs by adding either *ly* or *ally.*

a. He is _____ ill.
critic

b. She moved each object _____.
automatic

c. The proposal benefits each side _____.
specific

d. The owner reacted _____.
drastic

e. He announced his intentions _____.
public

## REVIEW

a. advisably
b. considerably
c. sensibly
d. basically
e. responsibly
f. publicly
g. automatically
h. reliably
i. terribly
j. apologetically
k. irritably
l. probably

**17.** Add *ly* or *ally* as appropriate.

a. advisable    _____

b. considerable  _____

c. sensible    _____

d. basic     _____

e. responsible   _____

f. public     _____

g. automatic    _____

h. reliable    _____

i. terrible    _____

j. apologetic   _____

k. irritable    _____

l. probable    _____

*ally*

**18.** Most words ending in *ic* add (*ly, ally*). _____

public

**19.** What one word ending in *ic* adds *ly?* _____

whole   simple
due    true

**20.** Most words ending in silent *e* simply add *ly* to the root. Four words are exceptions: _____  _____  _____
_____.

hungrily
*y* is preceded by a con-
sonant, so *y* is changed
to *i*; the *y* has the long
sound of *e*.

**21.** Choose the correct spelling and then state your reasons for this choice: hungryly hungrily. _____
_____

## OUS

**22.** Most words ending in a consonant add *ous* to form the adjective meaning full of. To the word *marvel* (which ends in the consonant *l*) you add *ous: marvelous.* If words end in the consonant *f,* however, you change the *f* to *v* before the *ous.* For instance, the word *grief* becomes *grievous.* Now from this list check the words whose last consonant must be changed to *v* before adding *ous:*

a. humor _____    e. mischief _____

b. peril _____    f. hazard _____

c. danger _____    g. grief _____

d. riot _____    h. mountain _____

e.  g.

**23.** Add *ous* to all the words in the preceding frame.

a. _____    e. _____

b. _____    f. _____

c. _____    g. _____

d. _____    h. _____

a. humorous
b. perilous
c. dangerous
d. riotous
e. mischievous
f. hazardous
g. grievous
h. mountainous

**24.** Now look at and pronounce these words:

continue        advantage        space

All end in a silent *e,* but the second ends in *ge* and the third in *ce.* Both the *g* and *c* have the soft sound (as in *gem* and *city*). Generally, words ending in silent *e* drop the *e* before a suffix beginning with a vowel, so before adding *ous* to a word like *continue,* you would drop the *e: continuous.* With *advantage,* you must preserve the soft sound of *g* by keeping the *e: advantageous.* Otherwise you would get the hard sound of *g* as in "advantag ous."
    The soft sound of *c* presents a slightly different problem. Here you must change the *e* in *space,* for example, to *i,* not only to preserve the soft sound but also the pronunciation of the last syllable: "shus" in *spacious.* If you kept the *e* you would have to pronounce the word like this: spa  ce  ous, which, of course, is wrong.
Here are six words. Apply these guidelines and add *ous* correctly to them.

a. humorous
b. perilous
c. dangerous
d. riotous
e. mischievous
f. hazardous
g. grievous
h. mountainous

a. desirous
b. outrageous
c. spacious
d. adventurous
e. troublous
f. gracious

a. desire _____

b. outrage _____

c. space _____

d. adventure _____

e. trouble _____

f. grace _____

a. grievous
b. poisonous
c. courageous
d. libelous
e. continuous
f. spacious
g. marvelous
h. mischievous

**25.** Now add *ous* to this list of words.

a. grief _____

b. poison _____

c. courage _____

d. libel _____

e. continue _____

f. space _____

g. marvel _____

h. mischief _____

a. victorious
b. plenteous
c. injurious
d. piteous

**26.** Let us look at these words:

vary        beauty

Both end in *y,* with a consonant preceding it: an *r* in *vary* and a *t* in *beauty.* When you add a suffix beginning with a vowel, like *ous,* to words ending in *y* preceded by a consonant, you usually change the *y* to *i. Vary* follows this rule: *various.* You cannot change the *y* in beauty to *i,* however, because you will change the pronunciation. The sound of the *y* is a long *e* (beautee), and to keep that sound you must change the *y* to *e: beauteous.* Changing the *y* to *i* would change the last syllable to "tious" (or "shus"), which, of course, would be wrong.
Add *ous* to these words.

a. victory _____

b. plenty _____

c. injury _____

d. pity _____

*e*
*i*

**27.** So as not to get the "shus" sound in pit___ous, you drop the *y* from *pity* and add _____. On the other hand, to keep the "shus" sound in spac___ous, you change the *e* to _____ and then add *ous.*

*t*

**28.** Before adding *ous* to words ending in a final *y,* check to see which consonant precedes the *y.* Change the *y* to *e* if the consonant is _____.

a. spacious
b. piteous
c. gracious

**29.** Add *ous* to these roots and write the complete words.

a. space _____

b. pity _____

c. grace _____

## REVIEW

a. ridiculous
b. vigorous
c. gracious
d. courageous
e. mountainous
f. desirous
g. various
h. grievous
i. plenteous
j. dangerous
k. spacious
l. bounteous
m. mischievous
n. riotous
o. advantageous
p. porous

**30.** Now test your skill by adding *ous* to these words and writing the complete words.

a. ridicule  _____
b. vigor  _____
c. grace  _____
d. courage  _____
e. mountain  _____
f. desire  _____
g. vary  _____
h. grief  _____
i. plenty  _____
j. danger  _____
k. space  _____
l. bounty  _____
m. mischief  _____
n. riot  _____
o. advantage  _____
p. pore  _____

drop

**31.** In adding *ous* to *desire,* you (drop, keep) the *e.* _____

keep
e retains soft *g.*

**32.** In adding *ous* to *advantage,* or *courage,* you (drop, keep) the silent *e.* _____
State the reason why. _____

*i*

**33.** *Space* and *grace* have a soft *c.* But instead of keeping the *e,* you must change it to __ before *ous.*

*v*

**34.** Words ending in *f* change the *f* to __ before *ous.*

*e*

**35.** The following words end in a long *e* sound: *plenty, bounty, pity.* So that this sound is not changed before *ous,* you must drop the *y* and add __.

## POSTTEST

A. Choose the correctly spelled word in each pair and write it in the blank.

1. hungryly, hungrily  _____
2. accidently, accidentally  _____

3. advantagous, advantageous _____

4. heavily, heavyly _____

5. publicly, publickly _____

6. continueous, continuous _____

7. practicly, practically _____

8. sincerely, sincerly _____

9. temporaryly, temporarily _____

10. carefully, carefuly _____

11. appropriately, appropriatly _____

12. gracious, graceous _____

13. extremly, extremely _____

14. courageous, couragous _____

15. mischievious, mischievous _____

16. injuryous, injurious _____

17. annualy, annually _____

18. truely, truly _____

19. physicly, physically _____

20. academically, academicly _____

B. Have someone dictate the following words for you to write.

21. certainly _____

22. entirely _____

23. desirous _____

24. marvelous _____

25. piteous _____

26. ridiculous _____

27. various _____

28. morally _____

29. considerably _____

30. easily _____

# CHAPTER
# SIXTEEN
## PLURALS

There are just two plural endings, but not knowing when to use one or the other can present some problems. In this chapter you will learn specific rules for each ending, apply the rules to a number of words and write these plurals in context, recognize the exceptions and spell them correctly. You will also change various plurals back to the singular so that you will not misspell either form.

**PRETEST**

Write the plurals of the following nouns.

1. display _____
2. penalty _____
3. gas _____
4. veto _____
5. zoo _____
6. monarch _____
7. inquiry _____
8. crisis _____
9. Negro _____
10. melody _____
11. perch _____
12. thief _____
13. potato _____
14. Tommy _____
15. wish _____

16. buzz _____
17. university _____
18. Tory _____
19. discrepancy _____
20. grief _____
21. half _____
22. society _____
23. gulf _____
24. elegy _____
25. datum _____
26. hero _____
27. wife _____
28. study _____
29. decoy _____
30. tax _____

a. princesses
b. airships
c. clutches
d. seedlings
e. crashes
f. concerts
g. wishes
h. screens
i. pitches
j. addresses
k. matches

**1.** Two suffixes are used to form the plural from the singular: *s* and *es*. Most words take just *s*. For instance, the plural of *table* is *tables,* of *book* is *books,* and of *chair* is *chairs.* Certain other words need *es* to form the plural because just an *s* would make them difficult or impossible to pronounce. Take *dress* or *gas,* which already end in *s*. Another *s* would only extend the original "s" sound, not make another syllable that is needed to pronounce the plural: *dress es, gas es.* The same problem applies to words ending in *sh* and *tch*. If you try pronouncing *dish* and *ditch* with just another *s* (as in *dishs* and *ditchs*) you will hear just an "s" sound after the *sh* or *tch,* not a distinct syllable, as in *dish es* or *ditch es.*

Apply these rules to make the plural forms of the nouns below.

a. princess _____          g. wish _____

b. airship _____          h. screen _____

c. clutch _____          i. pitch _____

d. seedling _____          j. address _____

e. crash _____          k. match _____

f. concert _____

taxes  buzzes

**2.** Like those words ending in *s, sh,* and *tch,* those ending in *x* and *z,* like *tax* and *buzz,* need more than the *s* to form a pronounceable plural ending. How would you write the plurals of tax and buzz? _____ _____

a. S    d. S
b. S    e. H
c. H    f. S
• • • • • • • • • • • • •
arches  lurches
monarchs  peaches
epochs  porches

**3.** The plural ending for a word ending in *ch* depends on the sound of the *ch*. If it has the soft sound (as in *church*) you add *es*. If it has the hard sound (as in *epoch*) you add *s*.

Indicate by S (soft) or H (hard) which sound of *ch* these words have.

a. arch _____          d. peach _____

b. lurch _____          e. epoch _____

c. monarch _____          f. porch _____
• • • • • • • • • • • • • • • • • • • • • • • • • • • • • • • • • •
Now add the correct plural endings to the above words.

_____     _____     _____

_____     _____     _____

*s  sh  ch (soft sound)*
*tch  x  z*

**4.** Now we have another general rule for forming plurals. Using this list as a guide, write the consonant endings that require *es:* _____

dress      bush      porch      match      fox      waltz

*es*

**5.** Words ending in *s*, *sh*, *ch* (soft), *x*, and *z* take _____ to form the plural.

a. matches
b. transplants
c. bungalows
d. dishes
e. monarchs
f. organs
g. taxes
h. splashes
i. stairs
j. compresses
k. bookcases
l. pitches
m. waltzes
n. lurches

**6.** Apply the rules presented thus far and form the plurals.

a. match _____         h. splash _____

b. transplant _____    i. stair _____

c. bungalow _____      j. compress _____

d. dish _____          k. bookcase _____

e. monarch _____       l. pitch _____

f. organ _____         m. waltz _____

g. tax _____           n. lurch _____

a. *s*
b. *es*
c. *s*
d. *es*
e. *es*
f. *s*
g. *s*
h. *es*
i. *es*
j. *s*
k. *es*
l. *s*

**7.** Nouns ending in *y* preceded by a vowel usually take *s* to form the plural. For example, *attorney* ends in *y* preceded by *e*, so its plural is *attorneys*. On the other hand, most nouns ending in *y* preceded by a consonant take *es* and the *y* is changed to *i* before the *es*. *Party* ends in *y* preceded by *t*, so its plural is *parties*.
From the list below decide which words take *s* and which take *es*.

a. decoy _____         g. pulley _____

b. lullaby _____       h. dormitory _____

c. tray _____          i. tragedy _____

d. clergy _____        j. display _____

e. melody _____        k. duty _____

f. bay _____           l. attorney _____

a. studies
b. ploys
c. days
d. elegies
e. dailies
f. replies
g. buoys
h. inquiries
i. frays
j. cemeteries
k. trolleys
l. joys

**8.** Now write the plurals for these singular nouns.

a. study _____         g. buoy _____

b. ploy _____          h. inquiry _____

c. day _____           i. fray _____

d. elegy _____         j. cemetery _____

e. daily _____         k. trolley _____

f. reply _____         l. joy _____

a. Bettys   Tonys
b. Kellys

**9.** Proper names (first and last) ending in *y* preceded by either a vowel or consonant take *s* so that the name will not be changed. For instance, the Kennedy family can be called the Kennedys. More than one Libby would be Libbys and more than one boy named Harry would be Harrys. Some proper nouns, however, take *es* because they are not names of specific individuals. The plural of *Tory* (a member of a British political party in the seventeenth century) would be *Tories*. Note that the *y* is changed to *i* before adding *es*.

a. If you wrote about several girls named Betty and several boys named Tony, how would you write the plurals?

_____  _____

b. All the members of the Kelly family would be called the

_____.

a. deputies
b. Anthonys
c. properties
d. Crosbys
e. Tories
f. societies

**10.** Write the correct plurals for these words.

a. deputy  _____   d. Crosby  _____

b. Anthony  _____   e. Tory  _____

c. property  _____   f. society  _____

a. drays
b. Sibleys
c. countries
d. envoys
e. Henrys
f. plays
g. treaties
h. counties

**11.** Now apply all the rules about plurals you have learned thus far and write the correct forms for these words ending in *y*.

a. dray  _____   e. Henry  _____

b. Sibley  _____   f. play  _____

c. country  _____   g. treaty  _____

d. envoy  _____   h. county  _____

a.  d.  e.  f.
b.  c.

**12.** Sometimes the singular form is incorrectly formed from the plural. So that you do not make this mistake, let us practice forming the singular. As you remember, you form the plural of words ending in *y* preceded by a vowel by adding *s*. The singular is formed by subtracting the *s*. For words endings in *y* preceded by a consonant you must subtract *es* and change the *i* back to the original *y*.
Which of the following would end in *y* preceded by a consonant in the singular? _____

a. discrepancies   d. bullies

b. holidays   e. cemeteries

c. chimneys   f. lobbies

To form the singular which ones would have the *s* subtracted?

_____

a. discrepancy
b. bully
c. cemetery
d. lobby

**13.** Write the singular forms for each word below.

a. discrepancies  _____

b. bullies  _____

c. cemeteries _____

d. lobbies _____

a. societies
d. lobby
f. tries
g. tragedy

**14.** The endings of some words below are misspelled. By applying the rules, identify the incorrect words and spell them correctly.

a. societys _____     e. chimneys _____

b. surveys _____     f. trys _____

c. studies _____     g. tragedie _____

d. lobbie _____

## REVIEW

a. valleys
b. Woodburys
tragedies
c. addresses
d. taxes
e. waltzes
f. Februarys
g. columns
h. comedies
i. ditches

**15.** Now test your skill by writing the plural noun(s) for each sentence.

a. The ranches were built only in the _____.
 valley

b. The _____ have suffered many _____.
 Woodbury  tragedy

c. How many _____ does he have?
 address

d. The legislature is trying to reduce _____.
 tax

e. For the next orchestra concert the conductor has selected two _____.
 waltz

f. Minnesota _____ are usually cold.
 February

g. The auditorium has six Doric _____.
 column

h. The last two Broadway hits are both _____.
 comedy

i. The farmers are busy digging irrigation _____.
 ditch

es

**16.** Which plural ending do you use with words ending in *s*, *sh*, *ch* (soft), *tch*, *s*, and *z*? _____

Change the *y* to *i*
and add *es*—cries.

**17.** How do you form the plural of *cry*? _____
_____

displays

**18.** Write the plural of *display*. _____

a. zoos
b. tomatoes
c. photos
d. radios
e. echoes
f. potatoes
g. Negroes
h. boos
i. vetoes
j. silos
k. heroes
l. torpedoes

**19.** Most nouns ending in *o* preceded by either a vowel or a consonant take *s.* Seven words, however, are exceptions: *echo, hero, Negro, potato, tomato, torpedo,* and *veto.* Write the plurals of these "o" words.

a. zoo _____          g. Negro _____

b. tomato _____          h. boo _____

c. photo _____          i. veto _____

d. radio _____          j. silo _____

e. echo _____          k. hero _____

f. potato _____          l. torpedo _____

a. Negroes
b. heroes  potatoes
tomatoes
c. Echoes  vetoes
d. torpedoes

**20.** Perhaps an easy way to remember the exceptions is to place them in a context. Read the sentences below and supply the plural forms.

a. Some blacks prefer to be called _____.
                                                                    Negro

b. The _____ like _____ and _____.
              hero                    potato                  tomato

c. _____ of the speeches condemning the
          Echo

governor's _____ rang through the corridors.
                            veto

d. The 20-year-old sailor fired the decisive _____.
                                                                        torpedo

a. silos
b. sopranos
c. potatoes
d. torpedoes
e. pianos
f. vetoes
g. bassos
h. ratios
i. Negroes
j. altos
k. rodeos
l. heroes
m. zoos
n. echoes

**21.** Now test your skill in writing the plurals for these words.

a. silo _____          h. ratio _____

b. soprano _____          i. Negro _____

c. potato _____          j. alto _____

d. torpedo _____          k. rodeo _____

e. piano _____          l. hero _____

f. veto _____          m. zoo _____

g. basso _____          n. echo _____

Negro
hero
potato
tomato
echo
veto
torpedo

**22.** Name the seven words ending in *o* that do not take *s* to form the plural.

_____          _____

_____          _____

_____          _____

_____

a. rodeo
b. tomato
c. piano
d. veto
e. Negro
f. kangaroo
g. torpedo
h. ratio
i. hero
j. potato

**23.** Because it is important to spell the singular as well as the plural correctly, let us reverse the procedure and write the singular from the plural. For example, to reduce *zoos* you simply take off the *s: zoo. Echoes* has the *es* ending, so the singular would be *echo*. Now reduce these plurals to their singular forms.

a. rodeos _____         f. kangaroos _____

b. tomatoes _____       g. torpedoes _____

c. pianos _____         h. ratios _____

d. vetoes _____         i. heroes _____

e. Negroes _____        j. potatoes _____

a. griefs
b. sheriffs
c. fifes

**24.** To form the plural of nouns ending in *f, fe,* or *ff,* you usually add *s.* For instance, the plural of *belief* is *beliefs,* of *strife* is *strifes,* and of *tariff* is *tariffs.* What would be the plurals for these?

a. grief _____         c. fife _____

b. sheriff _____

a. elves
b. shelves
c. halves
d. leaves
e. thieves
f. wolves

**25.** Certain words ending in *f* or *fe* change their ending to *ves* to form the plural. Write the plurals of these words:

a. elf _____         d. leaf _____

b. shelf _____       e. thief _____

c. half _____        f. wolf _____

a. wolves
b. leaves
c. halves
d. thieves
e. elves
f. shelves

**26.** To remember these particular words, let us put them in a context. Read the sentence first, then supply the plural form.

a. Every night _____ roam the countryside.
                    wolf

b. In the fall trees shed their _____ .
                                   leaf

c. Jack cut the apples into _____ .
                              half

d. The basement was broken into by _____ .
                                      thief

e. Medieval folklore is filled with stories of _____ .
                                                  elf

f. The clerk filled the _____ .
                          shelf

lives
wives
knives

**27.** *Life, wife,* and *knife* are treated like the previous exceptions. How would you write the plurals of these words?

life _____ wife _____ knife _____.

wives
lives
thieves
knives

**28.** Supply the plural forms.

The _____ fled for their _____ when the
　　　　wife　　　　　　　　　　　　life

_____ came after them with _____.
　　thief　　　　　　　　　　　　knife

a. mischiefs
b. halves
c. wives
d. cliffs
e. leaves
f. griefs
g. lives
h. gulfs
i. strifes
j. proofs
k. sheriffs
l. thieves
m. knives
n. elves

**29.** Write the plurals of these words.

a. mischief _____　　h. gulf _____

b. half _____　　i. strife _____

c. wife _____　　j. proof _____

d. cliff _____　　k. sheriff _____

e. leaf _____　　l. thief _____

f. grief _____　　m. knife _____

g. life _____　　n. elf _____

elf　elves
shelf　shelves
half　halves
leaf　leaves
thief　thieves
wolf　wolves
life　lives
wife　wives
knife　knives

**30.** You have studied nine words ending in *f* or *fe* that are exceptions to the general rule of adding *s* to form the plural. Write these nine words and then write their plurals. Here is *elf* as a starter.

elf _____　　　　　　_____

_____　　　　　　_____

_____　　　　　　_____

_____　　　　　　_____

_____

crises

**31.** Plurals of some words, Greek in origin, are formed by changing the ending *is* to *es*. Take *crisis,* for instance. The plural would be _____.

a. analyses
b. diagnoses
c. bases

**32.** Form the plural of similar words of Greek origin:

a. analysis _____
b. diagnosis _____
c. basis _____

data

**33.** Plurals of some words, Latin in origin, are formed by changing the ending *um* to *a*. Take *datum,* meaning a fact. The plural of this word is dat___.

**34.** Other words of Latin origin follow the same pattern:

a. addendum ____________________

b. memorandum ____________________

c. compendium ____________________

a. addenda
b. memoranda
c. compendia

**35.** Write the correct plural forms for each sentence.

a. Three scientists made separate ________________ (analysis) of the new theory.

b. The educator stated that the students had not presented sufficient ________ (datum) to prove their ________________ (hypothesis).

c. The proprietor agreed to use all the ________ (medium) of advertising.

d. Almost every person experiences several ______ (crisis) during a lifetime.

a. analyses
b. data
hypotheses
c. media
d. crises

## REVIEW

**36.** What is the plural ending for most nouns ending in *o?* ____ in *fe?* ____ in *ff?* ____

*s s s*

**37.** Test your skill by writing the plurals of these nouns.

| | | | |
|---|---|---|---|
| a. piano | ____________ | i. tomato | ____________ |
| b. belief | ____________ | j. hero | ____________ |
| c. wife | ____________ | k. cliff | ____________ |
| d. potato | ____________ | l. grief | ____________ |
| e. zoo | ____________ | m. veto | ____________ |
| f. auto | ____________ | n. thief | ____________ |
| g. half | ____________ | o. tariff | ____________ |
| h. radio | ____________ | | |

a. pianos
b. beliefs
c. wives
d. potatoes
e. zoos
f. autos
g. halves
h. radios
i. tomatoes
j. heroes
k. cliffs
l. griefs
m. vetoes
n. thieves
o. tariffs

**38.** Write the singular form of the following plurals.

| | | | |
|---|---|---|---|
| a. wishes | __________ | f. thieves | __________ |
| b. potatoes | __________ | g. kangaroos | __________ |
| c. halves | __________ | h. lives | __________ |
| d. heroes | __________ | i. Negroes | __________ |
| e. photos | __________ | j. echoes | __________ |

a. wish
b. potato
c. half
d. hero
e. photo
f. thief
g. kangaroo
h. life
i. Negro
j. echo

a. hypotheses
b. bacteria
c. oases
d. media
e. bases
f. data
g. addenda
h. analyses

**39.** Write the plural forms of these words of Latin and Greek origin.

a. hypothesis _____     e. basis _____

b. bacterium _____     f. datum _____

c. oasis _____     g. addendum _____

d. medium _____     h. analysis _____

## POSTTEST

A. Write the plurals of these "f" words.

1. rebuff _____     7. giraffe _____

2. thief _____     8. wolf _____

3. life _____     9. dwarf _____

4. brief _____     10. shelf _____

5. self _____     11. fife _____

6. chief _____

B. Fill in every plural form.

The _____ ruled their _____ with iron hands.
　　　monarch　　　　　　　　　　country

They allowed no foreigners to cross the borders and repelled all _____
　　　　　　　　　　　　　　　　　　　　　　　　　　　　　　　overture

from neighboring states to negotiate _____.
　　　　　　　　　　　　　　　　treaty

C. Write the plurals of these words of Latin or Greek origin.

16. parenthesis _____     19. axis _____

17. thesis _____     20. neurosis _____

18. compendium _____     21. oasis _____

D. Test your skill further by writing the correct plural forms of these words.

22. appendix _____     32. sphinx _____

23. halo _____     33. sinus _____

24. hero _____     34. rally _____

25. rodeo _____     35. battery _____

26. volley _____     36. shampoo _____

27. tornado _____     37. lurch _____

28. piano _____     38. chimney _____

29. tragedy _____     39. Friday _____

30. leaf _____     40. studio _____

31. crutch _____

# CHAPTER SEVENTEEN
## THE APOSTROPHE

The apostrophe has two main uses: to indicate the omission of one or more letters in a contraction and to show possession. Contrary to what you may think, the possessive form is an important part of spelling, and even though the apostrophe can be omitted in expressions like "at wits end," for the most part current usage requires the use of the apostrophe to show possession. In working through this chapter you will (1) recognize both singular and plural forms; (2) apply the rules for using ' or 's to a number of nouns and compound nouns; (3) distinguish between indefinite pronouns and the possessive form of the personal pronouns, and (4) use the apostrophe in correctly forming contractions.

**PRETEST**

Write the appropriate possessive form or contraction.

1. Yesterday was the end of the _____ reign.
   king

2. Someone stole the _____ bicycles.
   boys

3. _____ catalog is
   Brannon and Butterworth (joint ownership)
   not in print.

4. _____ poetry is fascinating.
   John Donne

5. The _____ reports are inaccurate.
   secretary and the treasurer (single ownership)

6. He _____ realize his true strength.
   <br>does not

7. All the _____ hats were red.
   <br>women

8. The two women watched _____ movements closely.
   <br>each other

9. _____ reforms were medi-
   <br>Louis the Thirteenth
   <br>ocre.

10. The canary fluffed _____ feathers.
    <br>it

11. _____ strange that _____ ideas were accepted.
    <br>It is    nobody

12. I'm tired of hearing my _____ complaints.
    <br>friend

13. Let me see your _____ painting.
    <br>father-in-law

14. In the experiment a _____ delay can be crucial.
    <br>minute

15. The house is _____ to sell, not _____.
    <br>their    our

b. Harry's
c. baby's
e. soprano's
g. family's
h. class' or
class's

**1.** To form the possessive of a singular noun, simply add *'s* (my friend's hat), unless the word ends in *s*. Then you can add either *'* or *'s*—both are correct today (the princess' crown or the princess's crown). Very often the sound will determine which form is better. Pick out the singular nouns in this list and form the possessive for those words only.

a. cooks          e. soprano

b. Harry          f. sisters

c. baby           g. family

d. men            h. class

a. women's
b. duchesses'
c. monkeys'
e. sheep's
h. writers'

**2.** Here is the second rule: To form the possessive of a plural noun, simply add *'s* (men's) unless the word ends in *s*. But this time you have no choice—just add the apostrophe (my friends' hats, the princesses' crowns). Pick out the plural nouns in this list and write the possessive of those words only.

a. women          e. sheep

b. duchesses      f. goat

c. monkeys        g. dentist

d. farm           h. writers

a. people's
b. babies'
c. Andy's
d. government's
e. fishermen's
f. enemy's
g. daughters'
h. thieves'

's
s
' or 's
's
s
'

a. Ruth's
b. Simmons' or
Simmons's
c. Frost's
d. students'
e. actress' or
actress's
f. Joneses'
g. children's
h. church's

a. sister-in-law's
b. secretary's
treasurer's
c. jack-o-
lantern's
d. Dunn and
Numeier's
e. passer-by's

**3.** Write the possessive for each noun in this list.

a. people            e. fishermen

b. babies           f. enemy

c. Andy            g. daughters

d. government     h. thieves

**4.** To form the possessive of singular nouns you add _____ unless the word ends in _____; then you add either _____ or _____. To form the possessive of plural nouns you add ___ unless the word ends in _____. Then you just add _____.

**5.** Read each sentence carefully. Then supply the correct possessive.

a. Put _____ coat on the chair.
              Ruth

b. Tom _____ name was called first.
             Simmons

c. Although I like John Keats' poetry, I prefer Robert

_____.
       Frost

d. The _____ musical program was ex-
            students
ceptional.

e. The _____ embroidered handkerchief
            actress
is missing.

f. The _____ farm is for sale.
         Joneses

g. Put the _____ names in a separate
            children
list.

h. The _____ spire towered above the other
         church
buildings.

**6.** To form the possessive of a compound noun (two or more words joined to form a single noun), you add ' or 's to the last element of the noun. For example, the 's would be added to *law* in *father-in-law*. In a compound expression, like *Sears and Roebuck,* you add the ' or 's to the last noun to show *joint* ownership (they own it together): Sears and Roebuck's catalog. For *single* ownership, you add ' or 's to each noun: *Mary's* and *James'* (or *James's*) reports on ecology (each prepared a report separately.)

Now identify the part of the underlined compound noun or expression that requires the possessive and then write the complete word(s).

a. <u>sister-in-law</u> cottage _____

b. <u>the secretary and the treasurer</u> position papers (the two the's give you a clue whether it is single or joint ownership)

_____

c. the <u>jack-o-lantern</u> light _____

d. <u>Dunn and Numeier</u> property (joint ownership) _____

_____

e. the <u>passer-by</u> heckling _____

**7.** Fill in the missing possessive form.

a. employee's

a. Today I received the new _____
Diller and Dollar

brochure.

b. She hung her _____
brother-in-law

raincoat on the rack.

c. We listened attentively to the _____
secretary-treasurer

speech.

d. For a while the judge could not find the _____
runner-up

medal.

e. Jim and Joe bought a used Ford, so you would speak of

it as _____ car.
Jim and Joe

f. Tom Davis bought five acres of lakeshore property on which his brother Richard built a house. Tom owns the land and Richard owns the house. Whenever friends speak of the Davis property, they refer to _____
Tom and Richard

property.

## REVIEW

**8.** Test how skillful you are in forming the possessive.

a. The supervisor criticized the _____
employee

work.

b. I doubt the veracity of the _____
Secretary

statement.

Left margin answers (Exercise 7):
a. Diller and Dollar's
b. brother-in-law's
c. secretary-treasurer's
d. runner-up's
e. Jim and Joe's
f. Tom's and Richard's

Left margin answers (Exercise 8):
a. employee's
b. Secretary's
c. Bliss' or Bliss's
d. friends'
e. Williams' or Williams's
f. mother-in-law's

g. people's
h. men's
i. mayor's
and governor's
j. bosses'
k. Smith and
Butler's
l. woman's
women's

c. A fence separates our property from the _____ property.
<br>Bliss

d. All of my best _____ parents are separated.
<br>friends

e. Joe _____ house is right on the highway.
<br>Williams

f. I am using my _____ drapes.
<br>mother-in-law

g. He is a staunch advocate of a _____ government.
<br>people

h. They painted the _____ locker room bright green.
<br>men

i. How many of the _____ mayor and governor (single ownership) _____ analyses do you have?

j. Both secretaries are complaining about their _____ strict rules.
<br>bosses

k. Let's have supper at _____ Smith and Butler (joint ownership) _____ department store.

l. One _____ dissatisfaction with a product will hardly be recognized, but many _____ complaints may force a manufacturer to take appropriate action.
<br>woman
<br>women

a. P
b. P
c. I
d. P
e. I
f. I  P

**9.** Indefinite pronouns also take ' or 's for the possessive: *one's* belief, *another's* ideas, or the *others'* receipts. But the possessive forms of the personal pronouns never include the apostrophe: *his, hers, its, ours, yours, theirs.* Indicate by I or P whether the underlined words are indefinite or possessive personal pronouns.

a. The bird preened *its* feathers. _____

b. I'll bring my records if you'll bring *yours.* _____

c. *Somebody's* hat is on the table. _____

d. I've already had my turn; now it's *hers.* _____

e. *Nobody's* suggestions were accepted. _____

f. The *others'* proposals were illogical; *ours* were not. _____

a. everybody's
b. hers
c. its
d. others'
e. theirs
f. anybody's
g. another's

**10.** Now write the correct possessives for these sentences.

a. Don't believe _____ statements.
   everybody

b. This is _____.
   her

c. The hawk eyed _____ prey.
   it

d. The _____ proposals are innovative.
   others

e. The property is _____.
   their

f. It's _____ guess.
   anybody

g. Many times one person's opinion is as good as _____
   _____.
   another

you're
isn't
weren't
he's
they're
I'm
we're

**11.** Another function of the apostrophe is to take the place of letters omitted. To put it another way, words are contracted and the apostrophe stands for one or more missing letters. Take the expressions *do not* and *would not.* If we omit the vowel *o* in *not,* we have do n__t and would n__t. In each case, joining the two words and inserting an apostrophe to represent the missing *o* produces the contractions *don't* and *wouldn't.* It is your turn now—write contractions for these expressions.

| you are | _____ | they are | _____ |
|---------|------------|----------|------------|
| is not  | _____ | I am     | _____ |
| were not| _____ | we are   | _____ |
| he is   | _____ |          |            |

a. It's
b. its
c. Whose
d. There's

**12.** Some contractions sound exactly like the possessive form of the personal pronoun and are often mistaken for them. For example, *it's* and *its.* You will never make a mistake, however, if you remember that the apostrophe stands for a missing letter: it(i)s. In no way could you write "The dog wagged it's (it is) tail."
Choose the correct version for each sentence.

a. _____ going to rain today.
   It's, Its

b. When the cat raced around Bobby, he inadvertently stepped on _____ tail.
   it's, its

c. _____book is this?
   Whose, Who's

d. _____a burglar downstairs.
   Theirs, There's

a. won't
b. didn't
c. isn't theirs
d. hers
e. It's yours

**13.** Choose the correct word(s) for each sentence.

a. Why (wont', won't) you come? _____

b. They (didnt, didn't) know I was coming. _____

c. The decision (isnt, isn't)(theirs, there's) to make. _____
_____

d. The clock is (her's, hers). _____

e. (Its, It's)(yours, your's) to sell. _____

**REVIEW**

a. each other's
b. can't
c. yours
d. others'
e. its
f. wouldn't

**14.** Select the correctly spelled word or expression in each parentheses.

a. The two friends fell into (each others', each other's) arms.
_____

b. Don't tell me you (can't, cant) do it. _____

c. My sketches are simple compared to (your's, yours).
_____.

d. I read all the (others', others) manuscripts. _____

e. Why does the tiger keep licking (its, its', it's) paw? _____

f. Even if I could go to Canada, I (wouldnt', wouldn't)
_____.

**POSTTEST**

Locate every misspelled word and write the correct possessive form or contraction.

1. The cat ran around the table trying to catch it's tail. _____

2. I don't care who's coat it is. _____

3. This is my business, not your's. _____

4. Sandy didnt agree with the womans' remarks. _____

5. The council did not approve anyone's suggestions. _____

6. I put my books on the mantel. Tell Mary to put her's on the table. _____

7. Their about to leave for Chicago. _____

8. Hanging on the wall were the actresses' pictures. _____

9. Some questionable stories are called old wive's tales. _____

10. The president listened to all the others' opinions. _____

11. Isn't this Marnie's manuscript? _____

12. Did you ask to use your brother-in-law's car? _____

13. The assembly heard Jack and Linda's report on Monday—hers in the morning and his in the afternoon. _____

14. The supervisor criticized both employee's work records. _____

15. Whose going to the fair this year? _____

# TEST
## PART FOUR

A. Unscramble these *ie-ei* words and write them correctly.

1. iredw     _____
2. elseiur     _____
3. robghien     _____
4. rofgnie     _____
5. ietncfedi     _____

6. vedecie     _____
7. gesei     _____
8. htiheg     _____
9. zseei     _____
10. epeic     _____

B. Form the plural of these nouns or verb forms.

11. stretch     _____
12. artist     _____
13. waltz     _____
14. diagnosis     _____
15. handcuff     _____
16. woman     _____
17. foot     _____
18. knife     _____
19. tariff     _____
20. potato     _____

21. sandwich     _____
22. sister-in-law     _____
23. canary     _____
24. bluebird     _____
25. hero     _____
26. kangaroo     _____
27. notary     _____
28. shelf     _____
29. address     _____
30. mix     _____

C. Write the correct combination.

31. excel    *ent*     _____
32. benefit    *ing*     _____
33. compel    *ed*     _____
34. omit    *ing*     _____
35. occur    *ence*     _____
36. rebut    *al*     _____

37. drop      *ing*    _____
38. equip     *age*    _____
39. canoe     *ing*    _____
40. plot      *er*     _____
41. inhibit   *ing*    _____
42. chagrin   *ed*     _____
43. advise    *ing*    _____
44. enclose   *ure*    _____
45. service   *ing*    _____
46. preserve  *ation*  _____
47. amuse     *ing*    _____
48. nine      *th*     _____
49. care      *ful*    _____
50. lively    *hood*   _____
51. drunken   *ness*   _____
52. friendly  *ness*   _____
53. argue     *ment*   _____
54. tan       *ing*    _____
55. begin     *ing*    _____

D.  Check each misspelled word and write it correctly.

56. advantagous  _____     66. publicly       _____
57. drastically  _____     67. graceous       _____
58. courageous   _____     68. coolly         _____
59. laughably    _____     69. duely          _____
60. mischievous  _____     70. economically   _____
61. continueous  _____     71. carefuly       _____
62. spacious     _____     72. adventurous    _____
63. accuratly    _____     73. occasionally   _____
64. basicly      _____     74. miscellanous   _____
65. wholely      _____     75. accidently     _____

# FINAL

# TEST

A. Test your knowledge of the guidelines and rules you have studied in this text. Indicate whether each sentence is true or false by writing T or F in the right-hand column.

1. *Cieling* is spelled correctly. _____

2. In adding *ence* to *refer, prefer,* and *confer,* you double the *r* at the end of the word. _____

3. *Suggestible* is spelled correctly. _____

4. The *es* plural ending is added to *wish, tax, pitch,* and *porch.* _____

5. The plural ending for *crisis* is *es.* _____

6. *Heighth* is misspelled. _____

7. *Lives, wives,* and *knives* are spelled correctly. _____

8. *Due, true,* and *whole* are examples of "silent *e*" words that keep the *e* before *ly.* _____

9. In each of these words—*cemetery, tragedy, inquiry,* and *country*—you change the *y* to *i* before adding the plural ending *s.* _____

10. *Panic, frolic, mimic,* and *traffic* add a *k* before *ing* and *ed.* _____

11. *Hero, tomato,* and *potato* take *s* to form the plural. _____

12. The word in italics is correctly spelled: The bird preened *it's* feathers. _____

13. *Brilliance* is an exception to the tendency of bases ending in *i* to take one of these suffixes: *ance, ence.* _____

14. *Shriek* is correctly spelled. _____

15. Before adding the suffix *ure,* the last *t* in *portrait* is doubled. _____

16. *Lobbys* is incorrectly spelled. _____

17. *Leisure, weird,* and *seize* are examples of the rule for the long *e* sound of *i* and *e.* _____

18. *Mane/main* and *peer/pier* are examples of homonyms. _____

19. The origin of *occur* (L. *currere*) tells you to double the *r* and add *ance*. _____

20. Incorrectly pronounced words contribute to incorrectly spelled words. _____

B. For each word, write the corresponding noun (*ation, ion*) and the adjective (*able, ible*).

21. communicate _____ _____

22. access _____ _____

23. cancel _____ _____

24. exhaust _____ _____

25. dispense _____ _____

26. corrupt _____ _____

27. import _____ _____

28. digest _____ _____

29. interpret _____ _____

30. flex _____ _____

C. Find the misspelled word in each sentence and write it correctly.

31. He had a recurence of the high fever. _____

32. Come here immediatly. _____

33. My washer is garanteed for a year. _____

34. I tried to pursuade my cousin to stop smoking. _____

35. Some days the scar tissue is quite noticable. _____

36. The visiting choirmaster lead the congregational singing. _____

37. The new teacher is very agressive. _____

38. To everyones relief, the play finally ended. _____

39. His face certainly looks familar. _____

40. He is known everywhere as an exploitter of the poor. _____

41. How many theorys did you propose? _____

42. The little leaguer is called "Sluger Dan." _____

43. The horses gallopped across the field. _____

44. Try to spell each word accuratly. _____

45. The army withstood a ten-day seige. _____

46. She is dying her dress purple to match her shoes. _____

47. He has been studing for hours. _____

48. The evening was indeed pleasureable. _____

49. The porcelain doll is considered a rareity. _____

50. Joey is known for his mimickry. _____

D. Choose the correct ending and write the complete word.

51. correspond  (*ant, ent*)  _____

52. domin  (*ance, ence*)  _____

53. preval  (*ance, ence*)  _____

54. persist  (*ence, ance*)  _____

55. repel  (*ant, ent*)  _____

56. experi  (*ence, ance*)  _____

57. tend  (*ancy, ency*)  _____

58. assist  (*ent, ant*)  _____

59. depend  (*ent, ant*)  _____

60. relev  (*ence, ance*)  _____

E. Supply the correct ending and write the full word.

61. tempor  (*ary, ery*)  _____

62. critic  (*ize, ise*)  _____

63. station  (*ary, ery*)  _____
    (writing material)

64. homogen  (*ize, ise*)  _____

65. secret  (*ery, ary*)  _____

66. paral  (*ize, yze*)  _____

67. prelimin  (*ery, ary*)  _____

68. enterp  (*ise, ize*)  _____

69. libr  (*ary, ery*)  _____

70. bound  (*ary, ery*)  _____

71. recogn  (*ise, ize*)  _____

72. real  (*ise, ize*)  _____

73. Febru  (*ary, ery*)  _____

74. surpr  (*ise, ize*)  _____

75. anal  (*yze, ize*)  _____

F. From this list of words, select the one that fits the context of each sentence and write it in the blank.

76. We need a standard _____ for office practices.

77. Doug addressed the high school _____.

78. His ideas were _____.

79. The committee gave verbal _____ to the chairman's plan.

80. The police quickly _____ the crowd.

81. Willy was fed _____ly for a week.

82. From what _____ are you looking at the picture?

83. What did the physician _____?

84. She didn't cast a _____.

85. It's _____ for me to see him this afternoon.

86. We need first-class _____.

87. I tried to _____ her fears.

88. Meteorological conditions prevailing in a particular region are called _____ conditions.

89. Greg has no _____ for his actions.

90. A _____ of angry citizens stormed the capitol.

allay
horde
ballot
prescribe
irrational
accommodations
intravenous
explanation
assembly
procedure
assent
angle
convenient
dispersed
climatic

G. Fill in the troublesome middles.

91. Wed_____day

92. ter_____ble

93. ac_____mulate

94. bull__tin

95. aud__ble

96. ex_____ibit

97. cyl_____der

98. exag_____ate

99. envi_____ment

100. fin_____cial

101. fun_____mental

102. par_____el

103. in_____est

104. lab_____tory

105. math__matics

106. ath_____ics

107. nec_____ary

108. pron_____ciation

109. op_____tunity

110. lo_____liness

H. Select the correctly spelled word in each sentence.

111. She (accidently, accidentally) spilled the coffee.  _____

112. You won't be (admited, admitted) free.  _____

113. How much (experiance, experience) do I need?

_____

114. The doctors made two separate (diagnosis, diagnoses) of her ailments.

_____

115. Bill invested in a (franchize, franchise) for a hamburger stand.

_____

116. I wish I had made different (arrangements, arrangments)

_____

117. Louis was (chagrined, chagrinned) over his sister's despondency.

_____

118. The old man scarcely ekes out an (existance, existence).

_____

119. The reviewer's (criticism, critacism) was unfair.

_____

120. What course of study are you (pursuing, pursueing)?

_____

121. He received only thirty (replys, replies) to his questionnaire.

_____

122. Betty was hired as an (accompanyist, accompanist).

_____

123. Do you have any (colateral, collateral) to put up for this loan?

_____

124. I don't have a driver's (licence, license).

_____

125. He announced his decision (publically, publicly).

_____

126. The actor's (performance, preformance) was exceptional.

_____

127. Does the team have enough (releif, relief) pitchers?

_____

128. Too much (repitition, repetition) in your writing makes it boring.

_____

129. Her handwriting is (illegible, illegable).

_____

130. Mike is very (susceptable, susceptible) to colds.

_____

I. These specific combinations do not appear in the text. See how well you can apply what you have learned.

131. align + *ment* =

_____

132. govern + (*ance, ence*) =

_____

133. god + *ess* =                    _____

134. industry + *al* =               _____

135. mystery + *ous* =               _____

136. maintain + *ing* =              _____

137. practical + (*ly, ally*) =      _____

138. *preced* + (*ence, ance*) =     _____

139. scarce + *ly* =                 _____

140. take + *ing* =                  _____

141. outrage + *ous* =               _____

142. approve + *al* =                _____

143. perspire + *ation* =            _____

144. shine + *ing* =                 _____

145. recover + (*able, ible*) =      _____

146. sure + *ty* =                   _____

147. try + *es* =                    _____

148. *dis* + *ease* =                _____

149. evolution + (*ary, ery*) =      _____

150. rocket + *ry* =                 _____

151. worry + *ing* =                 _____

152. define + (*able, ible*) =       _____

153. consult + (*ant, ent*) =        _____

154. remorse + *ful* =               _____

155. excite + (*able, ible*) =       _____

J. To prove to yourself how well equipped you are to tackle words not covered in *Spelling Improvement,* here is a list of words arbitrarily drawn from various fields. Apply your five-step method and write the syllables for each word. You are on your honor to write the word from memory. Check your dictionary for meanings.

156. symmetry      _____

157. appendicitis  _____

158. foreclosure   _____

159. metronome     _____

160. curriculum    _____

161. decoupage     _____

162. molecule      _____

163. baccalaureate _____

164. nucleus _____

165. nomenclature _____

166. invertebrate _____

167. catalyst _____

168. lithography _____

169. pollination _____

170. denominator _____

171. demagnetize _____

172. conciliation _____

173. prorate _____

174. insolvency _____

175. fraudulent _____

176. bankruptcy _____

177. debenture _____

178. aeronautics _____

179. codicil _____

180. malfeasance _____

# APPENDIX
## TEST ANSWERS

### DIAGNOSTIC TEST

#### PART TWO

1. C
2. C
3. environment
4. maintenance
5. C
6. athletics
7. laboratory
8. pronunciation
9. C
10. mischievous

11. comparative
12. C
13. C
14. similar
15. C
16. sophomore
17. C
18. category
19. C
20. separate

21. C
22. C
23. rhythm
24. C
25. C
26. C
27. C
28. psychology
29. Wednesday
30. C

31. existence
32. C
33. C
34. permanent
35. C
36. noticeable
37. analyze
38. C
39. C
40. license

#### PART THREE

41. description
42. C
43. dissolution
44. C
45. disappoint
46. C
47. commence
48. C
49. C
50. despise

51. C
52. exceed
53. succeed
54. C
55. intercede
56. C
57. concede
58. proceed
59. C
60. C

61. led
62. C
63. latter
64. compliment
65. C
66. C
67. stationary
68. C
69. breathe
70. principal

71. C
72. advise
73. discuss
74. effect
75. C
76. lose
77. C
78. C
79. angel
80. humane

## PART FOUR

81. foreigner
82. C
83. C
84. C
85. siege
86. C
87. weird
88. C
89. C
90. friendship
91. C
92. rebuttal
93. C
94. C
95. occurrence
96. beginning
97. C
98. benefited

99. C
100. stopper
101. C
102. C
103. C
104. adequately
105. desirous
106. C
107. writing
108. C
109. shiny
110. C
111. C
112. C
113. replies
114. C
115. C
116. certifiable

117. accompanying
118. dutiful
119. C
120. studying
121. C
122. truly
123. immediately
124. C
125. copious
126. C
127. sincerely
128. C
129. wholly
130. grievous
131. calves
132. Negroes
133. heroes
134. C

135. batteries
136. elves
137. C
138. C
139. C
140. crises
141. don't
142. you're
143. C
144. C
145. C
146. it's
147. C
148. C
149. man's
150. women's

# CHAPTER 1   GUIDELINES TO SYLLABICATION

### PRETEST

1. nec  es  sar  y
2. man  u  fac  ture
3. vow  el
4. ac  com  mo  date
5. car  pen  ter

6. rap  id
7. con  sid  er  a  tion
8. an  tip  a  thy
9. ge  ol  o  gy
10. rub  ble

11. ref  er  ence
12. ac  cu  mu  late
13. de  lude
14. pi  lot
15. soph  o  more

16. an  ti  bod  y
17. con  so  nant
18. ap  pear  ance
19. trib  u  la  tion
20. ri  val  ry

### POSTTEST

1. con  tro  ver  sy
2. res  tau  rant
3. re  cur  rence
4. pre  cede
5. dis  ap  point  ment

6. tre  men  dous
7. un  nec  es  sar  y
8. de  scrip  tion
9. op  por  tu  ni  ty
10. ad  van  tage  ous

11. in  ci  den  tal
12. doc  u  men  ta  ry
13. knowl  edge
14. Wed  nes  day
15. psy  chol  o  gy

16. ri  dic  u  lous
17. a  chieve  ment
18. for  got  ten
19. gov  ern  ment
20. pro  ce  dure

# CHAPTER 2   A FIVE-STEP METHOD FOR SPELLING

### PRETEST

A.
1. interest
2. embarrass
3. irrelevant
4. sergeant
5. villain
6. experience
7. acquire
8. immediately

9. dissatisfaction
10. vacuum
11. apparent
12. convenience
13. procedure
14. occasionally
15. disappoint
16. loneliness

17. opportunity
18. financier
19. discrimination
20. parallel
21. accumulate
22. disappear
23. interrupt
24. restaurant

25. appreciate
26. acquaintance
27. explanation
28. accomplishment
29. possession

## POSTTEST

1. vacuum
2. villain
3. interest
4. sergeant
5. embarrass
6. acquire
7. disappear
8. experience
9. immediately
10. procedure
11. occasionally
12. loneliness
13. financier
14. apparent
15. discrimination
16. accumulate
17. opportunity
18. convenience
19. interrupt
20. acquaintance
21. dissatisfaction
22. restaurant
23. appreciate
24. disappoint
25. explanation
26. accomplishment
27. parallel
28. possession
29. irrelevant

B. Check your dictionary for correct syllabication.

## TEST   PART ONE

1. per   cep   tion
2. bril   liant
3. fas   ci   nate
4. per   se   ver   ance
5. me   di   o   cre
6. bi   og   ra   phy
7. en   cy   clo   pe   di   a
8. tran   si   tion
9. in   hab   i   tant
10. pen   i   cil   lin
11. rem   i   nisce
12. vac   ci   nate
13. mo   men   tum
14. cat   e   go   ry
15. ex   ag   ger   ate
16. spe   cif   i   cal   ly
17. rec   on   cile
18. trace   a   ble
19. phys   i   cal
20. en   dorse   ment

## CHAPTER 3   PRONUNCIATION AND ENUNCIATION

### PRETEST

1. hindrance
2. recognize
3. athlete
4. mischievous
5. lightening
6. tragedy
7. chimney
8. temperature
9. athletics
10. liable
11. finally
12. disastrous
13. vegetable
14. lightning
15. prejudice
16. federal
17. remembrance
18. grievous
19. temperament
20. quantity
21. government
22. environment
23. background
24. gratitude
25. hundred
26. aggravate

If you had 23 of 26 correct, you may bypass this chapter. But before you do, look up any misspelled words in the Index and review the section pertaining to those words.

### POSTTEST

A.
1. environment   liable   federal   boundary

B.
2. background
3. chocolate
4. government
5. twelfth
6. surprise
7. library
8. quantity
9. recognize
10. temperament
11. temperature
12. vegetable
13. finally
14. hundred
15. aggravate
16. tragedy
17. prejudice
18. locale
19. striped
20. rationale
21. hypercritical
22. suite
23. solder
24. corral
25. liter
26. deprecate
27. tortuous
28. naive
29. resume
30. allay

For any wrong answers, check the Index and review the section pertaining to those words. You do not want to leave the chapter without spelling every word accurately. For any word not listed in the Index, check your dictionary.

## CHAPTER 4 THE UNSTRESSED VOWEL

### PRETEST

| | | | |
|---|---|---|---|
| 1. competent | 9. dominant | 17. controversy | 25. fascinate |
| 2. grammar | 10. warrant | 18. criticism | 26. particular |
| 3. optimism | 11. candidate | 19. separate | 27. privilege |
| 4. familiar | 12. sentence | 20. linen | 28. peculiar |
| 5. humorous | 13. semester | 21. calendar | 29. bulletin |
| 6. comparative | 14. dormitory | 22. legitimate | 30. intelligence |
| 7. eliminate | 15. mathematics | 23. category | |
| 8. similar | 16. sacrifice | 24. probably | |

If you had 27 of 30 correct, you may bypass this chapter. But before you do, look up any misspelled words in the Index and review the section pertaining to those words, or check your dictionary for those not listed.

### POSTTEST

A.

| | | | |
|---|---|---|---|
| 1. calendar | 5. ballot | 9. separate | 13. freshman |
| 2. peculiar | 6. privileges | 10. comparative | 14. benefit |
| 3. bulletin | 7. sensitive | 11. dormitory | 15. maintenance |
| 4. humorous | 8. warrant | 12. category | |

B.

| | | | |
|---|---|---|---|
| 16. epidemic | 19. tolerate | 22. aluminum | 25. discrepancy |
| 17. murmuring | 20. apology | 23. voluntary | |
| 18. offend | 21. permanent | 24. competition | |

For any wrong answer, check the Index and review the section pertaining to those words. You do not want to leave the chapter without spelling every word accurately. For any word not listed in the Index, check your dictionary.

## CHAPTER 5 "SILENT" LETTERS

### PRETEST

| | | | |
|---|---|---|---|
| 1. Wednesday | 5. wry | 9. debris | 13. herb |
| 2. debt | 6. psychology | 10. subtle | 14. khaki |
| 3. condemn | 7. mortgage | 11. gnaw | 15. jeopardy |
| 4. guardian | 8. numb | 12. doubt | |

If you had 12 of 15 correct, you may bypass this chapter. But before you do, look up any misspelled words in the Index and review the section pertaining to those words, or check your dictionary for those not listed.

### POSTTEST

| | | | |
|---|---|---|---|
| 1. guard | 6. rhythm | 11. numb | 16. khaki |
| 2. undoubtedly | 7. mortgages | 12. debt | 17. answer |
| 3. Wednesday | 8. debris | 13. fluoridation | 18. science |
| 4. subtle | 9. rhinoceros | 14. gnaw | 19. columns |
| 5. exhaust | 10. guardian | 15. rhubarb | 20. Psalm |

For any wrong answers, check the Index and review the section pertaining to those words. You do not want to leave the chapter without spelling every word accurately. For any word not listed in the Index, check your dictionary.

# CHAPTER 6   SOUND-ALIKE SUFFIXES

## PRETEST

A. *able-ible*
1. permissible
2. acceptable
3. estimable
4. changeable
5. admirable
6. marketable
7. inevitable
8. eligible
9. considerable
10. passable
11. possible
12. perishable
13. defensible
14. repressible
15. reducible
16. educable

B. *ary-ery*
1. boundary
2. stationery
3. secretary
4. library
5. cemetery
6. February
7. contemporary
8. stationary

C. *ise-ize-yze*
1. advise
2. analyze
3. criticize
4. summarize
5. surprise
6. emphasize
7. paralyze
8. exercise
9. advertise
10. realize

D. *ance-ence (ant-ent)*
1. intelligent
2. resistance
3. equivalent
4. accident
5. defendant
6. prominence
7. existent
8. confidence
9. science
10. consequent
11. experience
12. magnificence
13. maintenance
14. excellent
15. guidance
16. influence
17. extravagance
18. insistent
19. attendance
20. dominant
21. prevalence
22. delinquent
23. brilliance
24. significant

If you had 14 of 16 in A, 7 of 8 in B, 9 of 10 in C, and 21 of 24 in D correct, you may bypass this chapter. But before you do, look up any misspelled words in the Index and review the section pertaining to those words, or check your dictionary for those not listed.

## POSTTEST

A.
1. debatable
2. indestructible
3. anniversary
4. exercise
5. paralyzed
6. surprised
7. sense
8. references
9. occurrences
10. preference

B.
11. inoperable
12. collectibles
13. analyze
14. superintendent
15. noticeable
16. infirmary
17. equalize
18. difference
19. permanent
20. excellence
21. prominent
22. admittance
23. desirable
24. manageable
25. impressionable

C.
27. marriageable
28. resistant
32. authorize
33. negligence
34. irritable
36. license
38. persistent
42. generalize
43. deference
44. comprehensible
48. dominant
50. cemetery

For any wrong answers, check the Index and review the section pertaining to those words. You do not want to leave the chapter without spelling every word accurately. For any word not listed in the Index, check your dictionary.

# TEST PART TWO

A.
1. criticism
2. controversial
3. legitimate
4. humorous
5. exhaust
6. admissible
7. appreciable
8. experience
9. cemetery
10. liable

B.
11. e. abundance
12. g. congregation
13. f. satellite
14. a. accumulate
15. i. exhilarate
16. j. impediment
17. c. chauvinism
18. h. rival
19. d. villain
20. b. derivation

C.
21. mortgage
22. psychiatry
23. guardian
24. predictable
25. stationary
26. incident
27. preference
28. preferred
29. conscience
30. eliminate
31. salary
32. separate
33. psalm
34. quantity
35. definite
36. condemn
37. solemn
38. warrant
39. pneumonia
40. hymn

D.
41. eminent
42. diffident
43. subsidize
44. insurgence
45. divisible
46. responsible
47. commentary
48. vulcanize
49. resistible
50. perceptible
51. recognize
52. interference
53. reversible
54. sensible
55. imaginary
56. literary
57. ancient
58. naturalize
59. endurable
60. legalize

E.
61. hindrance
62. factory
63. library
64. tragedy
65. twelfth
66. temperature
67. chimney
68. mischievous
69. probably
70. vegetables
71. cruel
72. hundred
73. sophomore
74. perspire
75. chocolate

F.
76. standardize
77. interesting
78. introduced
79. Angles
80. northern

# CHAPTER 7   PREFIXES

## PRETEST

A.
1. acquaint
2. committee
3. disturb
4. ability
5. innocence
6. unnecessary
7. connection
8. irrational
9. address
10. persuade
11. professor
12. extraordinary
13. disappoint
14. success
15. except

B.
16. infect
17. disinfect
18. defect
19. perfect
20. affect
21. effect
22. distract
23. protract
24. attract
25. contract
26. abstract
27. subtract

If you had 25 of 27 correct, you may bypass this chapter. But before you do, look up any misspelled words in the Index and review the section pertaining to those words, or check your dictionary for those not listed.

## POSTTEST

A.

| | | | |
|---|---|---|---|
| 1. irregular | 7. disappearance | 13. excavate | 19. absent |
| 2. contradiction | 8. postgraduate | 14. unnatural | 20. proclamation |
| 3. inoculate | 9. translation | 15. supernatural | 21. departure |
| 4. effect | 10. extraordinary | 16. intravenous | 22. ineligible |
| 5. perception | 11. precaution | 17. circumstances | 23. explanation |
| 6. dissatisfaction | 12. reorganize | 18. immodest | 24. assembly |

B.

| | | | |
|---|---|---|---|
| 25. ad | 28. disreputable | 31. acquit | 34. persuaded |
| 26. attract | 29. prefer | 32. away | 35. acquaintance |
| 27. away | 30. through | 33. perspire | |

For any wrong answers, check the Index and review the section pertaining to those words. You do not want to leave the chapter without spelling every word accurately. For any word not listed in the Index, check your dictionary.

# CHAPTER 8 "SEED" ROOTS

## PRETEST

A.

| | | | |
|---|---|---|---|
| 1. accede | 4. secede | 7. antecede | 10. intercede |
| 2. proceed | 5. exceed | 8. recede | |
| 3. concede | 6. succeed | 9. supersede | |

B.

| | | | |
|---|---|---|---|
| 11. supersede | 14. precede | 17. exceed | 20. recede |
| 12. accede | 15. succeed | 18. secede | |
| 13. proceed | 16. intercede | 19. concede | |

If you had 18 of 20 correct, you may bypass this chapter. But before you do, look up any misspelled words in the Index and review the section pertaining to those words, or check your dictionary for those not listed.

## POSTTEST

| | | |
|---|---|---|
| 1. supersede | 3. intercede | 5. exceed |
| 2. proceed | 4. succeed | |

For any wrong answers, check the Index and review the section pertaining to those words. You do not want to leave the chapter without spelling every word accurately. For any word not listed in the Index, check your dictionary.

# CHAPTER 9   HOMONYMS

### PRETEST

| | | | |
|---|---|---|---|
| 1. compliment | 6. principal | 11. cite | 16. capital |
| 2. there | 7. council | 12. passed | 17. horde |
| 3. already | 8. altogether | 13. too | 18. ascent |
| 4. its | 9. stationery | 14. their | 19. led |
| 5. coarse | 10. capitol | 15. site | 20. mantle |

If you had 18 of 20 correct, you may bypass this chapter. But before you do, look up any misspelled words in the Index and review the section pertaining to those words, or check your dictionary for those not listed.

### POSTTEST

A.

| | | | |
|---|---|---|---|
| 1. course | 4. sight | 7. two | 10. principles |
| 2. all together | 5. stationary | 8. already | 11. alter |
| 3. council | 6. Capitol | 9. led   lead | 12. its |

B.

| | | | |
|---|---|---|---|
| 13. assent | 17. fair   fare | 21. forward | 25. currant |
| 14. grated | 18. jibe | 22. raze | |
| 15. borne | 19. sheer   shear | 23. steak   stake | |
| 16. discrete | 20. caret | 24. while   wiled   wiles | |

For any wrong answers, check the Index and review the section pertaining to those words. You do not want to leave the chapter without spelling every word accurately. For any word not listed in the Index, check your dictionary.

# CHAPTER 10   SIMILAR WORDS

### PRETEST

A.

| | | | |
|---|---|---|---|
| 1. quite | 5. prophesy | 9. thorough | 13. loose |
| 2. access | 6. accept | 10. weather | |
| 3. lose | 7. than | 11. personnel | |
| 4. casual | 8. effects | 12. advise | |

B.

| | | | |
|---|---|---|---|
| 14. *f* | 19. *q* | 24. *s* | 29. *m* |
| 15. *t* | 20. *b* | 25. *d* | 30. *l* |
| 16. *n* | 21. *o* | 26. *e* | 31. *k* |
| 17. *g* | 22. *r* | 27. *c* | 32. *j* |
| 18. *p* | 23. *h* | 28. *a* | 33. *i* |

If you had 30 of 33 correct, you may bypass this chapter. But before you do, look up any misspelled words in the Index and review the section pertaining to those words, or check your dictionary for those not listed.

## POSTTEST

A.
1. casual
2. morale
3. ingenious
4. thorough
5. loose
6. advise
7. personal
8. latter

B.
9. angel
10. breathe
11. disburse
12. instance
13. formerly
14. elicit
15. delusion
16. clothes
17. flaunt
18. conscious
19. perspective
20. climactic

For any wrong answers, check the Index and review the section pertaining to those words. You do not want to leave the chapter without spelling every word accurately. For any word not listed in the Index, check your dictionary.

## TEST   PART THREE

A.
1. promotion
2. declassified
3. discredits
4. performed
5. appalled
6. disease
7. predictions
8. preface
9. collection
10. commences
11. irrevocable
12. detestable
13. progress
14. illegal
15. admittance

B.
16. effect
17. council
18. alter
19. capital
20. immigrants
21. accept
22. later
23. site
24. loose
25. led
26. principal
27. your
28. past
29. complemented
30. boarders

C.
31. description
32. proposal
33. acclaimed
34. immediately
35. difference
36. unnumbered
37. intercede
38. courses
39. stationery
40. border
41. irrelevant
42. restaurant
43. acquaintance
44. embarrass
45. explanation
46. dissatisfaction
47. procedure
48. accomplishments
49. convenience
50. loneliness

## CHAPTER 11   *IE-EI*

### PRETEST

1. relieve
2. conceit
3. receive
4. seizures
5. deficient
6. weighed
7. chief
8. piece
9. weird
10. counterfeit
11. height   weight
12. achieve
13. foreign
14. neighborhood
15. leisure

If you had 13 of 15 correct, you may bypass this chapter. But before you do, look up any misspelled words in the Index and review the section pertaining to those words, or check your dictionary for those not listed.

## POSTTEST

| | | | |
|---|---|---|---|
| 1. believe | 6. forfeit | 11. weigh | 16. heinous |
| 2. siege | 7. reindeer | 12. deficient | 17. friend |
| 3. sovereign | 8. efficient | 13. leisure | 18. heifer |
| 4. freight | 9. yield | 14. weird | 19. surveillance |
| 5. receive | 10. seize | 15. thief | 20. sieve |

For any wrong answers, check the Index and review the section pertaining to those words. You do not want to leave the chapter without spelling every word accurately. For any word not listed in the Index, check your dictionary.

# CHAPTER 12   DOUBLING THE FINAL CONSONANT

## PRETEST

| | | | |
|---|---|---|---|
| 1. planner | 8. beginning | 15. instilling | 22. chagrined |
| 2. witty | 9. occurrence | 16. equipped | 23. vexing |
| 3. streaked | 10. dimly | 17. omitted | 24. delightful |
| 4. plugger | 11. repealed | 18. dimmer | 25. trafficker |
| 5. taxing | 12. transferring | 19. excellent | |
| 6. exploiter | 13. propellant | 20. conference | |
| 7. dropped | 14. gossipy | 21. benefited | |

If you had 22 of 25 correct, you may bypass this chapter. But before you do, look up any misspelled words in the Index and review the section pertaining to those words, or check your dictionary for those not listed.

## POSTTEST

A.

| | | | |
|---|---|---|---|
| 1. acquittal | 6. exceeding | 11. development | 16. mimicry |
| 2. propeller | 7. balloting | 12. summary | 17. different |
| 3. trafficking | 8. admittance | 13. womanish | 18. relaxing |
| 4. allotment | 9. repellent | 14. allotted | 19. stoppage |
| 5. dependable | 10. gossipy | 15. equipment | 20. mannish |

B.

| | | | |
|---|---|---|---|
| 21. beginner | 25. blotter | 29. beggar | 33. regrettable |
| 22. omitting | 26. dropping | 30. propeller | 34. rebellion |
| 23. compelled | 27. swimmer | 31. planning | |
| 24. bagging | 28. excellent | 32. drummer | |

C.

35. equipped   equipping   equipage
36. deferred   deferrer   deferring   deference
37. skimmed   skimmer   skimming
38. bagged   bagging   baggage
39. blotted   blotter   blotting
40. begged   begging   beggar
41. occurred   occurring   occurrence
42. omitted   omitting
43. preferred   preferrer   preferring   preference
44. transferred   transferring   transference
45. referred   referrer   referring   reference
46. stopped   stopper   stopping   stoppage

For any wrong answers, check the Index and review the section pertaining to those words. You do not want to leave the chapter without spelling every word accurately. For any word not listed in the Index, check your dictionary.

# CHAPTER 13   THE FINAL *E*

## PRETEST

1. desiring
2. useless
3. serviceable
4. duly
5. density
6. ninth
7. coming
8. received
9. argument
10. writing
11. truly
12. wholesome
13. advertisement
14. losing
15. rarity
16. singeing
17. arguing
18. adventurous
19. diner
20. canoeist
21. enforcing
22. wholly
23. indispensable
24. ninety
25. accurately

If you had 23 of 25 correct, you may bypass this chapter. But before you do, look up any misspelled words in the Index and review the section pertaining to those words, or check your dictionary for those not listed.

## POSTTEST

A.
1. losing
2. manageable
3. issuable
4. pursuing
5. sincerely
6. arguing
7. remoteness
8. judging
9. disbursement
10. pleasurable
11. desirous
12. truly
13. advantageous
14. hopeful
15. aching
16. canoeing
17. wholly
18. argument

B.
19. challenged   challenger   challenging   challengeable
20. pronounced   pronouncer   pronouncing   pronounceable   pronouncement
21. accused   accuser   accusing
22. believed   believer   believing   believable
23. acknowledged   acknowledging   acknowledgeable   acknowledgment
24. dyed   dyer   dyeing
25. advised   adviser   advising   advisable   advisement
26. traced   tracer   tracing   traceable
27. amused   amuser   amusing   amusable   amusement
28. opposed   opposer   opposing   opposable
29. arranged   arranger   arranging   arrangement
30. dined   diner   dining

For any wrong answers, check the Index and review the section pertaining to those words. You do not want to leave the chapter without spelling every word accurately. For any word not listed in the Index, check your dictionary.

# CHAPTER 14   THE FINAL Y

## PRETEST

| | | | |
|---|---|---|---|
| 1. accompanying | 9. happiness | 17. pitiful | 25. pitying |
| 2. hurries | 10. disobeying | 18. prayer | 26. copyist |
| 3. occupying | 11. identifiable | 19. stories | 27. payee |
| 4. studies | 12. dutiful | 20. shinier | 28. reliable |
| 5. employment | 13. luxurious | 21. denial | 29. companies |
| 6. counties | 14. tragedies | 22. liveliest | 30. studying |
| 7. burial | 15. business | 23. employable | |
| 8. beautiful | 16. daily | 24. trial | |

If you had 27 of 30 correct, you may bypass this chapter. But before you do, look up any misspelled words in the Index and review the section pertaining to those words, or check your dictionary for those not listed.

## POSTTEST

A.

| | | | |
|---|---|---|---|
| 1. conveying | 3. conveyers | 5. relied | 7. reliance |
| 2. conveyed | 4. conveyance | 6. relies | 8. reliable |

B.

| | | | |
|---|---|---|---|
| 9. dissatisfied | 11. replies | 13. unjustifiable | 15. paid |
| 10. discrepancies | 12. controversial | 14. X-rayed | |

For any wrong answers, check the Index and review the section pertaining to those words. You do not want to leave the chapter without spelling every word accurately. For any word not listed in the Index, check your dictionary.

# CHAPTER 15   *LY* AND *OUS*

## PRETEST

A. *ly-ally*

| | | | |
|---|---|---|---|
| 1. basically | 6. publicly | 11. finally | 16. coyly |
| 2. morally | 7. accidentally | 12. accurately | 17. dryly or drily |
| 3. truly | 8. angrily | 13. vaguely | 18. safely |
| 4. frequently | 9. chiefly | 14. wholly | 19. simply |
| 5. continuously | 10. duly | 15. easily | 20. slyly |

B. *ous*

| | | | |
|---|---|---|---|
| 21. various | 24. mischievous | 27. mountainous | 30. grievous |
| 22. perilous | 25. libelous | 28. adventurous | 31. victorious |
| 23. advantageous | 26. piteous | 29. troublous | 32. spacious |

If you had 18 of 20 in A and 10 of 12 in B, you may bypass this chapter. But before you do, look up any misspelled words in the Index and review the section pertaining to those words, or check your dictionary for those not listed.

## POSTTEST

A.
1. hungrily
2. accidentally
3. advantageous
4. heavily
5. publicly

6. continuous
7. practically
8. sincerely
9. temporarily
10. carefully

11. appropriately
12. gracious
13. extremely
14. courageous
15. mischievous

16. injurious
17. annually
18. truly
19. physically
20. academically

B.
21. certainly
22. entirely
23. desirous

24. marvelous
25. piteous
26. ridiculous

27. various
28. morally
29. considerably

30. easily

For any wrong answers, check the Index and review the section pertaining to those words. You do not want to leave the chapter without spelling every word accurately. For any word not listed in the Index, check your dictionary.

# CHAPTER 16    PLURALS

## PRETEST

1. displays
2. penalties
3. gases
4. vetoes
5. zoos
6. monarchs
7. inquiries
8. crises

9. Negroes
10. melodies
11. perches
12. thieves
13. potatoes
14. Tommys
15. wishes
16. buzzes

17. universities
18. Tories
19. discrepancies
20. griefs
21. halves
22. societies
23. gulfs
24. elegies

25. data
26. heroes
27. wives
28. studies
29. decoys
30. taxes

If you had 27 of 30 correct, you may bypass this chapter. But before you do, look up any misspelled words in the Index and review the section pertaining to those words, or check your dictionary for those not listed.

## POSTTEST

A.
1. rebuffs
2. thieves
3. lives

4. briefs
5. selves
6. chiefs

7. giraffes
8. wolves
9. dwarfs

10. shelves
11. fifes

B.
12. monarchs

13. countries

14. overtures

15. treaties

C.
16. parentheses
17. theses

18. compendia
(also compendiums)

19. axes
20. neuroses

21. oases

D.

| | | | |
|---|---|---|---|
| 22. appendixes | 27. tornadoes | 32. sphinxes | 38. chimneys |
| 23. halos | (or tornados) | 33. sinuses | 39. Fridays |
| (or haloes) | 28. pianos | 34. rallies | 40. studios |
| 24. heroes | 29. tragedies | 35. batteries | |
| 25. rodeos | 30. leaves | 36. shampoos | |
| 26. volleys | 31. crutches | 37. lurches | |

For any wrong answers, check the Index and review the section pertaining to those words. You do not want to leave the chapter without spelling every word accurately. For any word not listed in the Index, check your dictionary.

# CHAPTER 17   THE APOSTROPHE

## PRETEST

1. king's
2. boys'
3. Brannon and Butterworth's
4. John Donne's
5. secretary's and the treasurer's
6. doesn't
7. women's
8. each other's
9. Louis the Thirteenth's
10. its
11. It's   nobody's
12. friend's
13. father-in-law's
14. minute's
15. theirs   ours

If you had 13 of 15 correct, you may bypass this chapter. But before you do, look up any misspelled words in the Index and review the section pertaining to those words, or check your dictionary for those not listed.

## POSTTEST

| | | | |
|---|---|---|---|
| 1. its | 5. C | 9. wives' | 13. Jack's and Linda's |
| 2. whose | 6. hers | 10. C | 14. employees' |
| 3. yours | 7. they're | 11. C | 15. Who's |
| 4. didn't   women's | 8. C | 12. C | |

For any wrong answers, check the Index and review the section pertaining to those words. You do not want to leave the chapter without spelling every word accurately. For any word not listed in the Index, check your dictionary.

# TEST   PART FOUR

A.

| | | | |
|---|---|---|---|
| 1. weird | 4. foreign | 7. siege | 10. piece |
| 2. leisure | 5. deficient | 8. height | |
| 3. neighbor | 6. deceive | 9. seize | |

B.

| | | | |
|---|---|---|---|
| 11. stretches | 16. women | 21. sandwiches | 26. kangaroos |
| 12. artists | 17. feet | 22. sisters-in-law | 27. notaries |
| 13. waltzes | 18. knives | 23. canaries | 28. shelves |
| 14. diagnoses | 19. tariffs | 24. bluebirds | 29. addresses |
| 15. handcuffs | 20. potatoes | 25. heroes | 30. mixes |

C.
31. excellent
32. benefiting
33. compelled
34. omitting
35. occurrence
36. rebuttal
37. dropping

38. equipage
39. canoeing
40. plotter
41. inhibiting
42. chagrined
43. advising
44. enclosure

45. servicing
46. preservation
47. amusing
48. ninth
49. careful
50. livelihood
51. drunkenness

52. friendliness
53. argument
54. tanning
55. beginning

D.
56. advantageous
61. continuous
63. accurately

64. basically
65. wholly
67. gracious

69. duly
71. carefully
74. miscellaneous

75. accidentally

# FINAL TEST

A.
1. F
2. F
3. T
4. T
5. T

6. T
7. T
8. F
9. F
10. T

11. F
12. F
13. T
14. T
15. F

16. T
17. F
18. T
19. F
20. T

B.
21. communication    communicable
22. accession    accessible
23. cancelation or    cancelable or
cancellation    cancellable
24. exhaustion    exhaustible
25. dispensation    dispensable

26. corruption    corruptible
27. importation    importable
28. digestion    digestible
29. interpretation    interpretable
30. flexion    flexible

C.
31. recurrence
32. immediately
33. guaranteed
34. persuade
35. noticeable
36. led
37. aggressive
38. everyone's

39. familiar
40. exploiter
41. theories
42. Slugger
43. galloped
44. accurately
45. siege
46. dyeing

47. studying
48. pleasurable
49. rarity
50. mimicry
51. correspondent
52. dominance
53. prevalence
54. persistence

55. repellent
56. experience
57. tendency
58. assistant
59. preferred:
dependent
(also dependant)
60. relevance

E.
61. temporary
62. criticize
63. stationery
64. homogenize

65. secretary
66. paralyze
67. preliminary
68. enterprise

69. library
70. boundary
71. recognize
72. realize

73. February
74. surprise
75. analyze

F.
76. procedure
77. assembly
78. irrational
79. assent

80. dispersed
81. intravenously
82. angle
83. prescribe

84. ballot
85. convenient
86. accommodations
87. allay

88. climatic
89. explanation
90. horde

G.
91. Wednesday
92. terrible
93. accumulate
94. bulletin
95. audible

96. exhibit
97. cylinder
98. exaggerate
99. environment
100. financial

101. fundamental
102. parallel
103. interest
104. laboratory
105. mathematics

106. athletics
107. necessary
108. pronunciation
109. opportunity
110. loneliness

H.
111. accidentally
112. admitted
113. experience
114. diagnoses
115. franchise

116. arrangements
117. chagrined
118. existence
119. criticism
120. pursuing

121. replies
122. accompanist
123. collateral
124. license
125. publicly

126. performance
127. relief
128. repetition
129. illegible
130. susceptible

I.
131. alignment
132. governance
133. goddess
134. industrial
135. mysterious
136. maintaining
137. practically

138. precedence
139. scarcely
140. taking
141. outrageous
142. approval
143. perspiration
144. shining

145. recoverable
146. surety
147. tries
148. disease
149. evolutionary
150. rocketry
151. worrying

152. definable
153. consultant
154. remorseful
155. excitable

J.
156. sym  me  try
157. ap  pen  di  ci  tis
158. fore  clo  sure
159. met  ro  nome
160. cur  ric  u  lum
161. de  cou  page
162. mol  e  cule
163. bac  ca  lau  re  ate
164. nu  cle  us
165. no  men  cla  ture
166. in  ver  te  brate
167. cat  a  lyst
168. lith  og  ra  phy

169. pol  lin  a  tion
170. de  nom  i  na  tor
171. de  mag  net  ize
172. con  cil  i  a  tion
173. pro  rate
174. in  sol  ven  cy
175. fraud  u  lent
176. bank  rupt  cy
177. de  ben  ture
178. aer  o  nau  tics
179. cod  i  cil
180. mal  fea  sance

# INDEX